The Complete Guide To Successful Financial Markets Trading

Simon Watkins

Copyright © 2017 Simon Watkins
All rights reserved.
ISBN: 190875690X
ISBN-13: 978-1908756909 (ADVFN Books)

ADVFN BOOKS

This book is dedicated to my son, James Harper-Watkins

Contents

Why Trade In The First Place?	1
Taking Control Back From Apathetic Fund Managers	1
Ability To Short Is A Huge Advantage For Individuals	2
Opportunities For Smart Trading Around The Clock	3
Dealing Profits Are Tax-Free	4
Trading Towards A Better Lifestyle	4
The Basics Of Foreign Exchange Trading	5
The Biggest And Most Transparent Market In The World	5
The Conventions Of An FX Trade	6
Making A Trade (Applicable To Trading Any Asset)	9
Market Order Types (Applicable To All Asset Trading)	14
Important Fundamental Principles For FX Trading	18
Money Goes To Where It Is Best Rewarded...	18
For The Concomitant Risk Involved...	18
But Supply And Demand Dynamics Are Also Vital...	20
As Are Market Perceptions	20
Basic Models For FX Trading	21
Purchasing Power Parity (PPP)	21
Interest Rate Parity (IRP)	22
Key Economic Indicators For FX And Other Assets	22
Interest Rates And Inflation	22
Trade Flows (Including Manufacturing And Services Figures)	25
GDP	26
Employment	27
Personal Spending/Consumption	29
Business Confidence/Consumer Confidence Indices	29
Credit Ratings	30
The Basics Of Equities Trading	36
A Good Starter Market For Those New To Trading	36
Index Trading	37
Index Trading Utilises The First Components Of Top-Down Trading	38
Area-Specific Index Trading (Positive Paradigm Shifts)	38
Area-Specific Index Trading (Negative Paradigm Shifts)	41
Important Fundamental Principles For Top-Down Index Trading	45
Individual Stock Trading	50

The Complete Guide To Successful Markets Trading

The Kondratieff Wave	51
The Business Cycle	53
The Minsky Cycle	55
Specific Stock Sector Investment Implications Of The Cycles	58
The Basics Of Bottom-Up Investing	59
Comparables	60
Management	60
Value Investing Versus Growth Investing	63
Key Basic Metrics For Stock Investors	64
The Basics Of Commodities Trading	**66**
Trading Is Best Confined To Oil And Metals	66
Supply And Demand	67
The Oil Market	69
Saudi Arabia	71
The US	82
Iran	87
Iraq	95
The Metals Market	99
Gold	100
Silver	102
Other Metals	104
The Basics Of Bond Trading	**106**
A Key Part Of Any Investment Portfolio	106
Basic Terminology	109
Face Value ('Par')	109
Coupon	109
Maturity Date	110
Yield	110
Yield To Maturity	110
Duration	111
Different Types Of Bonds	112
Government Bonds	112
Corporate Bonds	112
Emerging Market Bonds	112
Mortgage-Backed Securities (MBS) And Asset-Backed Securities (ABS)	113
Non-Government Bonds	113
Basic Bond Trading Strategies	113
Passive ('Buy And Hold')	113
Indexing	114
Immunisation	115

Active	115
Developed Market Debt Versus Emerging Market Debt	116
Basic Convergence Premise	116
Emerging To Developed Market Progress Is Rarer Than Thought	118
The Current General Environment For Bonds	121
The Current Investment Balance Between DM And EM Bonds	123
Technical Analysis	**125**
Candlesticks	126
Resistance And Support Levels	130
Fibonacci Levels	133
Moving Averages	134
Relative Strength Index	141
Bollinger Bands	144
Elliott Wave Theory	146
Continuation Patterns	149
Ascending And Descending Triangles	150
Flags	152
Trend Reversals	154
Double Top And Double Bottom	155
Head And Shoulders Patterns	155
Ichimoku Kinko Hyo	157
The Cloud	157
The Basic Components Of Ichimoku	159
Key Trading Signals	161
Risk/Reward Management And Hedging	**163**
The Nature Of Risk	163
Greed And Fear	164
Orders Are The Cornerstone Of Risk Management	165
The Risk Curve	166
Net Margin/Trading Requirement (NMR/NTR)	167
Account Size And Setting Targets	168
Straight Averaging Up	170
Layered Averaging Up	172
Value Averaging	173
Trailing Stop Loss Orders	174
Hedging	174
Cross-Currency Hedging	175
Cross-Asset Hedging	179
Cross-Sovereign/Credit Rating Hedging	181
Options	182

Key Types	182
Key Terms	183
Key Legislation	185
Basic Structures (Long-Only Options)	186
Risk-On/Risk-Off And Other Correlations	**189**
What Is RORO?	189
Changing Bond And Equity Correlations	193
Equities Trading In A Rising US Interest Rates Scenario	203
Bond Trading In The Current Economic Environment	209
Oil In The Correlations Mix	211
Oil And The US Dollar	211
Oil And Other Currencies	213
Moving Along The Risk Curve, By Market- And Asset-Type	215
Risk Rotation Currently Reinforces US Economic Growth	218
Trading Strategies Off The Current Saudi Fix	218
Metals In The Correlations Mix	237
Gold	237
Silver	241
PGMs	242
Other Metals	244
Key Risks On The Horizon	**248**
The US	249
The Risk Of A Major Equities Correction	251
China	253
Huge And Growing Debt Leverage	254
Stockmarket Bubbles	257
Housing Bubbles	257
Mathematical Impossibility Of Current Debt Management / Growth Strategy	258
Catalyst For Catastrophe Could Be US Rates Rises	259
Brexit And The Eurozone	260
Brexit	260
The Eurozone	263
Black Swan Events	265
Reviews	**268**
About The Author	**270**
Also By Simon Watkins	**272**
More Books From ADVFN	**280**

Simon Watkins

Why Trade In The First Place?

Prior to the Global Financial Crisis that began in 2007 the general view was that trading the financial markets was too complicated for most people to become involved with. After the crisis, this perception is still commonplace, added to which financial markets' trading is now also widely regarded as being an extremely risky activity. In fact, neither of these assumptions is correct. **This book will go step-by-step through all aspects of trading all major asset classes so that, by the end of it, readers will be in a position to profitably trade whichever of them they wish. In the process they could significantly augment their day-to-day incomes or indeed become full-time financial markets' traders.** The reasons to take this step are compelling, as outlined below.

Taking Control Back From Apathetic Fund Managers

Based on the previously mentioned twin assumptions, the overwhelming majority of people with money available for investment decide to hand it over to 'professionals', most commonly in the form of ISAs (or equivalent) and/or pensions, on the basis that 'they know what they're doing and they will make good returns'. In fact, **even a cursory glance at the investment performance of the world's developed markets pension fund and investment fund managers over the past ten years at least shows that the vast majority of them have not even produced returns in line with those of their benchmark stock indices.** Indeed, a majority of them have not produced returns in line with the near-zero interest rates in their countries and a near-majority have actually lost money.

The stark fact is that to fund managers an individual's money does not matter at all. Provided that they retain the bulk of their customers – which they do, due to the two reasons mentioned above, together with a general apathy about switching investment providers and deterrent penalties on withdrawing funds – fund managers are happy to take their in-built rolling commission and not worry too much about making money.

In short, the individual cares a lot more about their money and their future than fund managers do, so they should take control of it. Moreover, **if a person knows what they are doing – as they will when they finish reading this book – then they are likely to generate returns on their money way above those of the benchmark stock indices and exponentially greater than those of virtually all developed markets pension fund and investment fund managers.**

Ability To Short Is A Huge Advantage For Individuals

A key reason why the majority of fund managers perform so poorly over time is quite simply that they cannot sell assets that they do not already hold (i.e. 'go short'), they can only buy assets (i.e. 'go long'). In markets that are broadly rising (i.e. 'bull markets') this is not a particular encumbrance to making money but in markets that are broadly falling (i.e. 'bear markets') it is a huge disadvantage and, for many of the fund managers trading through the height of the Global Financial Crisis – or any of the many major market downturns that we have seen in the past 50 years (e.g. the 1997 Asia Financial Crisis, the 1998 Russian Financial Crisis, the 1999 Dotcom Bubble Burst) – it was shown to be a generally catastrophic hindrance.

However, individual traders (i.e. 'retail traders') dealing over a trading platform, most commonly through a spread betting account, do not suffer from this disadvantage. **They can sell assets that they do not already hold as well as buy assets, so they can profit just as much from moves lower as from moves higher.**

This is a huge trading advantage that gives retail traders a massive trading edge over even the most experienced pension fund or investment fund manager, all other factors remaining equal. In fact, it is fair to say that, given the way markets move in a pervasive bear trading environment – that is, they often move much faster and with more momentum than markets that are in a broadly rising trend – profits can be much, much greater when assets are generally falling than when they are rising.

Opportunities For Smart Trading Around The Clock

All major pension fund and investment fund managers are big institutions and, like all such companies, it takes time – and a large degree of consensus amongst key decision makers – to effect meaningful change in overall strategy and even to make a quick decision of the type that are absolutely essential to trade effectively over time in the world's financial markets.

Individual traders, though, are under no such constraints: they are at liberty to make decisions quickly and to put them into effect immediately in a global trading marketplace that is open 24 hours six days a week.

Additionally, although individuals can seek advice from others about a trading idea, ultimately they are the key decision maker, allowing them to trade nimbly, quickly and smartly. This is precisely the type of trading required to optimise returns from the type of marketplace that has been particularly evident since the onset of the Global Financial Crisis in 2007.

Dealing Profits Are Tax-Free

For individuals in the UK trading on a spread betting platform, all profits made are completely exempt from Capital Gains Tax and do not attract stamp duty or commissions. The only exception is if an individual explicitly puts down on a tax return that spread trading is their main source of income.

Trading Towards A Better Lifestyle

Provided that traders adhere to the very basic rules of dealing – principally those surrounding managing risk and achieving rewards – then there is no reason at all why they cannot make life-changing amounts of money for as long as they keep trading. Life-changing not just in terms of having more money but also in terms of being able to work wherever and whenever they like for themselves and their families, not for other people they do not know. **In short, successful traders are entirely in charge of their own destiny and can shape their lives as they wish them to be.**

The Basics Of Foreign Exchange Trading

The Biggest And Most Transparent Market In The World

In broad terms, the global foreign exchange (FX) market is the biggest financial market in the world – larger than the equity, bond and commodity markets added together – with a daily average trading volume of USD5.1 trillion in 2016, according to that year's 'Triennial Central Bank Survey' by the Bank for International Settlements (BIS). In practical terms, this translates into it being **the most transparent of these markets to trade, less subject to manipulation by traders from leading banks and fund managers in the loop of information about deal orders and flows that is not available to retail traders.**

For many traders starting out, though, the FX market can appear a more daunting prospect than the equity market or even the commodity market as it involves simultaneously handling two assets and, in effect, two transactions in one trade (the bond market often appears almost as confusing, given the pricing structure to be discussed later in this section). However, this should not deter the trader, as the benefits of trading such a big, transparent and wide-ranging market far outweigh overcoming any initial difficulty in understanding the bare mechanics of FX trading.

The Conventions Of An FX Trade

If a trader thinks, for example, that the British pound is going to strengthen he cannot just 'buy the pound', he needs to buy it against another currency, which, at the same time as buying the pound, he must sell; it is an exchange of currencies. Alternatively, if a trader thinks that the British pound is going to weaken he cannot just 'sell the pound', he needs to sell it against another currency, which he buys at the same time as selling the pound. In fact, **all FX trades involve two currencies** (although the Dollar Index is the rate of the US dollar against a basket of other currencies), from which is derived the 'foreign exchange rate' for any currency pairing at a given point in time.

Looking at any FX rate in a newspaper, website or TV will show either of the following formats: e.g. £/$1.2441 or GBPUSD1.2441. In this case, the rate shown is for the British pound against the US dollar and is the 'mid-rate' price; that is the mean average price between the 'bid' price and the 'offer' price (see below). In the first format, symbols are used for each, but for the vast majority of currencies there are no easily recognisable symbols. Consequently, **every currency in the world has a currency code of three letters**, which generally is comprised of two key letters in the name of the country appearing first and then the first letter of the unit of currency. In this case, then, GBP is comprised of the 'G' from Great and the 'B' from Britain, plus the 'P' from pound, whilst USD is comprised of the 'U' from United and the 'S' from States, plus the 'D' from dollar. Other commonly trading currency codes are: JPY (Japanese yen), EUR (euro) and CHF (Swiss franc, with the 'CH' being derived from the Latin name for the country, Confoederatio Helvetica), but the trader can look up any currency code on the internet by just typing into the search engine the name of the country and 'currency code'.

Here are some of the most traded codes for currencies and a few others mentioned in this book, for convenience:

GBP = Great British pound
USD = US dollar
EUR = euro
JPY = Japanese yen
CHF = Swiss franc
AUD = Australian dollar
NZD = New Zealand dollar
CAD = Canadian dollar
HKD = Hong Kong dollar
RMB = Chinese renminbi

It is also essential for the trader to know two extra pieces of basic information regarding the way in which the FX market actually works in a trading scenario:

1. **All FX trades are quoted with a 'base currency' on the left hand side of the quote and the 'counter currency' on the right hand side of the quote.** The FX rate shows how much one unit of the counter currency is required to exchange it for one unit of the base currency. So, in the example above, GBPUSD1.2441, 1 US dollar and slightly over 24 cents are required in exchange for one British pound.

2. FX trading quotes (on, say, a trading platform, or from a bank) comprise two prices (as do all trading quotes, in fact): the one on the left is the price at which whomever the retail trader is trading with will buy the base currency (see below) and, therefore, sell the counter currency (see below) – known as the **'bid price'** – and the one on the right is the price at which whomever the retail trader is trading with will sell the base currency (see below) and, therefore, buy the counter currency (see below) – known as the **'offer price'**.

So, if a retail trader wants to sell the base currency then the trading platform will be buying the base currency, so the price on the left is the one that the trader needs to look at. If the retail trader wants to buy the base currency (which means the trading platform is selling the base currency), then the trader needs to look at the price on the right.

For example, on a trading platform, a retail trader will typically see the following:

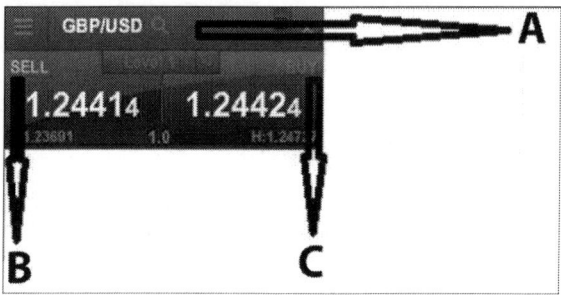

[Chart Key:
A= The British pound is the 'base currency' and the US dollar is the 'counter currency' – that is 'how many US dollars are equivalent to one British pound?'
B = 'Sell' is from the retail traders' perspective – that is, the retail trader is selling the British pound (and buying US dollars) to the trading platform (that is buying the British pound and selling US dollars)
C = 'Buy' is from the retail traders' perspective – that is, the retail trader is buying the British pound (and selling US dollars) to the trading platform (that is selling the British pound and buying US dollars)]

It is very important to note that this trade box shows the client's view (that is, the retail trader's view).

Making A Trade (Applicable To Trading Any Asset)

Given this, if a trader in this instance wants to sell the British pound (which automatically necessitates buying the US dollar) then he must complete the transaction as described step-by-step below (please note that FX prices move every second, so the above quote has also moved).

1. Pull up the price chart for the British pound (GBP) against the US dollar (USD)

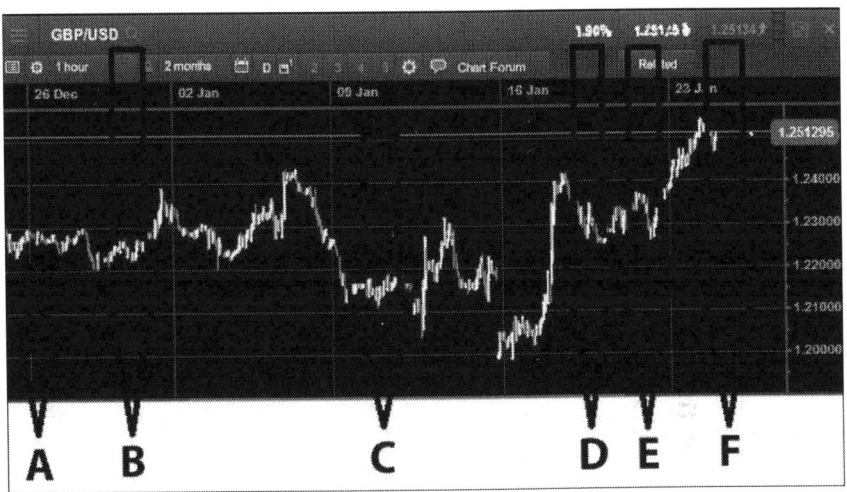

[Chart Key:
A = White (and red) line = number of US dollars required to exchange for one British pound over a set period of time
B = The letters are the currency codes selected by the retail trader: in this case the British pound (GBP) against the US dollar (USD)
C = The line with the red price on the right attached to it is the current market mean average price
D = The % shown is the rise or fall in the value of the GBP against the USD on the day

E = *The left hand price is the price at which the retail trader can sell GBP (and buy USD)*
F = *The right hand price is the price at which the retail trader can buy GBP (and sell USD)]*

2. Click on the left hand side price (in this case, 1.25125) if the trader wants to sell GBP (and buy USD) or the right hand price (in this case, 1.25134) if the trader wants to buy GBP (and sell USD), at which point a 'deal ticket' will appear on screen, as below. In this case, let us say that the trader wants to sell GBP (and buy USD), so he clicks on the left hand price.

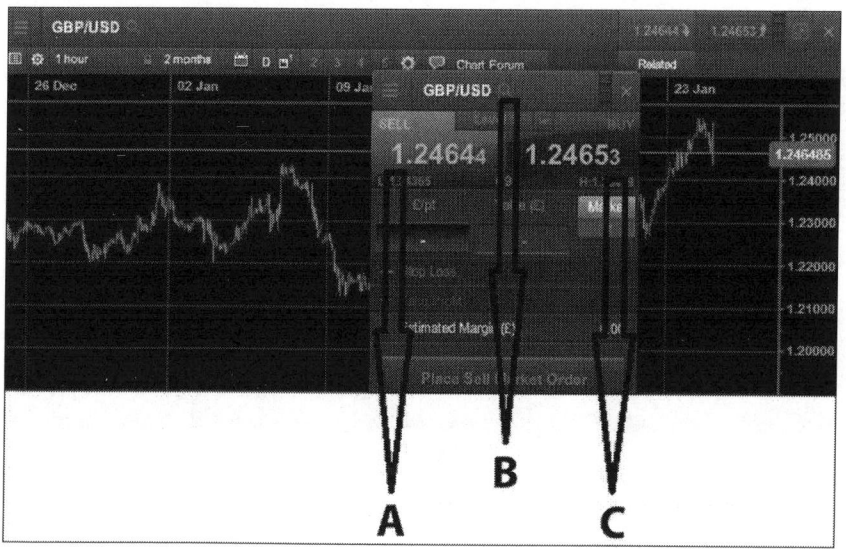

[Chart Key:
A = *Because the trader selected the left hand price, the ticket highlights the option for the trader to sell GBP (and buy USD)*
B = *The deal ticket*
C = *At any point until the trader clicks on the 'Place Sell Market Order' tab, though he can change his mind and decide to buy GBP (sell USD) by clicking on the 'Buy' tab]*

3. The trader then decides how much money he wishes to trade: on most trading platforms, this is expressed in amount per point. It is important to know to what decimal points the currency pair (e.g. GBPUSD) being traded is actually quoted for trading purposes. For the vast majority of currency pairs, the number of decimal points is four. There are some notable exceptions, such as USDJPY, which is quoted to two numbers after the decimal point.

However, in the example of GBP against USD, one point relates to the fourth number after the decimal point; in this case, 4 (i.e. 1.2464), with the fifth number after the decimal point being redundant for trading purposes. As a general rule of thumb on trading platforms, in fact, the last number that appears after the decimal point on the right is always redundant for trading purposes. It is simply there for trading platforms to show that their quotes are very tight (i.e. the difference in price between their bid price on the left and their offer price on the right – called 'the spread', from which platforms make an in-built profit – is very close numerically).

So, in this example, let us say that the trader wants to trade £1 per point. This means that if the GBPUSD rate goes up to 1.2465 then he makes a £1 profit (if it goes up to 1.2466, then a £2 profit etc; 2 points X £1 per point), and he makes a loss if it goes the other way in the same proportions.

[Chart Key:
A = Trader decides on trading £1 per point movement
B = This 'value' is not the amount that the trader has invested, it is purely a technical function that is used by the trading platform for internal accounting procedures; the trader has only risked £1 per point in this example]

4. At this point, **it is absolutely essential that the trader also places a 'stop loss' order. The reason why 90% of all retail traders lose all of their investable funds within the first 90 days of beginning to trade is almost entirely due to the fact that they do not put stop loss orders on at the same time as making a trade,** and then his potential loss on the trade is uncapped and he can lose everything; it is that simple (see *Risk Management* section later on).

The trader should decide how much in total he is prepared to lose if the trade does not go his way and it can be any amount that is a multiple of the amount per point that he has placed on the trade; it can be £1 or £1,000, it simply comes down to what level of loss the trader is comfortable with.

Although there is a whole section of this book dedicated to managing risk, it is apposite to say at this point that, as a general rule of thumb, a trader – whether retail or at a major bank for that matter – should never risk more than 1% of the total capital that he has on any single trade. So, if the trader has trading capital of £10,000, for example, then on any single trade he should never allow more than £100 to be lost if the trade goes against him.

In this example, then, the stop loss order should at maximum be placed 100 points away from the entry price, as below. To effect this stop loss, the trader should click on the stop loss tab and then enter either the exchange rate that equates to £100 maximum loss or just put in the £100 figure for the amount; the choice is his. Finally, click on the 'Place Sell Market Order' tab and the deal is done (the selling of GBP and buying of USD, and also initiating the stop loss order at exactly the same time).

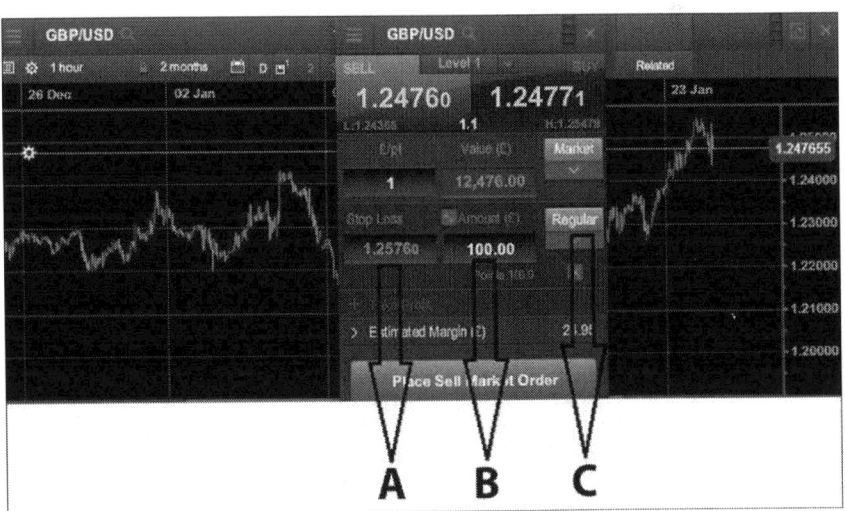

[Chart Key:
A = The trader can choose a specific price at which the stop loss order is activated
B = Or he can choose to just put a total amount in that he is prepared to lose should his trade go against him

C = 'Regular' here means that the order will be filled in most circumstances but may, in very busy markets, be filled at a slightly worse level (i.e. more loss)]

As highlighted in the above chart, the default stop loss order type is 'Regular'. This type of order means that in normal market conditions the trader's order will be filled at the price level or total amount that he has specified. However, in very busy market conditions – which often prevail – there may be some slippage on the level at which the order is filled, meaning a bigger loss than the trader bargained for.

My personal preference is to place stop loss orders on a 'Guaranteed Stop Loss Order' basis – done by simply clicking on the arrow below 'Regular' and clicking 'Guaranteed Stop Loss Order' instead. By doing this, although there is a small fee attached to it (dependent on the trading platform), the trader is absolutely guaranteed that his stop loss order will be filled at exactly the correct level, completely capping his loss at the required price level (or total amount).

Market Order Types (Applicable To All Asset Trading)

1. **Stop Loss (SL):** as described in detail above, this is without doubt the most important type of order, allowing traders to manage their risk entirely. No trade should ever be executed without a stop loss order also being effected at exactly the same time.

2. **Take Profit (TP):** the opposite of a stop loss, the take profit order, as the name suggests, allows a trader to close out his 'open position' (i.e. a trade that is still live) at a level selected by the trader in advance. So, using our GBPUSD trade example above,

the trader sold GBP (and bought USD) at a rate of 1.24760 (recall that the fifth number after the decimal point is irrelevant to the amount traded per point). Consequently a take profit order would be placed at a level (lower) that the trader expects it to reach and that he is happy to liquidate his position at; perhaps 1.24050. Therefore, at the same time that the trade is put on(or it can be done later), the trader puts on both his stop loss and his take profit.

The benefit of putting on a take profit order is that it allows the trader to lock-in his profit when he cannot or does not want to monitor his position on a real-time basis; that is, if he has a day job, or if he is called away from his screen for some other reason, or simply if he wants time away from watching his screen.

For traders just starting out (and indeed for those who have been in the business for some time), it also militates against fiddling around with positions – either because a trader begins to doubt his trade or because of boredom – which more often than not results in very poor trading.

3. **Limit (LMT):** this is an instruction to initiate the buying or selling of an asset when the price hits a certain level. Using the earlier GBPUSD example, then, it may be that the trader thinks it is more likely to go down than up but he thinks that this is much more likely to be a sustained downmove if it breaks a certain level (based on technical analysis or macro and political considerations, for example). Therefore, he puts a limit order in that effectively says 'if GBPUSD trades at 1.2450 then I sell GBP, £1 per point'. The trader should note that at the same time as putting on a limit order he should also put on a stop loss order as well, of course.

4. **Trailing Stop Loss (TSL):** As the name suggests, this is basically an order that allows the trader to completely limit his loss should his trade move against him. The key difference, though, is that if his trade is moving in the right direction (i.e. where he thought it

would, making him money) then the level of this stop loss moves as well in parallel at a distance in points specified by the trader. So, again using the GBPUSD example, let us say that the short GBP trade was done at the 1.24760 level and the stop loss was put on 20 points away at 1.24960 (meaning that the trader would lose a maximum of £20 if GBP starts going up instead of down). If GBP starts weakening (i.e. going down) as the trader thought it would then the trailing stop loss order follows it at a distance of 20 points. Consequently, if it goes to GBPUSD1.24200 then the trader's stop loss automatically re-adjusts to 1.2440 and so on. If it goes in the other direction then the original stop loss level is kept in place.

This type of order is extremely useful in allowing traders to lock-in profits in a market that is moving their way.

5. **One Cancels The Other (OCO):** This is useful again for occasions when the trader cannot or does not want to be in front of his screen monitoring positions live. It allows for the handling of a combination of orders to be placed into a trading platform: principally, initiating a position (limit order), protecting the downside (stop loss order) and closing out at a profit (take profit order). For example, with the GBPUSD trade a possibility in the trader's mind (not already executed), the trader could leave the following OCO order: if GBPUSD hits 1.24500 then sell GBP £1 per point with a stop loss at 1.24700 and a take profit at 1.24050 but if GBPUSD hits 1.24700 then buy GBP £1 per point with a stop loss at 1.24500 (i.e. it now becomes a buy GBP trade not a sell GBP trade) and a take profit at 1.24950 OCO.

OCO orders can be used in any combination that the trader wants: to remove a stop loss if a certain trade is done, or a take profit, or adjunct trades.

6. **Duration:** This is not, in and of itself, a type of thematic order but deals with timing of the above type of orders. However, when

considering the above types of orders thinking about timing is always useful and sometimes highly instructive.

a. Day – this type of order is only active for a regular trading session and then automatically expires
b. Good Til Cancelled (GTC) – this is valid either until the trader specifically cancels it, or it is executed (sometimes platforms cancel these if they have not been either executed or cancelled by the trader anywhere from 30 to 90 days, so traders need to check whether their trading platform has these restrictions before placing GTC orders).
c. Good Til Date (GTD) – as with GTC except the order is only valid until a certain date.
d. Immediate Or Cancel (IOC) – this requires that an order is filled, either wholly or in part, immediately or the order is automatically cancelled.
e. Fill Or Kill (FOK) – like the IOC, except all of the order has to be filled immediately (partial fills are not acceptable) or the order is automatically cancelled.
f. At The Opening (ATO) – as the name suggests, this order must be executed the second the market opens or it is automatically cancelled, whilst the 'At The Close' (ATC) order mist be done at the end of the market session as close to the closing price as possible or it is automatically null and void.
g. Minute – these are orders that exist for a pre-defined number of minutes only and then automatically cancel out. They are most effectively used if a trader anticipates the possibility of a sudden market move that might re-define market trend but he is not sure.

Important Fundamental Principles For FX Trading

Money Goes To Where It Is Best Rewarded...

This maxim and the next one are applicable to the investment universe as a whole. Clearly, if someone has £100 to freely invest, then that person is more likely to invest it in a place that provides him with 10% interest (or dividends in the case of stocks) per year rather than 0% interest per year. Exactly the same basic principle applies to investment in all asset classes, as investors are always looking for the best return.

For The Concomitant Risk Involved...

However, this is balanced against the concomitant risk involved in any single investment. For example, the yield on Zimbabwe bonds might be, say, 100% per year whilst the yield on US bonds might be, say, 5% per year. But a trader's chance of losing all of his money invested in Zimbabwe bonds is a lot higher than the chance of losing it from an investment in US bonds. This balancing act of reward against risk factors is the 'risk curve'; that is, the **worse an economy is perceived to be doing (gauged by the range of economic and fundamental indicators delineated below) the more reward investors will want as compensation to hold an asset of that country (either through interest rates or dividend payments).**

In very simple terms, returning to the £100 cash in the hand investment scenario, a simple risk curve can be viewed as follows:

- Keep it in **cash** where it cannot be found or lost = no risk/no reward.

- Keep it in a **bank in a 'safe' country** (a relative term nowadays, of course, but some developed market countries are obviously still safer than others, especially in emerging markets) = 1-3% reward/only risk is the bank going bust.

- Invest in **developed market government bonds** = slightly higher reward than a bank/slightly higher risk attached to potential uncertainty over government (e.g. Greek bonds during its crisis)

- Keep it in a **bank in a less safe country (an emerging or frontier market)** = 5% plus reward/higher risk of the bank going bust.

- Invest it into a **developed market index tracker** = potentially higher reward, if based on historical gains over the past 100 years/higher risk of a market slump, although this is spread over all of the shares in the index.

- Invest in **one particular developed market stock** = potentially even higher reward (dividend)/higher risk of something catastrophic happening to that one particular company (for example, BP's oil spill).

- Invest in **emerging markets index tracker** = potentially even higher reward (dividend)/higher risk of something catastrophic happening to that index (for example, dramatic change of a government etc).

- Invest in **commodities/non-government developed market bonds or FX** = potentially unlimited reward/unlimited risk (if not handled correctly, which is where education, training, strategy, order placing and risk management strategy come in).

- Invest in **one particular emerging markets stock** = potentially even higher reward (dividend)/higher risk of something catastrophic happening to that one particular company (for example, nationalisation of a major company by the government).

But Supply And Demand Dynamics Are Also Vital...

Each of the above serves to define the demand profile for all assets but there is also the **supply element** of the equation to factor in. So, therefore, a currency can also weaken if a country embarks on a 'quantitative easing' policy – that is, printing money (as the US's Fed, the Bank of Japan, the European Central Bank and the Bank of England, among the major central banks, did for a while) – or if the money supply figures start to rise for other reasons (if it is exporting a lot of goods then people are paying out lots of that currency for those goods and will then sell that currency back into their own currency for day to day living).

As Are Market Perceptions

The financial markets are a very small, insulated world, in which **it is not just what is real that counts and has trading resonance in currencies (and other asset classes) but what is perceived to be true or might happen.**

Consequently, it does not actually matter whether, for example, the Eurozone is actually going to break up and with it the EUR but whether dealers perceive that it may and to what degree that perception has taken hold. As such, most fundamental economic figures are not important so much for what they actually represent but rather for what they portend.

Basic Models For FX Trading

Purchasing Power Parity (PPP)

In basic terms, **this means that two currencies will find an equilibrium point at a level where the same product/service costs the same in each country, having taken into account the exchange rate.**

A commonly used example of this is the McDonalds' 'Big Mac' index. So, for example, if a Big Mac costs USD2 in the US and GBP1 in Great Britain then the exchange rate should be, according to the PPP measure, GBP1:USD2.

The PPP, then, also reflects inflationary data, as if inflation went up in Great Britain to a degree that it cost GBP2 for a Big Mac then the exchange rate would be parity between the two currencies – that is, GBP1:USD1.

Clearly the PPP, alongside other of these measures, are of longer-term use in discerning trading patterns.

Interest Rate Parity (IRP)

This is much more useful to know in the short term, as it occurs within a relatively quick time of interest rates being adjusted in a currency's country of origin.

IRP is simply a function of the notion that money goes to where it is best rewarded, as earlier. So if interest rates in both Great Britain and the US are at 1% and the price of a Big Mac is £1 in GBP and $2 in USD (so the exchange rate, according to PPP is GBPUSD2) if interest rates in Great Britain double to 2% then, all other things remaining equal, it would mean twice as many USD being held for every GBP than before. Therefore, on this basis alone, the exchange rate would be GBPUSD4.

Key Economic Indicators For FX And Other Assets

Interest Rates And Inflation

As alluded to above, **interest rates are perhaps the key determinant in FX rates globally.** All other factors remaining equal, if one country raises its interest rates to above those of another country then the former's currency will become stronger than the latter's as investment capital moves from the latter to the former.

Interest rates, in basic terms, are a key tool for a government in managing its economy. **Interest rates will go up when an economy is becoming overheated – i.e. inflation is increasing to beyond the point at which a government deems it healthy (a little inflation is a healthy thing, anything from 1% to 5% as a rule of thumb, depending on whether an economy is 'developed', 'emerging' or 'frontier').** This means in practical terms that money becomes more expensive, people spend less, demand decreases, manufacturers cannot increase their prices and thus prices stay the same and, of course, the converse is true.

The last few years in the West in the run-up to the Financial Crisis are instructive in this context. In the UK, for example, interest rates were low for many years, meaning that people could borrow money (from banks, on credit cards and so on) for very little in terms of interest repayments. As such, prices increased, the stock market boomed, house prices boomed and people had lots of 'things'. Eventually this resulted in a housing and stock market bubble, which then spent years bursting, and from which we are still seeing fallout.

In fact, this low interest rate scenario usually has the effect of increasing inflation – that is, more people are in a position to buy, for example, a DVD player, and thus the makers of DVD players raise their prices, increase supply or both.

If inflation is not contained in this scenario then there is the danger that it will spiral out of control, meaning that eventually the increasing price of DVD players would reach such a level that people would have to ask for pay rises. **More pay would mean more money in the economy, which would mean more DVD players being sold, which would mean prices going up further, which means more pay rises and so on and so forth: a never-ending upwards spiral. The logical conclusion of this was found in Weimar Germany where a wheelbarrow full of currency was eventually required to buy a loaf of bread,** or even today in countries such as Zimbabwe, in which the currency has become meaningless pieces of paper. Using the UK scenario, in the midst of such increasing supply of money, the value of GBP would collapse as a product of supply and demand. In this event, interest rates would have to rise to curtail price increases and the converse is true.

Consequently, **when figures are released showing that inflation in a country looks to be headed upwards, towards levels that a government will not tolerate (a little inflation is necessary to keep an economy expanding), dealers believe that the likelihood of interest rates being increased has been raised and thus the currency is likely to appreciate (money goes to where it is best rewarded) and the currency will be bought.** And, of course, the converse is true.

The chart below shows the effect that an anticipated increase in interest rates had on the NZD in June 2010; incidentally, this rise was due to growing inflationary pressures in the country. Speculation that the New Zealand government would raise rates began around 8 June; the actual rise was on 10 June.

NZDUSD (Historical)

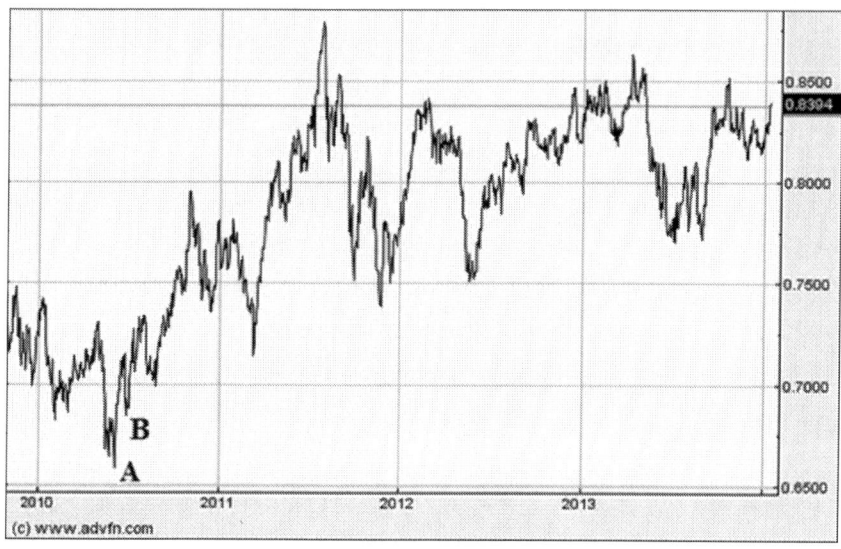

[Chart Key:
A = Market hears rumours that bolster expectations that the central bank will raise interest rates
B = Interest rates hikes are announced]

It is apposite to note here that there are **two key inflation figures released by most countries: the Consumer Price Index (CPI) and the Producers Price Index (PPI).** The UK also introduced the Retail Price Index, which includes items such as housing, which the government tends to play down, as it is often much worse for political purposes than the CPI.

The former can be viewed as prices relating to what people have to spend on a day to day basis to keep their lives ticking over: food, travel, clothing and so on, and this is the more important of the two inflation measures. The latter, in the meantime, deals with expenses that producers of the things people buy incur: machinery, fuel, staples and so on.

It is important to note that **rises or falls in the PPI are often a precursor to the same in the CPI.** This makes sense from the cost-push inflationary aspect as if the prices of raw materials/services used to make goods go up (PPI) then the price of goods/services will tend to go up (CPI).

Trade Flows (Including Manufacturing And Services Figures)

As it sounds, these are the **amounts of goods and services that are sold or bought between two countries,** and they have a major effect on currencies, as goods and services bought have to be paid for ultimately in the currency of the country manufacturing these goods or providing these services.

If a country (say, the US) buys more goods and services from another country (say, Japan) than the other country buys from it, then the latter's currency will be prone to rise against the former's. In practical terms, let us say that only Japan makes DVD players (which cost USD1 each in the US) and only the US makes baseball caps (which cost JPY100 each in Japan).

Citizens of the US buy 2 DVD players (JPY200 total), whilst those of Japan buy 1 cap (USD1 total). Japan will then have USD2 in the bank, which it will then sell, buying JPY that can be used in Japan. Conversely, the US will then have JPY100, which it will then sell, buying USD that can be used in the US. Clearly, then, in this case, twice as many USD are being sold and converted into JPY as the other way around. The logical conclusion of this is that the JPY will become in shorter supply than the USD and that, the laws of supply and demand being as they are, it will rise in value against the USD. In fact, **this is precisely why the JPY did not collapse during the many years it endured of complete domestic economic stagnation, as the country was for many years a net exporter (sells more goods and services to other countries than it buys).**

The apotheosis of this idea is in China (the ultimate net exporter), although here the effect on the currency is dampened because the government manages the CNY very carefully, and instead of allowing it to strengthen markedly (and thus make its goods more expensive relative to those of other exporters) it merely banks the excess foreign currencies in its central bank reserves (which are the largest in the world).

In real trading terms, these trade flows are summed up in a country's **Trade Balance** figure, which shows net exports minus net imports. Over time, an imbalance here will affect a country's currency, for the reason explained above.

In this context, the release of the indices by the US Institute for Supply Management's (ISM) on non-manufacturing businesses (which cover around 90% of the US economy) should be watched closely.

Exactly the same notion applies to a country's **capital flows,** which measures inflows of foreign capital entering a country in order to invest in its markets against outflows. Clearly again, if outflows are greater than inflows then a country's currency is prone to weaken.

GDP

This again is a **huge figure in trading terms, as it measures the rate of expansion or contraction in a country's economy.**

Although it is possible for a country's currency to rise in the absence of economic expansion (Japan, for example, during its long-running economic stagnation period), more commonly a currency will go down over time if it is either stagnant or contracting. Aside from anything else, an economy that is not growing will not produce sufficient goods and services to maintain its trade and capital flows and thus, for the reasons outlined above, is prone to decline.

The **real GDP figure is the one to look out for,** as it makes comparisons between different time periods easier, taking into account differing levels of inflation.

Additionally important to note is that **the real GDP figure will usually be lower than the CPI** figure, as the former also takes into account the extra portion of investment goods, which are not in the CPI and which tend to have lower inflationary levels than anything contained in the CPI.

Employment

This is often **a huge figure in trading terms,** with employment seen as a crucial sign of economic buoyancy, which finds its ultimate resolution and clarification in the GDP number, as above, and also in inflation (and thus in interest rates).

High unemployment will generally result in a lower level of goods and services being sold in a country, which, in turn, will affect its trade and capital flows and drive a currency down, all other factors remaining equal. Low unemployment will result in a burgeoning GDP, more positive trade balances and a currency moving up over time. High levels of employment, though, also bring with it the distinct possibility of rising inflation, as employed people have more money to spend than unemployed ones, and thus prices tend to rise in such an environment.

However, as mentioned earlier, **inflation only becomes a concern to the market if a government appears to be avoiding measures to tackle it,** whereas those governments that increase interest rates will likely benefit from a strengthening currency.

The unemployment figures of all major countries are a major trading factor, but perhaps the most important is the **US Non-Farm Payrolls** figure, as the US is the Western cornerstone of global economic growth (the Eastern one is China, of course). This is released by the US Department of Labor Statistics at 8:30 a.m. US Eastern time on the first Friday of every month. It estimates the total number of paid workers in the US, excluding those working in the Government, private household employees, non-profit organisations and farm workers. Together, 'non-farm' employees account for about 80% of US GDP.

As with all figures, major or minor, **it is not so much a case of what the figure actually is or what it means for an economy but rather how it compares to market expectations of what it should be.** Hence, if, as demonstrated below, the market believes that US employment is likely to increase at a certain level but the figure comes in at a level lower than those expectations then that country's currency will fall. The chart below shows the effect of the anticipation that previous estimates that employment conditions would continue to improve significantly were mistaken.

USDCHF (Historical)

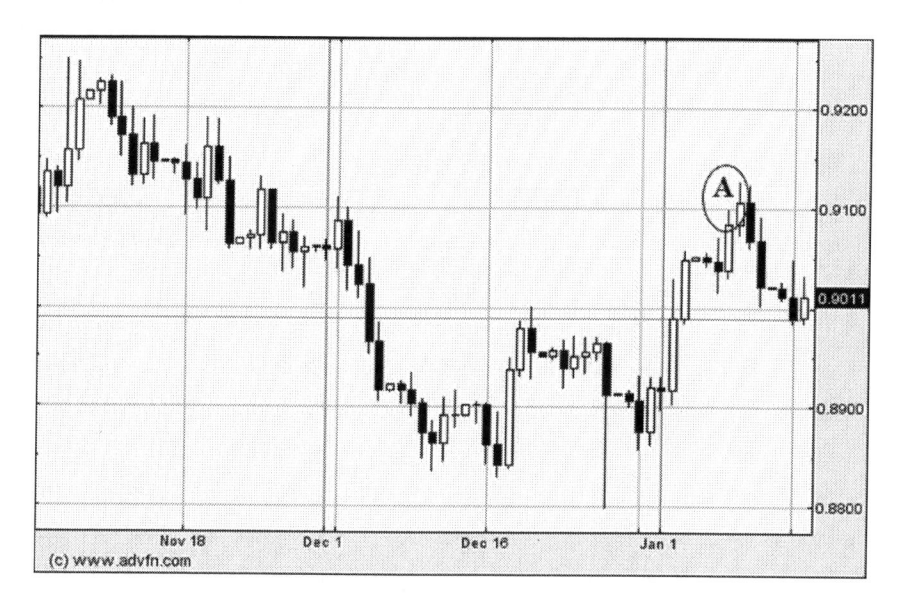

[Chart Key:
A = release of numbers showing that the rate of recent declines in the US unemployment figures slowed, raising some questions about the sustainability of the US Federal Reserve's intention to continue to taper down its buying of bonds for quantitative easing purposes]

Two problems of which to be aware in trading NFP figures are: first, that they **tend to be revised at various points close to the**

initial announcement (and thus, **a false move** is very common – e.g. a move down followed by a move up or vice-versa); and second, **they are released at a time when there are very few major market participants in the market** (London traders are generally down the pub by that time on a Friday, New York traders are probably making their way to their country houses in Connecticut and Asia is asleep), so these moves **tend to be very violent** one way and then the other.

Personal Spending/Consumption

This clearly will be reflected over time in one or other of the **CPI or RPI measurements,** but it is important to look at these indicators when they come out. The key ones that traders look out for are durable goods (those which are expected to last at least three years) and non-durable goods (those which are not). Spikes or dips in these will provide guidance as to whether or not a country's economy is expanding or contracting and thus the direction of inflation and then interest rates.

Housing figures are extremely important in this category, as, if an economy is looking poorly, people fear for their job security and thus will be less likely to undertake the single biggest purchase that most will make in a lifetime; and, of course, the reverse is true.

Often the housing figures (new homes sales, existing home sales and so forth) will act as a precursor to a rise/fall in CPI/RPI, as people tend to cut back/increase their lesser spending only after they have dealt with their immediate housing needs.

Business Confidence/Consumer Confidence Indices

Organisations and governments love to produce these indices (often on a scale of 0-100, where 100 reflects total confidence, 0 no confidence and anywhere above 50 shows overall optimism) for both of the above-mentioned categories.

The key ones are as follows, in no particular order, beginning with the **Philadelphia Fed Index,** which is a regional Federal Reserve Bank index based on a monthly survey of manufacturers located around the states of Pennsylvania, New Jersey and Delaware. Participants from companies which are voluntarily surveyed indicate the direction of change in their overall business activity. When the index is above 0 it indicates a factory-sector expansion and when below 0, it indicates contraction.

German IFO is again a business confidence index, which shows how confident or not businesses are of future prospects, on a scale of 0-100. This is especially important for the euro, given Germany's position as the powerhouse economy of the Eurozone.

The Chinese business confidence indices are the equivalent in terms of setting the tone for many emerging markets, as both of the above for their respective trading blocs.

Generally, any index that has a corporate name in it should be regarded as a second-tier indicator, if that.

Credit Ratings

As with people's individual credit ratings that allow them to buy a house or car on credit, a country's credit rating is a product of perception (in this case, the market's perception) of how able it is to generate sufficient income to cover its debts. Broadly speaking, the better the grade, the better a currency and all other assets of a country will be supported.

Of the three credit ratings agencies shown in the chart below, it is widely viewed that **Moody's and Standard & Poor's** (S&P) are the two most important, although Fitch ratings are well worth looking at as well. **The reason for looking at the first two is that these are the ratings that all major investors – hedge funds and 'real money' funds (pension funds, insurance companies and similar long-term horizon players) – look at in determining their broad investment risk parameters and consequent approaches.** For example, as a rule of thumb, the real money funds will be working under the auspices of an overarching investment mandate that governs all of their investment decisions, typically including provisions that allow them only to invest in assets that have a minimum (and high) credit rating, such as AA and upwards.

Credit Ratings Risk Profiles

Moody's		S&P		Fitch		
Long-term	Short-term	Long-term	Short-term	Long-term	Short-term	
Aaa		AAA		AAA		Prime
Aa1		AA+	A-1+	AA+	F1+	High grade
Aa2	P-1	AA		AA		
Aa3		AA-		AA-		
A1		A+	A-1	A+	F1	Upper medium grade
A2		A		A		
A3	P-2	A-	A-2	A-	F2	
Baa1		BBB+		BBB+		
Baa2	P-3	BBB	A-3	BBB	F3	Lower medium grade
Baa3		BBB-		BBB-		
Ba1		BB+		BB+		Non-investment grade speculative
Ba2		BB		BB		
Ba3		BB-	B	BB-	B	
B1		B+		B+		Highly speculative
B2		B		B		
B3		B-		B-		
Caa1	Not prime	CCC+				Substantial risks
Caa2		CCC				Extremely speculative
Caa3		CCC-	C	CCC	C	
Ca		CC				In default with little prospect for recovery
		C				
C		D	/	DDD	/	In default
/				DD		

The practical effect of this is broadly threefold. First, these trades will be fairly crowded, as there is a lot of money held in **real money funds** that have to find sufficiently well-rated assets in which to park their money. Second, these trades will tend to be priced to the high side, for the supply and demand reason just outlined. And third, they are usually less prone to quick, large moves (i.e. exceptional volatility), as the investors in them are not of the 'cut and run, churn and burn' variety.

This type of move is more associated with **hedge funds,** and for good reason. A large part of their returns are generated from big price swings, which often occur when an asset suddenly appears to be incorrectly rated (this relates to all asset markets, including currencies, although in this latter regard the 'rating' is not of the official variety but rather of the 'market perception' one). Often, hedge funds will be instrumental in causing a run on a particular asset, either by being nimble enough to invest quickly in an asset that is genuinely under- or over-valued and being the first ones in the trade in size, or simply by spooking the broader market into a trade that the hedge funds want simply by massive leveraged buying or selling of that asset, irrespective of the fundamental merits of the trade.

So, **knowing what the 'Big Two' ratings are and, more importantly, being cognisant of potential changes to them is a key to knowing what sort of money is likely to be the dominant investment in the asset and consequently how vulnerable it is to sudden shocks and how quickly it will move based on these. (All ratings agencies will broadcast, usually a relatively long time in advance, whether or not a rating is 'Under Review' and whether that is for a possible upgrade or downgrade.)**

Looking at Fitch's ratings is an important auxiliary to the Big Two as this agency has always tended towards taking a more realistic view towards its analysis of assets and countries than the others, for reasons outlined immediately below.

The Big Lie Behind Ratings

The major caveat to highlight at this point is that knowing what the ratings are is one thing – it is necessary in understanding how the institutional money is likely to be positioned in any asset, as mentioned – but **knowing that ratings are in reality often completely inaccurate is another, as this allows the investor to** act in the same manner as a hedge fund, pre-empting corrections in an asset's value based on reality hitting perception.

In this context, it is absolutely essential to know that – unbelievably to most people, whether a professional bank or fund trader or a retail one – **it is the owner of the asset that pays the ratings agencies to rate the asset! Each of the two big ratings agencies know that if they do not give the owner of the asset a rating that is in line with the owner's belief of what it should be then the owner will simply go to the other one and negotiate for a better rating.** More broadly, if one of the big two ratings agencies gets a reputation for 'being tough on ratings awards' then it will quite simply go out of business, as no asset owner will employ it to rate their products.

The Global Financial Crisis that hit in 2007/08 showed the Big Two credit ratings agencies to be at best incompetent and at worst collusive. Indeed, just prior to the Crisis, the Big Two agencies were still rating the big investment banks – for example Lehman Brothers and Bear Stearns – as AA or better, even as they were going bust. Even on a sovereign level, they continued to play the tune of the guys paying the piper, continuing to rate Iceland as a prime credit, even as its entire financial system unravelled.

The point here is that **being aware of the ratings of the Big Two is essential, as is knowledge that they are in many key cases fundamentally flawed and incorrect, as neither of them have changed their business procedures since the Crisis: their businesses still largely depend on being paid for ratings by the people who want the ratings.**

Only Foreign Currency Ratings Are Important

Also important to bear in mind is that it is **the foreign currency credit ratings of a country that are important,** not the local currency rating, as a country can always simply print more money to meet its local currency debts but cannot print more foreign currency to meet its foreign obligations.

The major global exception to the first point here is for the constituent countries of the Eurozone, which are dependent on the European Central Bank (ECB) for printing money. This dependence on a non-indigenous central bank, together with the fact that the euro's value does not reflect the inherent state of an individual member's economy in the same way that its former currency could, is at the heart of the essential problem in the alliance.

The importance of sovereign credit ratings to a country's currency can be seen below in the deleterious effect on the EUR of a four notch downgrade by Moody's of Greece's foreign currency debt profile, from A3 to Ba1. This pattern has been repeated whenever there is speculation that another of the Eurozone's fiscally-challenged members may about to be downgraded. The converse, of course, is true for an upgrade scenario.

EURUSD (Historical)

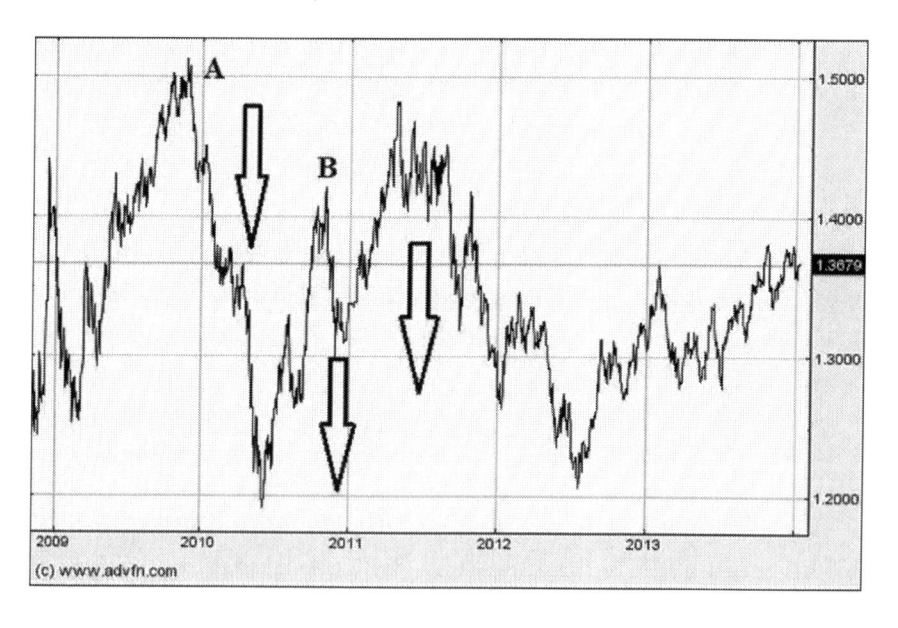

[Chart Key:

A = In October 2009, the newly elected government of Greece revealed that previous Greek governments had been underreporting the country's budget deficit. The underreporting was exposed through a revision of the forecast for the 2009 budget deficit from 6%-8% of GDP (no greater than 3% of GDP was a rule of the Maastricht Treaty that underpinned membership of the Eurozone) to 12.7%. Markets learned that Greece's debt was well over EUR400bn and that France owned 10% of that debt, highlighting the risk of bad debt contagion across the Zone and raising questions about other 'weaker' countries in the Zone, including Ireland, Portugal, Italy and Spain, and, by extension, the security and creditworthiness of the entire European banking system.

B = On 23 April 2010, the Greek government requested an initial loan of EUR45bn from the EU and International Monetary Fund (IMF) to cover its financial needs for the remaining part of 2010. A few days later S&P slashed Greece's sovereign debt rating to BB+ or 'junk' status amid fears of default, in which case investors were liable to lose 30–50% of their money].

The Basics Of Equities Trading

A Good Starter Market For Those New To Trading

Although not as large as the FX market, **the equities market does have two advantages over FX for the new retail trader:** first, it is probably **more familiar to most people than FX,** given that many primetime news bulletins often contain stories or updates about the FTSE100 and occasionally the US, Japanese and European equities markets; and second, it **involves just one trade,** either buying or selling an index (i.e. the aggregate value of a country's listed stocks, like the FTSE 100 in the UK, the Dow Jones Industrial Average in the US, the Nikkei 225 in Japan and the DAX in Germany, for example) or individual stocks.

It is true that, despite a swathe of regulation around the globe, these markets are prone to more manipulation than the FX market by those in possession of market-moving information ahead of the vast majority of others trading them – especially in the case of individual stocks – but for the most part, the playing field is relatively level, particularly when it comes to **trading indices, which is the best thing to trade to begin with.**

In looking at a selection of the various key equities investment styles to begin with, a useful analogy would be that of shooting a movie: the opening shot might be a wide-angle of a street ('top-down' trading, particularly applicable in index trading, as below), then the angle is narrowed to the door of a particular house ('bottom-up' trading, especially apposite to individual stock trading, as below), then to the inhabitants inside (management-focussed trading considerations, for individual stock trading) and then to one particular tight angle shot (key investment ratios, applicable to both index trading and individual stock trading).

Index Trading

A basic point that many people outside the financial markets do not know is that **the level of a stock index actually does mean something; is not just a relative indication of strength or weakness.** When a commentator says that the FTSE 100, for example, is trading at 7,000 this number is the market quotation of each of its listed companies' shares added together. Literally, if one had the time and inclination, one could go through every single stock quoted in the FTSE 100 (and every other country's benchmark stock index), adding up the price of each stock, and it would total the benchmark index's quote.

There are two reasons why it is important to know this: first, it means that **actual or expected changes in big economic and political factors (i.e. 'macro' factors) can affect the value of these indices** (like changes in interest rates, inflation, employment, manufacturing levels and so on), irrespective of the individual performance of key companies listed in an index; and, second, that **individual companies can be subject to moves in the opposite direction to the way in which the benchmark index is moving at any given time, providing separate trading opportunities.**

The mechanics of trading an index are exactly the same as those pertaining to the FX market, as described above, but there are important nuances in what drive these markets, as described below.

Index Trading Utilises The First Components Of Top-Down Trading

'Top Down' trading is an **investment approach that involves looking at the big picture** (a wide-angle, using the movie analogy), beginning with the area in which a country is located, then the economic and political dimensions of that country, where it is in its business cycle (see dedicated section on *Business Cycles* later), then the various sectors of the economy and then the specific details pertaining to a target company including management and key investment numbers and ratios.

For Index Trading, though, the focus is on just the first three elements of this mix, and a number of the greatest stock investors in history have used this style of trading to outperform all others in the market, notably including George Soros and his partner Jim Rogers in their early days at Soros Fund Management.

Area-Specific Index Trading (Positive Paradigm Shifts)

When they first began, whilst George was working through the numbers on his computer, Jim would be on his motorbike attempting to spot small changes at ground level in countries that were possibly on the cusp of major changes, through seeing tiny changes in general economic behaviour. Typically this might involve Jim stopping off at a cafe in Hungary in the early 1990s and noticing that the locals were suddenly happy to spend a dollar (equivalent) on a cappuccino.

In Jim's mind this indicated the following rationale: people have more money to spend on small luxuries following Hungary's departure from the umbrella of the USSR in 1989 – therefore, people are earning more money as a whole – therefore, companies must be making more money – therefore, their earnings per share ratios will increase – therefore, current stock values will look cheap – therefore, domestic companies will attract more foreign investment – therefore, their share price will continue to go up – therefore, more companies will float on the domestic stock exchange – therefore, the aggregate value of the index is likely to rise – therefore, more money will enter into the economy – and so on in the process of creating a 'virtuous investment cycle'.

As can be seen from the chart below, buying into a nation's changing broad economic architecture – in this case moving from the confines of the Soviet-style system to that of free enterprise and the increased consumerism that this entails – yielded exceptional results for Soros and Rogers. This example can often be seen in areas that similarly undergoing such **a shift in their behavioural paradigm,** as the same investment curve can be seen across the board, for example, in every country that broke away from the former Soviet Union (Poland, Czech Republic Baltic States etc).

Hungary – Budapest Stock Exchange (BUX) After Leaving USSR (Historical)

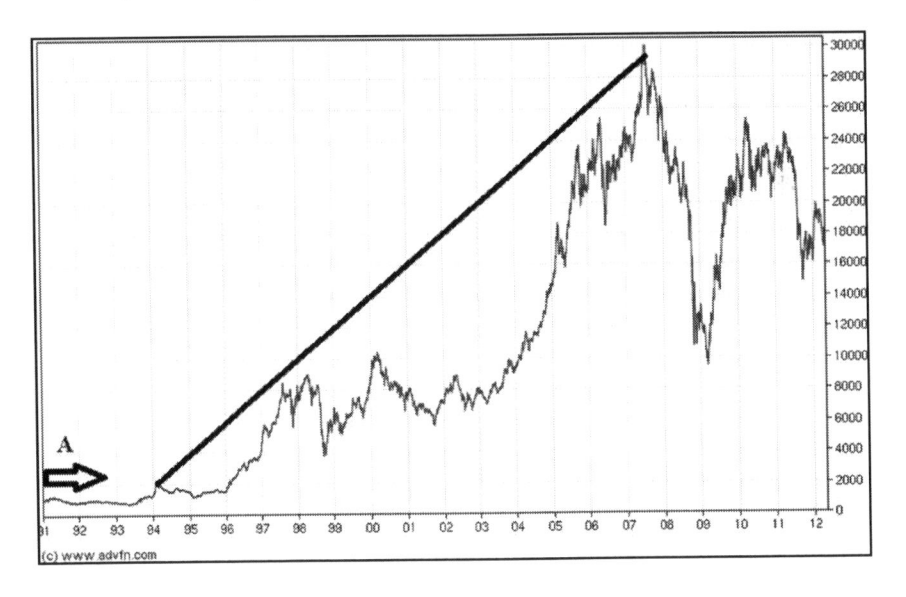

[Chart Key:

A = Straight line constant price of BUX during transition phase from leaving the USSR]

In the case of the former Soviet Union itself exactly the same theory applied as well, although with a delayed effect to those of its former satellite states, as a break with centralised state control occurred only later on, under the presidency of Boris Yeltsin, which began in December 1991.

For those Index investors who had learned the lesson from what happened to stocks (which are, after all, simply investment in companies that are, in turn, an investment on the most basic level in a country's prosperity) in the former satellite nations of the USSR then the opportunity for the next phase of investment was obvious. This opportunity was available through the Russian Trading System (RTS) Index initially, which was merged in December 2011 with the Moscow Interbank Currency Exchange (MICEX).

Russian Stock Exchange (RTS, later MICEX) After Yeltsin Took Power (Historical)

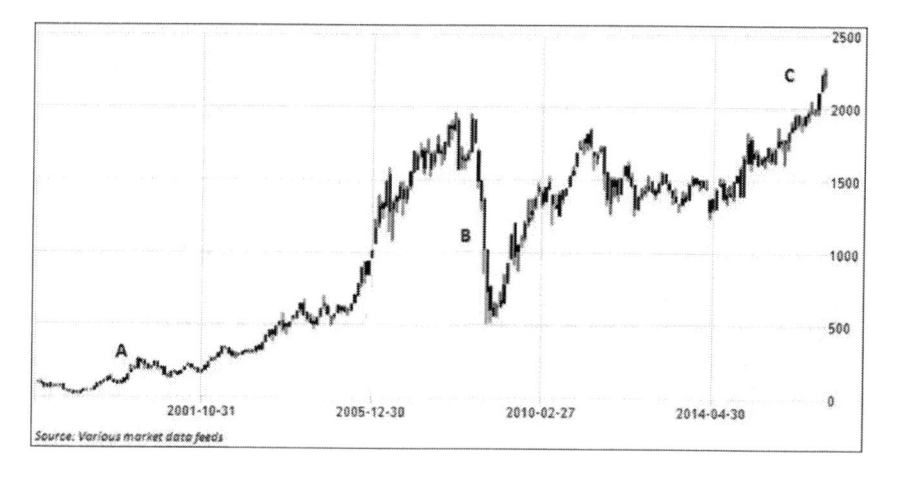

[Chart Key:
A = Yeltsin becomes President

B = 1998 Russia Crisis
C= Continued index growth]

Area-Specific Index Trading (Negative Paradigm Shifts)

At the time that the euro came into play on 1 January 1999, it was obvious to many that had been trading for many years through up and down economic and business cycles that it was a fundamentally flawed currency because the Eurozone was a fundamentally flawed idea itself.

The reasons for this notion now are exactly the same as they were at the beginning: unlike the USA, which could be regarded as a similar basic concept as the Eurozone – that is, a group of separate state economies with one currency (the USD) – the Eurozone lacked a true centralised fiscal policy (the use of taxation and expenditure to influence economic prospects), banking system or political vision. The lack of a central tax framework meant that taxes in each of the member countries of the Eurozone were set at different rates and were collected with a varying degree of efficiency (the southern states of the Eurozone were much laxer in collection than the wealthier than the northern states). Additionally, money was spent according to very different methodologies, and economies performed at very different levels.

Moreover, different member states benefited or not in vastly different ways. For Germany, the benefits of Eurozone membership were immediately extremely positive, by dint of the effective devaluation of its currency (the deutschemark) to the euro, thus making its exports significantly cheaper, leading to massive growth in exports. This can be seen in the chart below showing the country's Balance of Trade (the difference between the monetary value of exports and imports in an economy over a certain period of time).

Germany: Balance Of Trade (EUR And Equivalent)

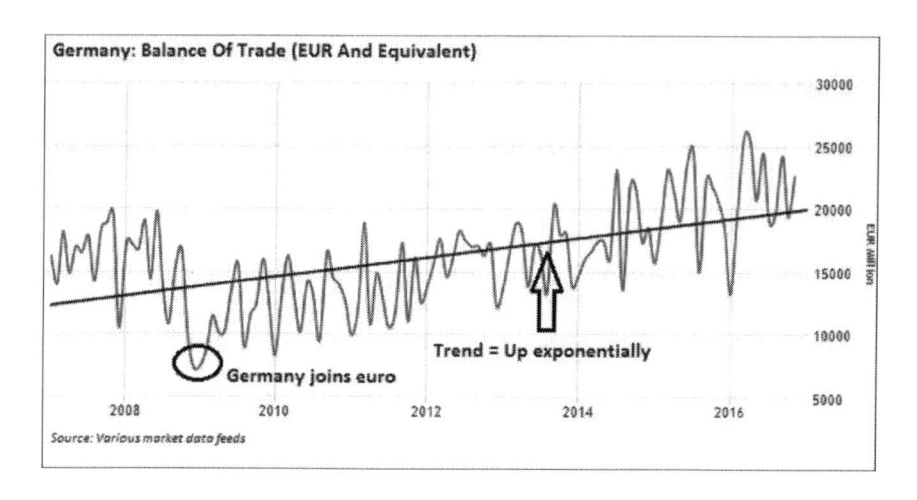

[Chart showing Germany's balance of trade from 2008 to 2016, with values ranging from 5000 to 30000 EUR millions. Annotations: "Germany joins euro" circled near 2008-2009, and "Trend = Up exponentially" with an upward arrow around 2013.]

Source: Various market data feeds

Contrast this to a country for which the introduction of the euro made its products and services more expensive than they were under their previous native currency: Greece (with the drachma formerly) is a notable newsworthy example, but any of the southern Eurozone states would show the same pattern, which is either no improvement or a decline over the period from January 1999.

In stock trading terms then this had very clear implications, worsened by the **conceptual difference between those living in the USA and those living in the Eurozone:** that is, that although those living for example in New York would view themselves firstly perhaps as New Yorkers they would also see themselves as Americans, whereas those living in, say, Spain would be unlikely to view themselves as Europeans to such a degree.

Of course, even worse for the dichotomy lying at the very heart of the Eurozone is the fact that **although the euro currency now adopted by the southern states was more expensive relative to their previous currencies, borrowing became a lot cheaper,** as the debt of countries such as Greece, Spain, Italy, Ireland and Portugal, for example, was classed alongside the debt of Germany in terms of its risk profile. This allowed the weaker states to borrow enormous sums at much lower costs than would have been the case before the introduction of the euro, which was spent largely on capital-intensive public sector ventures (and private sector property developments) and led to a huge debt pile. At the same time, the lack of real economic growth in these southern states meant that servicing the debt pile became increasingly difficult. Moreover, because the central bank of the Eurozone was not in the control of these countries as their own central bank had been, they could not simply print more of their native currency to devalue it and make exports cheaper, or reduce their interest rates to boost growth, or in fact, undertake any economic measure that would have led to a balancing of their budgets.

Because this basic discrepancy was evident across all southern states, the crisis of confidence in Greece then spread, exactly the same way as happened in the former Soviet Union states (but negatively in this case), to the remainder of the countries that were seen as bad credit risks (generally in order of how bad their vulnerability to indebtedness was viewed by the markets).

The markets are a place where traders look for signs of weakness to exploit: 'there's blood in the water' was a common refrain during the sterling currency crisis under Norman Lamont.

So the trick with Top-Down Index trading is to look beyond the immediate catastrophe for a country – for example Greece or Italy – and look to sell the indices of the countries that look like they are next in line for the sharks. This is the way traders make serious money. Below, can clearly be seen the effect of this contagion on selected markets, from late 2009 when fears about Greece's debt burden started to grow.

Greece Stock Exchange (ASE) Sparked The Hunt For Weak Indices To Sell (Historical)

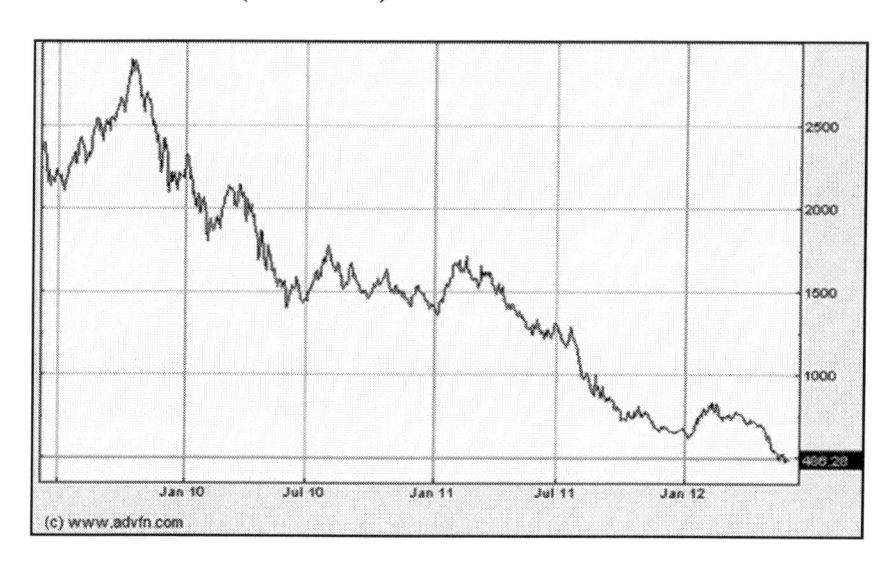

The following indices fitted the bill perfectly.

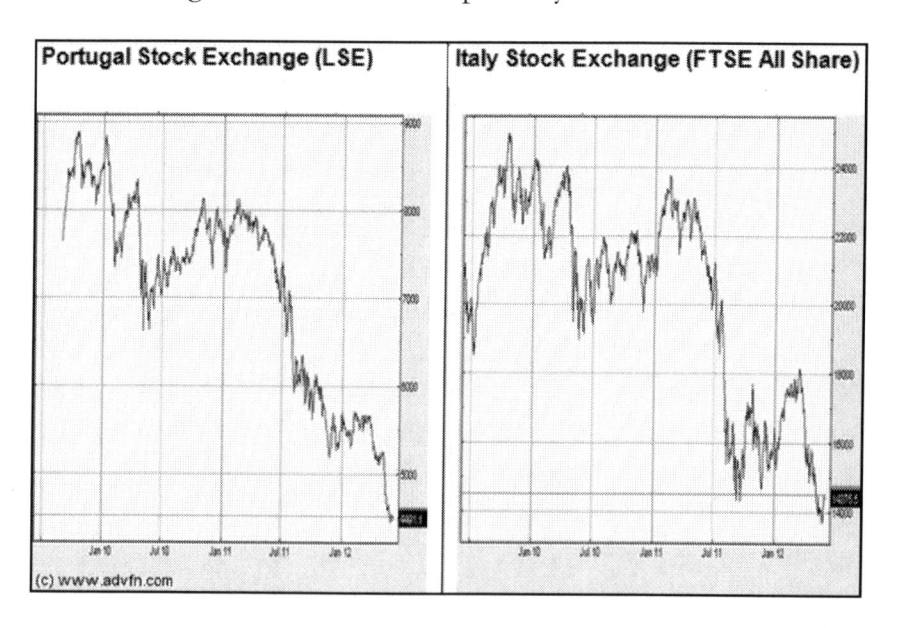

Important Fundamental Principles For Top-Down Index Trading

Interest Rates

As a basic guide to global investor flows both across regions, countries, markets and asset classes is that money flows to where it is best rewarded (via interest rate compensation or a substitute compensation, such as stock dividends) whilst taking into account the risk involved.

As an adjunct to this, interest rates are perhaps the key determinant in stocks globally (and thus the reason why inflation data is looked at so keenly as, if inflation is rising, then interest rates generally are set to rise, as an increase in rates reduces the use of credit and this spending declines).

Conversely to currencies, though, **individual domestic equities and benchmark indices will tend to go down as local interest rates are raised** for four main reasons:

1. As lower-risk investments (bank deposit accounts, savings bonds and so on) increase their return so higher risk investments (equities) will appear less marginally attractive (as highlighted above, money flows to where it is best rewarded whilst factoring in the relative risk involved).

2. Companies that have borrowed money (for expansion, or to cover cashflow requirements or whatever) will have to pay more of their overall capital back in loan repayments and interest thereupon, which means that they may be less profitable.

3. If the cost of borrowing has gone up for companies then it means that they are less likely to borrow money for corporate expansion, which again means over time that they will be less likely to grow and thus increase profits.

4. As interest rates rise, the general population are less likely to want to borrow money (either through overdrafts or credit cards or whatever) and will broadly spend less, which will hit the revenues of companies.

Australia Stock Exchange – Effect Of Expectations On Interest Rates (Historical)

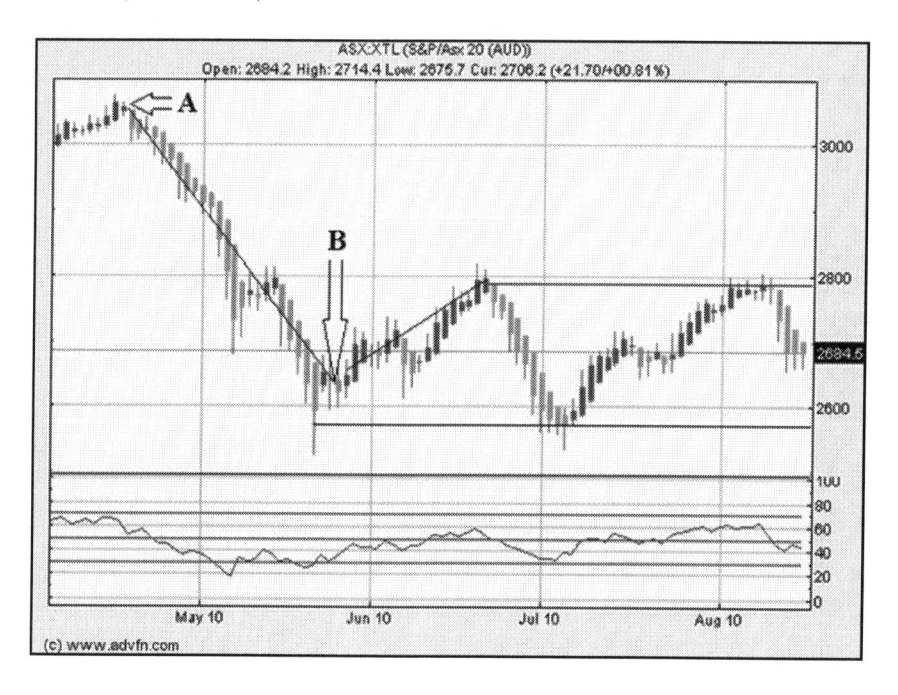

[Chart Key:
A = Australia raises interest rates to 4.5% (back in 2010)
B = Central bank signals that rates will remain steady for the foreseeable future]

Interest rates, in basic terms, are a key tool for a government in managing its economy. **If an economy is becoming overheated (i.e. inflation is increasing to beyond the point at which a government deems it healthy) then interest rates will go up.** This means in practical terms that money becomes more expensive, people spend less, demand decreases, manufacturers cannot increase their prices and thus prices stay the same (of course, the converse is true if inflation is spiralling down and interest rates are lowered).

The last few years in the West in the run-up to the Great Financial Crisis are instructive in this context. In the UK, for example, interest rates were low for many years, meaning that people could borrow money (from banks, on credit cards and so on) for very little in terms of interest repayments. As such, prices increased, the stock market boomed, house prices boomed and people had lots of 'things'. Eventually this resulted in something of a housing and stock market bubble which burst, with effects with which we are still living.

Credit Ratings

As mentioned earlier in relation to FX trading, credit ratings are a key gauge that investors use to determine the risk/reward balance by a country and, consequently, they feed through into the benchmark valuations of that sovereign state – these being its currency, its leading stock market index and its foreign currency government bonds.

Below shows the deleterious effect on the Greek Stock Exchange of a four notch (grade) downgrade by Moody's on Greece's foreign currency debt profile, to Ba1 from A3.

Athens Stock Exchange (Historical)

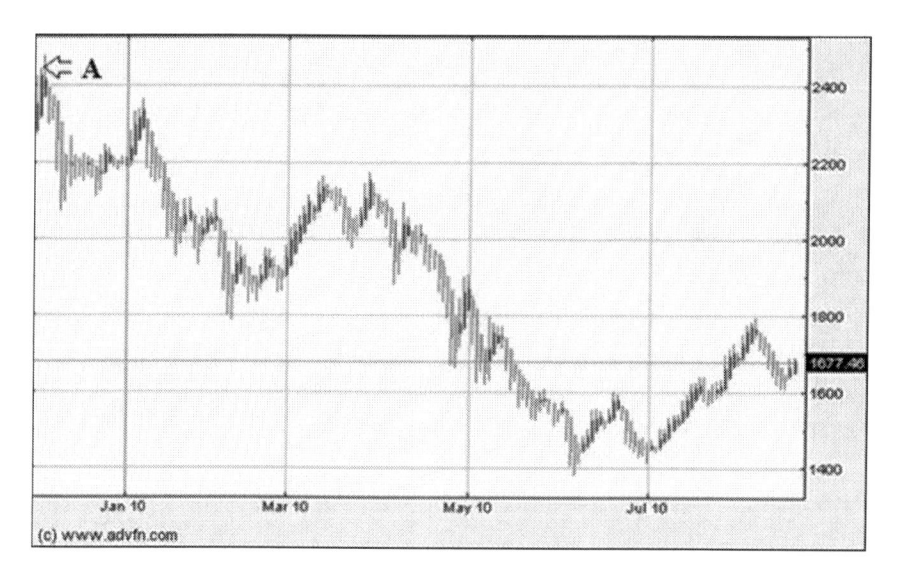

[Chart Key:
A = Point at which Fitch cuts Greece's sovereign credit rating to BBB+ and S&P puts it A- rating on watch for a possible downgrade]

This pattern has been repeated whenever there is speculation that another of the Eurozone's fiscally-challenged members may about to be downgraded. The converse, of course, is true for an upgrade scenario.

In the current still nervous global investment environment, of course, credit ratings are a major pre-occupation for investors of all kinds, not just in equities. This skittishness was reinforced as the IMF has been keen to highlight numerous times, the previous financial crisis that began in July 2007 was preceded by the considerable overrating, and hence mispricing, of safety. In this respect, high credit ratings were applied too often, both for private and sovereign issuers, and they did not sufficiently differentiate across assets with different underlying qualities (see chart below).

Historical Overview Of S&P Sovereign Debt Ratings Of Selected OECD Countries (1970-end Jan 2012)

Country	Year of First Rating	1970	1975	1980	1985	1990	1995	2000	2005	2010	2011	2012 (End-January)
Austria	1975	NR	AAA	AAA	AAA	AAA	AAA	AAA	AAA	AAA	AAA	AA+
Belgium	1988	NR	NR	NR	NR	AA+	AA+	AA+	AA+	AA+	AA	AA
Canada	1949	AAA	AAA	AAA	AAA	AAA	AA+	AA+	AAA	AAA	AAA	AAA
Denmark	1981	NR	NR	NR	AA+	AA	AA+	AA+	AAA	AAA	AAA	AAA
Finland	1972	NR	AAA	AAA	AAA	AAA	AA-	AA+	AAA	AAA	AAA	AAA
France	1975	NR	AAA	AAA	AAA	AAA	AAA	AAA	AAA	AAA	AAA	AA+
Germany	1983	NR	NR	NR	AAA	AAA	AAA	AAA	AAA	AAA	AAA	AAA
Greece	1988	NR	NR	NR	NR	BBB-	BBB-	A-	A	BB+	CC	CC
Iceland	1989	NR	NR	NR	NR	A	A	A+	AA-	BBB-	BBB-	BBB-
Ireland	1988	NR	NR	NR	NR	AA+	AA	AA+	AAA	A	BBB+	BBB+
Italy	1988	NR	NR	NR	NR	AA+	AA	AA	AA-	A+	A	BBB+
Japan	1959	NR[1]	AAA	AAA	AAA	AAA	AAA	AAA	AA-	AA	AA-	AA-
Luxembourg	1994	NR	NR	NR	NR	NR	AAA	AAA	AAA	AAA	AAA	AAA
Netherlands	1988	NR	NR	NR	NR	AAA	AAA	AAA	AAA	AAA	AAA	AAA
Norway	1958	NR[1]	AAA	AAA	AAA	AAA	AAA	AAA	AAA	AAA	AAA	AAA
Portugal	1988	NR	NR	NR	NR	A	AA-	AA	AA-	A-	BBB-	BB
Spain	1988	NR	NR	NR	NR	AA	AA	AA+	AAA	AA	AA-	A
Sweden	1977	NR	NR	AAA	AAA	AAA	AA+	AA+	AAA	AAA	AAA	AAA
Switzerland	1988	NR	NR	NR	NR	AAA	AAA	AAA	AAA	AAA	AAA	AAA
Turkey	1992	NR	NR	NR	NR	NR	B+	B+	BB-	BB	BB	BB
United Kingdom	1978	NR	NR	AAA	AAA	AAA	AAA	AAA	AAA	AAA	AAA	AAA
United States	1941	AAA	AAA	AAA	AAA	AAA	AAA	AAA	AAA	AAA	AA+	AA+

Source: IMF, S&P

Legend: AAA, AA, A, BBB, Noninvestment grade

As it now stands, in the current uncertain environment, **relative asset safety can be seen by considering a continuum of asset characteristics, composed of:** (1) low credit and market risks, (2) high market liquidity, (3) limited inflation risks, (4) low exchange rate risks and (5) limited idiosyncratic risks.

The first criterion, **low credit and market risks, is clearly pivotal to asset safety,** as a lower level of these risks tends to be linked with higher liquidity. However, high market liquidity depends on a wider array of factors, including ease and certainty of valuation, low correlation with risky assets, an active and sizable market and low market correlation, among others.

Importantly, as the IMF has underlined many times, different investors place a different emphasis on each of these criteria. For example, investors with long-term liabilities – such as pension funds and insurance companies – place limited emphasis on market liquidity and thus consider less liquid, longer maturity assets as safe. If their potential payoffs are linked to inflation and no inflation indexed securities are available, pension funds emphasise the real capital preservation aspect of safe assets.

Meanwhile for retail investors the same sort of analysis also holds true, and in this respect the idea that credit ratings agencies are all-knowing should be regarded as a highly dubious proposition to say the least.

Individual Stock Trading

There are three key elements to be considered when looking for a stock or stocks to buy or sell:

1. How the **countries in which the company firstly is based and secondly sells most of its products or services look from the macro perspective,** and this has been covered above.

2. How the **sector in which it operates is currently placed in the relevant business cycle.**

3. How the **company is performing on a basic level (principally, finances and management – known as the 'bottom-up' investment approach).**

To begin with the second point, there are broad-based long-term cycles that have important ramifications for overall portfolio structuring, with both broad and sectoral-specific implications, as delineated below.

The Kondratieff Wave

In global terms, the trader needs to be aware of the Kondratieff Wave ('K-Wave') – named after a Russian economist active in the 1920s named Nikolai Kondratieff – which seeks to show that **there are long-term cycles in the entire global capitalist economy of between 45 and 60 years – and even much longer – each that are self-correcting and evolving and are defined by the emergence of new industries in ongoing technological revolutions.** As an adjunct of this, each major cycle involves the destruction of much of the past cycle and the concomitant evolution of new innovation.

Kondratieff's theory has been refined/distorted – however you want to look at it – by various people since, but the consensus of the major examples over the past few hundred years would be:

- 1770s – the Industrial Revolution
- 1820s – the Steam and Railways age beginning
- 1870s – the Steel and Heavy Engineering move
- 1900s – the era of Oil, Electricity, Automobiles and Mass Production
- 1970s – the shift to the age of Information and Telecommunications.

It is interesting to note at this point that – arguably, although not much – **the world's most successful stock investor ever, Warren Buffett, bases his investment strategy on such fundamental paradigmatic shifts; seeking to identify the onset of a new cycle (or 'wave'), buying shares in as many solid new cycle-related businesses as he can and just sitting on them.**

In any event, the correlations between the K-Waves and key asset markets are evident from the charts below.

US Government 10-Year Yields 1790 to 2015

Kondratieff Waves

1845 1896 1949

1790 1826 1862 1898 1934 1970 2008

Source: Various market data inputs

US Stock Market In Gold Terms 1790-2015

Kondratieff Waves

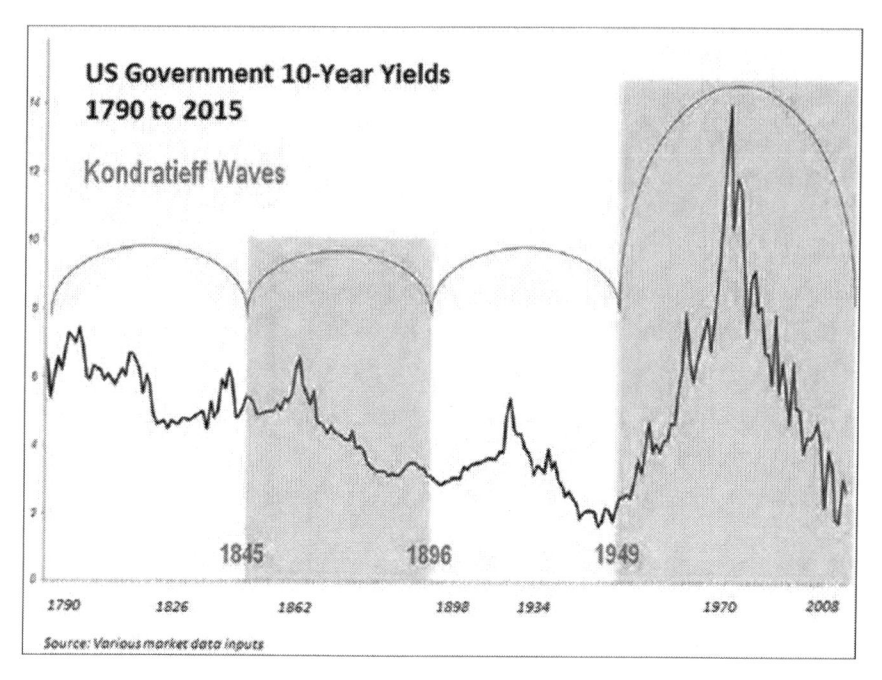

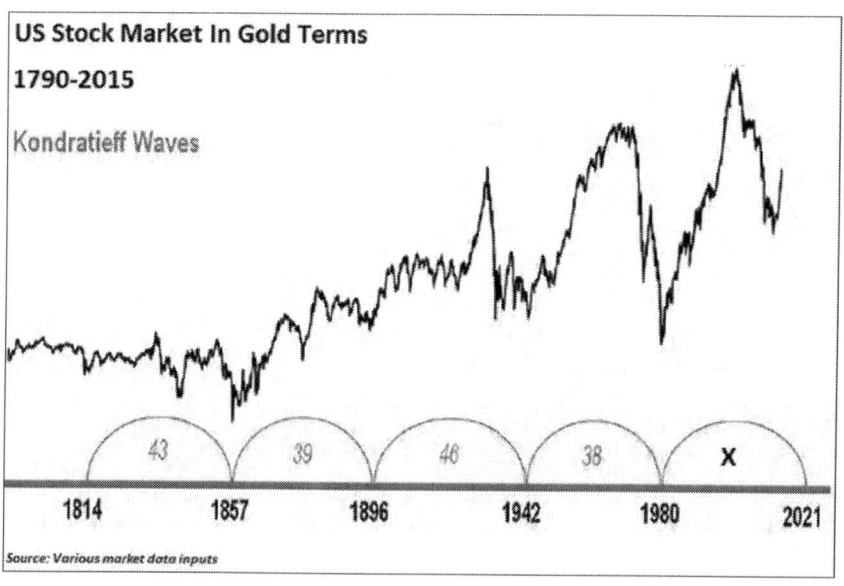

43 39 46 38 X

1814 1857 1896 1942 1980 2021

Source: Various market data inputs

In broad terms, there are four stages to the cycle described by the K-Wave:

1. At the onset of a long-term economic cycle there is likely to be a lack of confidence and a fear of falling back into slump or depression, before inflation, interest rates and credit slowly start to rise as confidence in the new age increases.

2. As the economy expands (indicated in this instance by inflation) and interest rates increase as an adjunct to this, then so business and consumer confidence grows further and credit is extended more.

3. As we enter into the final up-phase of the move, confidence levels morph into over-exuberance and extraordinary loose 'bubble-like' credit conditions, with interest rates also declining.

4. Finally, rising concerns over loose credit, inflationary upward spiral and bad debt causes business and consumer reticence to embark on new projects (in business terms, expansion and in consumer terms, new purchases), default rates increase, credit is squeezed, the economic outlook turns negative, unemployment rises, disinflation turns into deflation and we have a negative world view.

The Business Cycle

Within these long cycles, though, there are other shorter-time patterns manifesting themselves in the classic business cycle, which is the recurrent level of business activity that changes in an economy over a period of time. Here again, there are four stages of a cycle (although some maintain that there are five): full scale recession, early recovery, late recovery and early recession.

Since the Second World War, most business cycles have lasted between three and five years from peak to peak, with the average duration of an expansion being nearly four years and the average length of a recession being just under a year, although as we have seen in the most recent recession (and in the Great Depression era) recessions can last a lot longer.

According to the USA's National Bureau of Economic Research (NBER), the US has experienced 12 recessions (including the most recent one) and 11 expansions since the end of the Second World War, as shown in the chart below.

US Business Cycles Since 1857 (NBER)

BUSINESS CYCLE REFERENCE DATES		DURATION IN MONTHS			
Peak	Trough	Contraction	Expansion	Cycle	
Quarterly dates are in parentheses		*Peak to Trough*	*Previous trough to this peak*	*Trough from Previous Trough*	*Peak from Previous Peak*
June 1857(II)	December 1854 (IV)	--	--	--	--
	December 1858 (IV)	18	30	48	--
October 1860(III)	June 1861 (III)	8	22	30	40
April 1865(I)	December 1867 (I)	32	46	78	54
June 1869(II)	December 1870 (IV)	18	18	36	50
October 1873(III)	March 1879 (I)	65	34	99	52
March 1882(I)	May 1885 (II)	38	36	74	101
March 1887(II)	April 1888 (I)	13	22	35	60
July 1890(III)	May 1891 (II)	10	27	37	40
January 1893(I)	June 1894 (II)	17	20	37	30
December 1895(IV)	June 1897 (II)	18	18	36	35
June 1899(III)	December 1900 (IV)	18	24	42	42
September 1902(IV)	August 1904 (III)	23	21	44	39
May 1907(II)	June 1908 (II)	13	33	46	56
January 1910(I)	January 1912 (IV)	24	19	43	32
January 1913(I)	December 1914 (IV)	23	12	35	36
August 1918(III)	March 1919 (I)	7	44	51	67
January 1920(I)	July 1921 (III)	18	10	28	17
May 1923(II)	July 1924 (III)	14	22	36	40
October 1926(III)	November 1927 (IV)	13	27	40	41
August 1929(III)	March 1933 (I)	43	21	64	34
May 1937(II)	June 1938 (II)	13	50	63	93
February 1945(I)	October 1945 (IV)	8	80	88	93
November 1948(IV)	October 1949 (IV)	11	37	48	45
July 1953(II)	May 1954 (II)	10	45	55	56
August 1957(III)	April 1958 (II)	8	39	47	49
April 1960(II)	February 1961 (I)	10	24	34	32
December 1969(IV)	November 1970 (IV)	11	106	117	116
November 1973(IV)	March 1975 (I)	16	36	52	47
January 1980(I)	July 1980 (III)	6	58	64	74
July 1981(III)	November 1982 (IV)	16	12	28	18
July 1990(III)	March 1991 (I)	8	92	100	108
March 2001(I)	November 2001 (IV)	8	120	128	128
December 2007 (IV)	June 2009 (II)	18	73	91	81
Average, all cycles:					
1854-2009 (33 cycles)		17.5	38.7	56.2	56.4*
1854-1919 (16 cycles)		21.6	26.6	48.2	48.9**
1919-1945 (6 cycles)		18.2	35.0	53.2	53.0
1945-2009 (11 cycles)		11.1	58.4	69.5	68.5

* 32 cycles
** 15 cycles
Source: NBER

The Minsky Cycle

Within each of the two above cycles fits the 'Minsky Cycle' as another important element in the understanding of where one is in the overall global investment mix (which means, in practical terms, narrowing down the best trading options further).

The Minsky Cycle – coined around the time of the 1998 Russian financial crisis by a guy from PIMCO (Pacific Investment Management Company) – is a key part of the general psychology of trading (see later) and **seeks to chart the nature of the normal life cycle of an economy with particular reference to speculative investment bubbles.**

The idea here is that in times of prosperity, when the cashflow of banks and corporates moves to excess levels (over and above that which is needed simply to pay off debt), a 'speculative euphoria' develops, which soon exceeds that which borrowers can pay off. This in turn leads to tighter credit conditions etc etc. It is the slow pace at which the financial system moves to at first realise this and then seek to accommodate it that produces a financial crisis, known as the 'Minsky Moment'.

It is interesting to note here that knowing where one is in the cycle is crucial to making long-term, informed and extremely profitable positions, as is illustrated below in the shift along the Minsky Curve of what is propitious and what is not.

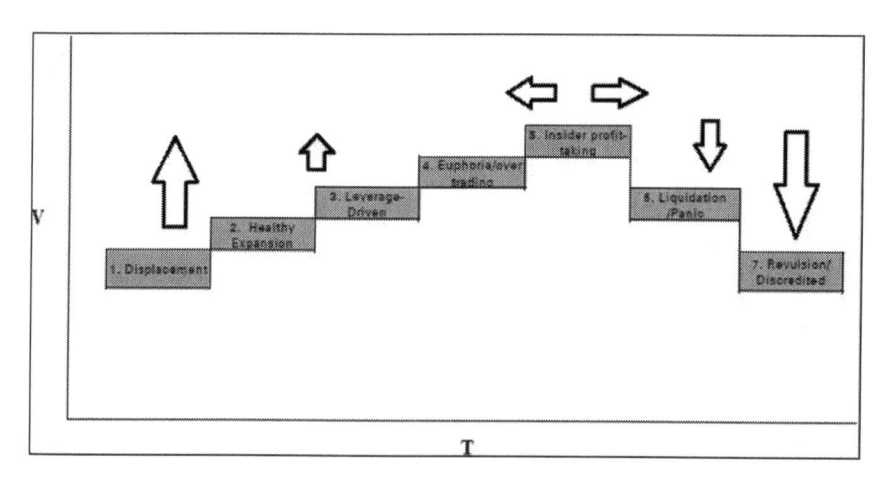

[Chart Key:
V = Values, various assets
T = Time]

So, looking at the above chart, for example, **in the immediate 'displacement' aftermath of the Great Financial Crisis, in the middle or so of 2011, one might have identified nascent pockets of value in Asian FX as various of the countries continued to show exceptional performance.** As the cycle progressed, the major beneficiaries of leverage became certain high-yielding currencies (such as the AUD) and certain commodities (notably, gold).

As credit became easier, so investors became less discerning about the underlying fundamentals of the assets into which they invested, and in the 'euphoria/over-trading' phase, for example, money poured into various of the already over-performing equities markets (China springs to mind). As ever in the markets, key insiders began to twig that a new indiscriminate phase of investment had manifested itself (the 'when my barber is talking to me about stocks then I know it's time to get out' concept), so liquidated out of things like Japanese government bonds and toppish currency positions. And of course, once this has occurred there is a much broader liquidation of assets (at this point it included things like selling USD and gold). Given the need to make good on losses in margin calls, this actually involves selling a much broader base of assets than would otherwise be merited.

Finally, the markets reach a point where investors are ultra-cautious in spending their money and regard any asset that is not seen as absolutely solid as being, in fact, abhorrent, with the main loser at the end of this particular cycle being the debt and other assets of Eurozone periphery countries (and there is an even larger corollary move into safe-haven assets at this point).

Looking at where we were in the middle of 2014, we can see that the displacement macro-shock had been negative rates announced by the ECB, the long and low easing policy of the US Fed appearing to be drawing to an end and a broad-based acceptance of an enduring economic slowdown in China gathering pace.

Within this, different asset classes are at different points along that cycle: for example, the USD may be entering a new long-term uptrend, as mentioned earlier; the JPY appears to be nearing the 'discredited' phase (as dealers cannot see what more can be done to weaken the currency, given what has already been implemented to do so); whilst there has been a generalised liquidation of being long volatility (volatility can be bought or sold, like any other aspect of the market, either directly – say through the VIX and similar indices – or indirectly through proxies).

Specific Stock Sector Investment Implications Of The Cycles

Given such an identification of which part of the cycle forms the backdrop to your current investment environment, **there are some general inferences that you can make regarding which sectors within stock markets may prove the most beneficial at a particular point in time,** as delineated below:

- *Full Scale Recession* (characterised by contracting GDP q-o-q, falling interest rates, increasing unemployment, declining consumer expectations, among others). Sectors that do well in this environment tend to be: **Cyclicals** (a company's revenues are generally higher in periods of economic prosperity and expansion and lower in periods of economic downturn and contraction, but they can cope easily by reducing wages and workforce during bad times and include companies that produce durable goods, such as raw materials and heavy equipment), **Transports, Technology and Industrials.**

- *Early Recovery* (consumer expectations are rising, unemployment is falling, industrial production is growing and interest rates have bottomed out): **Industrials, Basic materials industry and Energy firms.**

- *Late Recovery* (interest rates can be rising rapidly, consumer expectations are beginning to decline and industrial production is flat): **Energy, Staples and Services.**

- *Early Recession* (Consumer expectations are at their worst, industrial production is falling and interest rates are at their highest): **Services, Utilities, Cyclicals and Transports.**

The Basics Of Bottom-Up Investing

In contrast to Top-Down investing, **this approach attaches much less significance to the broader investment backdrop of economic and political factors than to a drilled-down-deep analysis of individual stocks,** although knowing where the sector in which it operates is placed in the specific investment cycles mentioned above is a good starting point.

The **advantage of this approach is that the investor can spend far less time looking at the multitude of factors that come into play when investing in a Top-Down style,** instead focussing on only one sector first and then on just one stock.

Another **major advantage is that by taking such a focussed approach this type of investor can identify overlooked opportunities that can generate major returns before the attention of Top-Down investors** has focussed on the stock by dint of a broad-based market re-assessment of sector, country or area. This means that Bottom-Up investors can catch the first part of a major move on a stock well ahead of the rest of the market in many cases.

Conversely, of course, **the downside is that Bottom-Up investors can be regarded as pioneers in the market, not benefitting from broad-based bull or bear markets** (the trend is not the friend of the Bottom-Up investor) and often has to plough his own furrow.

Having said that, there are a number of factors that can help you maximise returns and minimise risk, and we go into these below.

Comparables

Even the most die-hard Bottom-Up trader would be well-advised to look at the comparable performance of companies operating in the same business space as the company that is being assessed for investment.

In general terms, it is **wise to analyse earnings and revenue data, seek to identify trends in both areas and to look at market indicators – such as price/earnings ratio and dividend yield – and compare this data with that for comparable companies in order to see whether a stock offers good value.**

In addition, **looking at a stock's free cash flow** (operating cash flow minus capital expenditures, representing the cash that a company is able to generate after laying out the money required to maintain or expand its asset base) and **forward orders** is also useful, as is looking out for **new products/services** that the company has in the pipeline and at the **company's management history.**

Management

Many of the best **professional global fund managers talk to a company's senior management every six to eight weeks,** and often, as a result of these conversations, their allocation of available assets to a company can fall well short or in excess of a reasonable benchmark.

The ramifications for a company and its stockholders in the choice of its senior management team are virtually always enormous and all the more so in times of broad-based economic adversity such as those that prevailed up until very recently and may well occur again shortly.

To begin with, the management needs to be able to **find a balance between having an over-arching vision for the future and possessing an eye for detail, including a very thorough understanding of the company's business and finances.**

In this context, Samir Brikho from AMEC Foster Wheeler, who took over as CEO in October 2006 until he later left the firm, was widely regarded as initially having done a good job of sorting out the company's legacy issues and refocusing the operations for the longer term on the natural resources and power markets.

In this respect, not only did Brikho almost immediately sell off the company's non-core businesses and implement a major cost reduction programme on a practical note but also focused employees' efforts on achieving a newly clarified company vision ('to be a leading supplier of high value consultancy, engineering and project management services within the world's energy, power and process industries').

A natural, and vitally important, adjunct of being able to **step inside and outside the business is to understand as many of its component elements as possible.** There is a school of thought that takes the view that if someone has successfully run one business then they can do the same with any other, whether or not it is in the same business sector or not, but it is increasingly evident that this cannot be optimally achieved without their taking time out to learn everything possible about the specifics of the firm.

This is true for Sir Terry Leahy, former CEO of Tesco, one of whose principal business tenets was 'keeping a small business mentality within a big business body: the importance of core purpose, values and strategy'. With this approach, Leahy transformed Tesco, over the ten years under his charge, into the number one supermarket in the UK and the third biggest in the world, to a point where it was estimated that one in every eight pounds in the UK was spent in Tesco stores. After he left? Well . . .

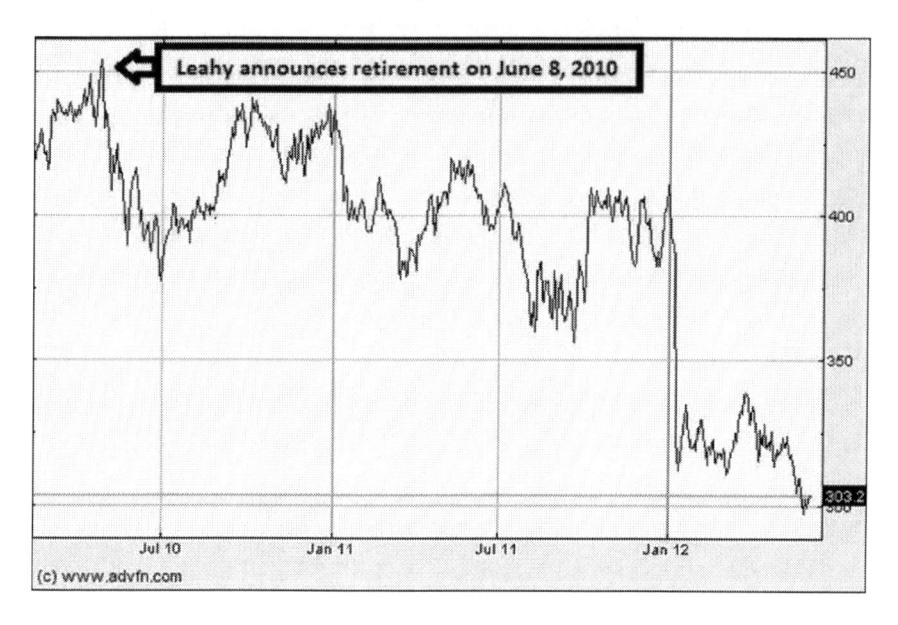

Tesco Share Price After Leahy Announces Retirement

[Chart: Tesco share price from Jul 10 to Jan 12, with annotation "Leahy announces retirement on June 8, 2010" and ending value 303.2. Source: (c) www.advfn.com]

Catching investor attention for a company's senior management team, though, is not always a good thing, particularly given the media glare that surrounds high-profile business figures. Perhaps the most notorious example of this was the overnight destruction of his eponymous British High Street retail chain by the then CEO **Gerald Ratner** who, in 1991, joked (in a speech to the traditionally well-media-covered Institute of Directors get-together) that one of his firm's products was "total crap" and boasted that some of its earrings were "cheaper than a prawn sandwich."

Similarly catastrophic, albeit on a much more rounded basis (gross incompetence plus an arrogant air towards media and shareholders alike) was **George Simpson's** handling of the then Marconi UK giant in the early 1990s. Interestingly (in a car-crash sort of way), not only did he manage to reduce the company from one with a share price of £12.50 in September 2000 (putting a notional value on the company of £35 billion) to one with shares valued at £0.29 (and a notional value of just £807 million) in just one year but he also engineered to pocket a pay-off for himself of over £1 million upon his 'retirement' to a baronial castle in Scotland.

Many investors see a **CEO buying shares in the company of which they are head as a good sign.** This could well be the case – the converse is true, of course, for directors selling their shares in their company. To find out whether a director is investing in his own firm, simply visit the company's home page on the Barclays Stockbrokers website and select the 'Director Deals' tab.

Value Investing Versus Growth Investing

Value investing generally involves buying shares that appear underpriced by some form of fundamental analysis (not the same as trading fundamentals but rather specific ratios, such as discounts to book value, tangible book value, looking at high dividend yield firms, those with low price-to-earnings multiples, low price-to-book ratios, low price-to-cash flow or any combinations thereof).

Perhaps the most generally well-known of this type of investor is Warren Buffett and his Berkshire Hathaway fund. It is well worth quoting a few of his views here, as his success is founded upon them.

On stock market investment in general: "**Over the long term, the stock market news will be good.** In the 20th century, the United States endured two world wars and other traumatic and expensive military conflicts; the Depression; a dozen or so recessions and financial panics; oil shocks; a flu epidemic; and the resignation of a disgraced president. Yet the Dow rose from 66 to 11,497 [now it is around 20,000]."

On timing a buy: "The best thing that happens to us is when a great company gets into temporary trouble ... **We want to buy them when they're on the operating table.**"

On the other hand, **growth investing involves buying shares in companies that exhibit signs of above-average growth, even if the share price appears expensive in terms of specific metrics** such as those mentioned directly above and below.

Key Basic Metrics For Stock Investors

Dividend Yield

As we have seen earlier, generally a higher dividend yield has long been considered to be desirable among many investors (it is, after all, cash in the hand, quite aside from any other considerations).

Additionally, however, although a high dividend yield can be considered to be evidence that a stock is under-priced, it can also be viewed as evidence that a company's fortunes have deteriorated and that future dividends will not be as high as previous ones.

Similarly a low dividend yield can be considered evidence that the stock is overpriced or that future dividends might be higher.

The formula for calculating this is as follows:

Current dividend yield = most recent full year dividend/current share price.

Book Value

This is the value of an asset according to its account balance as shown on the balance sheet. The value is based on the original cost of the asset less any depreciation, amortisation or impairment costs made against the asset.

Historically, the book value is a company's total assets minus its intangible assets and liabilities. However, in practice and depending on the type of business involved and the type of calculation being employed, book value varies substantially, according to values attributed to goodwill or intangible assets or any combination thereof ('tangible book value' excludes both of the previous two factors).

Earnings Per Share (EPS)

This is simply the total amount of earnings for each outstanding share of the company. It does not include preferred dividends for categories outside continued operations and net income.

The formula therefore is:

EPS = profit/weighted average common shares.

Price To Earnings (P/E)

This is a measure of the relative price of a share to the annual net income or profit earned by the firm per share:

P/E = market price per share/annual earnings per share.

A lot of emphasis is placed on the P/E ratio by many investors, as it can be regarded as a prime indicator of the level of confidence that investors have in any given company: clearly, a low P/E would indicate that there is not much to look forward to in terms of growth in earnings, whereas the opposite could be true for a high P/E.

Having said that, there is a danger when P/Es become very high that a bubble is growing about a particular stocks or sector, such as happened in the case of the dot.com bubble (when the average global P/E for such firms was 32).

The average P/E for US equities from 1900 to 2005 was 16 (arithmetic mean), but in many emerging markets where expectations are high and a weight of money is looking for a home (China recently has been a good example of this trend) these P/Es are much higher.

EV/EBITDA

This is the enterprise value (EV, the sum of claims of all the security-holders: debt-holders, preferred shareholders, minority shareholders, common equity holders and others) of a company divided by its earnings before interest, tax, depreciation and amortisation (EBITDA) and is preferred by many to P/E because it is capital structure neutral.

The Basics Of Commodities Trading

Trading Is Best Confined To Oil And Metals

The commodities market is, without doubt, subject to a much greater degree of manipulation by major trading institutions, because of its relatively small size compared to the FX and Equities markets and the fact that a small number of banks and trading houses hold all of the potentially market-moving orders. **The degree of manipulation is even more profound in the less well-known and less well-traded of the commodities markets, particularly those centred around livestock (including lean hogs, pork bellies, live cattle and feeder cattle) and agricultural commodities (including corn, soybeans, wheat, rice, cocoa, coffee, cotton and sugar),** which, even worse for the retail trader, are also particularly subject to unpredictable weather patterns, diseases and other such Acts of God.

Having said that, **the other two major commodities sectors – energy (including crude oil, heating oil, natural gas and gasoline) and metals (including gold, silver, platinum and copper) – can provide excellent trading opportunities, provided that the trader rigidly employs the range of risk management techniques,** and also hedging tools for other positions in both the FX and Equities markets and for general economic market conditions, covered in depth in this book. This is why these two sectors of commodities trading – and only these two – are being discussed here.

Supply And Demand

The **price of all commodities is in very large part a function of the supply and demand balance, to a degree, not present in the FX and Equities markets** (it is true that QE, as mentioned, affects FX rates and that rights issues and similar actions affect equities values, but the import of these factors is nowhere near that which supply and demand plays on commodities).

Aside from the Acts of God factors that play a role periodically in the supply and demand balance, about which the trader can do little more than ensure that he has the correct risk management tools in place for all his open positions, **there are broader economic factors that the trader can predict** and from which he can make returns over and above benchmark performance (i.e. 'alpha returns'). A case in point – from the demand side – occurred with **China's growth pattern from the early 1990s to around 2010 that was based on a dramatic expansion in manufacturing, including massive state-sponsored infrastructure projects. These utilised enormous amounts of relevant metals (copper, for example, for pipes, aluminium and so on) and vast quantities of oil and gas for power associated with such projects.**

This led to the 'metals supercycle' in which all of these metals prices shot up in one direction only for well over a decade, and **the trader would have made exponential returns simply by buying them** based on this one macroeconomic factor. **Since 2010, if the trader had read anything on China, then he would have made similar returns by selling certain metals as China switched its growth strategy to one based on manufacturing-led economic expansion to one based on consumer-led growth** as it tried to build out the middle class section of its society. At the same time, the demand for oil and gas has continued to stay steady, as the expanded middle class buys more items that need powering.

China GDP And Copper Price

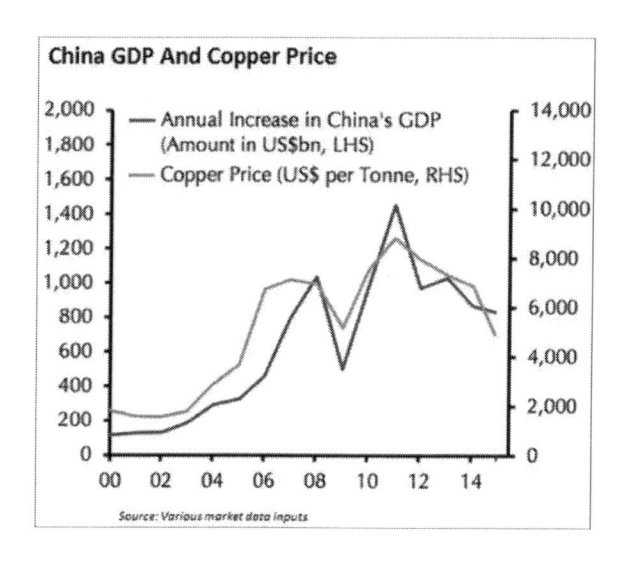

[Chart showing Annual Increase in China's GDP (Amount in US$bn, LHS) and Copper Price (US$ per Tonne, RHS) from 2000 to 2014]

Source: Various market data inputs

The same broad-based macro-economic play was specifically announced by Saudi Arabia in the oil sector at the beginning of 2014 – from the supply side – aimed at destroying the nascent North American shale energy industry, so again a trader simply following the news would have made alpha returns selling oil (and gas), from 2014 to when the Saudis decided that the strategy was not working (more of this below).

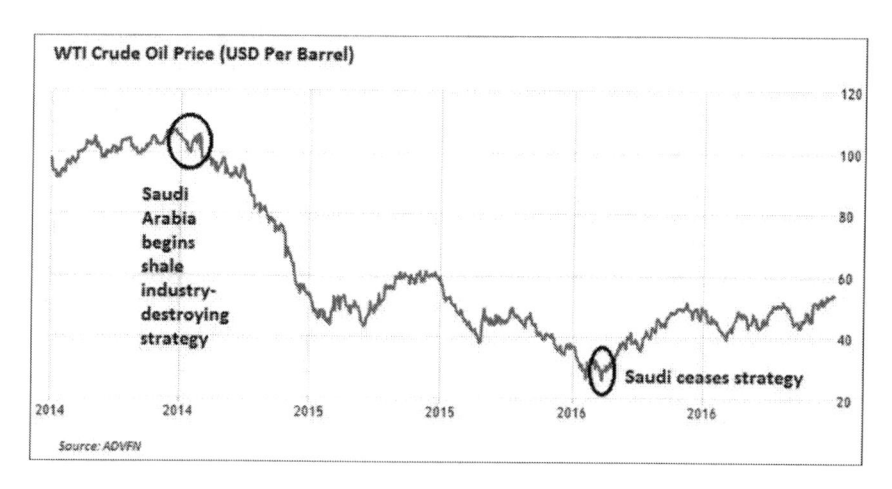

WTI Crude Oil Price (USD Per Barrel)

[Chart showing WTI Crude Oil Price from 2014 to 2016, marked with "Saudi Arabia begins shale industry-destroying strategy" and "Saudi ceases strategy"]

Source: ADVFN

Seeking to identify such shifts in macroeconomic policy, even if they are already underway, that will have a significant effect on the supply and demand balance in a particular commodity is absolutely key in making exceptional returns in the commodities markets as a whole. Below are more in-depth analyses of the oil and metals markets.

The Oil Market

As stated above, although there are opportunities to be had trading a number of the products in the energy sector mix, for the retail trader starting out or even for someone with a considerable degree of experience, **crude oil is the optimal product to trade in this sector,** and this will be the focus of this sub-section. The key reasons why it is the best of these energy products to trade is that it is the biggest of these sub-markets and major political and economic events that pertain to it are frequently mentioned in the mainstream media, which is useful for those who are trading on a part-time basis in building up their background knowledge. The trading correlations – both positive and negative – between oil and other asset classes are gone into in great depth later on in this book.

In terms of supply and demand in general, **there are two key numbers on the supply side that traders absolutely must watch in order to adjust short-term trades and to discern long-term trends.** The first of these is the US **Weekly Petroleum Status Report that is released every Friday.** This includes the total supply from this major producer, including data from the increasingly important shale energy sector. The second of these numbers is the **official release on a more ad hoc basis of the total supply coming from major oil producers that constitute the Organization of the Petroleum Exporting Countries (OPEC),** which has been the dominant cartel in the oil industry since its creation in 1960.

Indeed, OPEC was specifically founded to 'co-ordinate and unify the petroleum policies' of all of its member states; i.e. to align them and, consequently, to fix the oil price. Membership of this cartel comprises virtually all of the world's major oil and gas suppliers – in alphabetical order, not that of global oil significance: Algeria, Angola, Ecuador, Iran, Iraq, Kuwait, Libya, Nigeria, Qatar, Saudi Arabia, the United Arab Emirates (UAE) and Venezuela – with the most notable exception, perhaps, being Russia. Bearing in mind that Russia is currently the world's second biggest oil producer, its output also needs to be monitored by traders.

Although there are members that flout OPEC guidance, **this club sets the oil production targets of its members. With a collective 40% or so of the world's crude oil output produced by these countries and around 60% of the total petroleum traded internationally coming from their oil exports, what OPEC says and does plays a huge part in determining the global price not just of oil but of natural gas and related oil and gas products.**

World's Biggest Oil Producers (2016) In Barrels Per Day (bbl/d)

	Country	Production (bbl/day) Top 10 countries 2016
1	Saudi Arabia (OPEC)	10,625,000
2	Russia	10,254,000
3	United States	8,744,000
4	Iraq (OPEC)	4,836,000
5	People's Republic of China	3,938,000
6	Iran (OPEC)	3,920,000
7	Canada	3,652,000
8	United Arab Emirates (OPEC)	3,188,000
9	Kuwait (OPEC)	3,000,000
10	Brazil	2,624,000

Source: EIA

Clearly, in pure supply and demand terms, **if supply falls whilst demand stays the same or rises then the price of oil can be expected to increase, whereas if supply rises whilst demand**

stays the same or falls then the price of oil can be expected to fall. The reverse of both of these supply and demand equations, of course, also hold good.

It is wise also to keep an eye on sudden changes in supply from producers who have unrealised potential, as delineated below, which may have occurred due to a technical problem (rigs out of commission, problems with loading areas and so forth) or political problems (wars, changes of government and so on). In this context, there follows an examination of the key player in the oil industry currently – Saudi Arabia – plus those that are in the process of changing the longstanding dynamics of the oil market – the US, Iran and Iraq.

World's Largest Proved Reserve Crude Oil Holders (billion barrels)

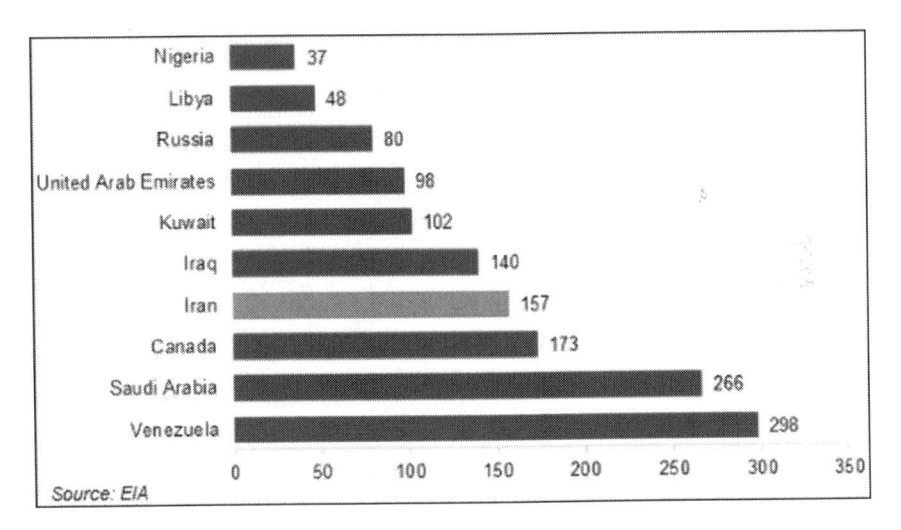

Country	Billion barrels
Nigeria	37
Libya	48
Russia	80
United Arab Emirates	98
Kuwait	102
Iraq	140
Iran	157
Canada	173
Saudi Arabia	266
Venezuela	298

Source: EIA

Saudi Arabia

Until 1973, the basis of the historical relationship between the US and OPEC (entirely driven at that point by Saudi Arabia) had been demarcated at a meeting on 14 February 1945 between then

American President, Franklin D Roosevelt and the Saudi King at the time, Abdulaziz. The first face-to-face contact between the two was held on board the US Navy cruiser Quincy in the Great Bitter Lake segment of the Suez Canal. The deal they agreed, which persisted unchallenged until 1973, was this: **the US would get all of the oil and gas supplies it needed for as long as Saudi had hydrocarbons reserves, in return for which the US would guarantee the security both of the country and of the ruling House of Saud.**

That said, **the key moment that would define the global oil market as it still stands today was the 1973 Oil Crisis.** This began in October of that year when OPEC members plus Egypt, Syria and Tunisia began an embargo on oil exports to the US, the UK, Japan, Canada and the Netherlands in response to the US's supplying of arms to Israel in the Yom Kippur War. By the end of the embargo in March 1974, the price of oil had risen from USD3 per barrel (pb) to nearly USD12 pb. As the Saudi Minister of Oil and Mineral Reserves at the time, Sheikh Ahmed Zaki Yamani, unequivocally highlighted at that point, the extremely negative effects on the global economy marked a fundamental shift in the world balance of power between the developing nations that produced oil and the developed industrial nations that consumed it.

Indeed, up until ten years ago, Saudi Arabia was the undisputed king of the global energy complex – the world's 'swing' producer – sitting atop OPEC, propped up by its own massive high quality oil reserves and able to extend its petro-powered influence into all areas of the world's economy; from the trajectory of the US dollar, through the price of gold, to the performance of the leading equities indices. **From 2004 to now, the oil price has to varying degrees been the product of the tune played from the pied pipes of Saudi:** rising from around USD50 pb of West Texas Intermediate (WTI) at the end of 2004, through the USD147 pb level in 2008 and back down again in 2014/15 to below the USD30 pb before rallying again over

USD50 pb on a supposed OPEC production cut agreed in November 2016.

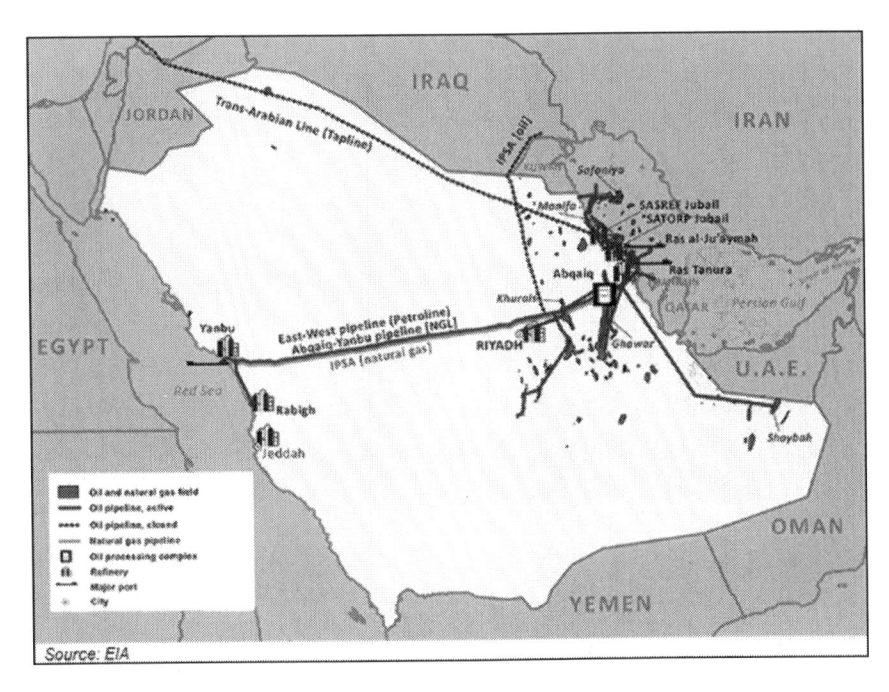

Saudi Arabia's Major Oil And Gas Infrastructure

However, **underlying the simple price movements, the global energy market has undergone fundamental complex changes that have cast doubts over Saudi's stature in the oil markets in the years to come, not just from the US-driven threat from shale oil and gas or from the increased geopolitical tensions in the Middle East as a whole but also from questions about precisely how much oil Saudi actually has** and consequently its ability to act effectively as a swing energy producer by manipulating its spare capacity.

According to the US's Energy Information Administration (EIA), Saudi Arabia has approximately 266 billion barrels (bbbl) of proved oil reserves, in addition to half of the 2.5 bbbl estimated in the Saudi-

Kuwaiti shared Partitioned Neutral Zone, over half of which is held in eight longstanding fields – 16% of total proved world oil reserves. However, **oil and gas (hydrocarbons) reserves figures are often nowadays a matter more of political expediency than of cold reality, with doubt having grown in recent years over the veracity of any figures produced anywhere, but especially perhaps in the Middle East.** For example, Abu Dhabi claimed reserves of 92.3 bbbl from 1988 to 2004 but, over that period, approximately 14 bbbl were extracted.

Similarly, back in 1989, Saudi Arabia claimed to be sitting on a total of 170 bbbl of oil, but only a year later and without the discovery of any major new oil fields the official reserve estimate somehow grew by 51.2% to 257 bbbl. **Now, again without any major discoveries and despite having pumped an average of nearly three billion barrels of oil every year from 1973 to the end of 2016 – which totals 129 billion barrels – official reserves stand at 266 bbbl, which is, of course, a mathematical impossibility.**

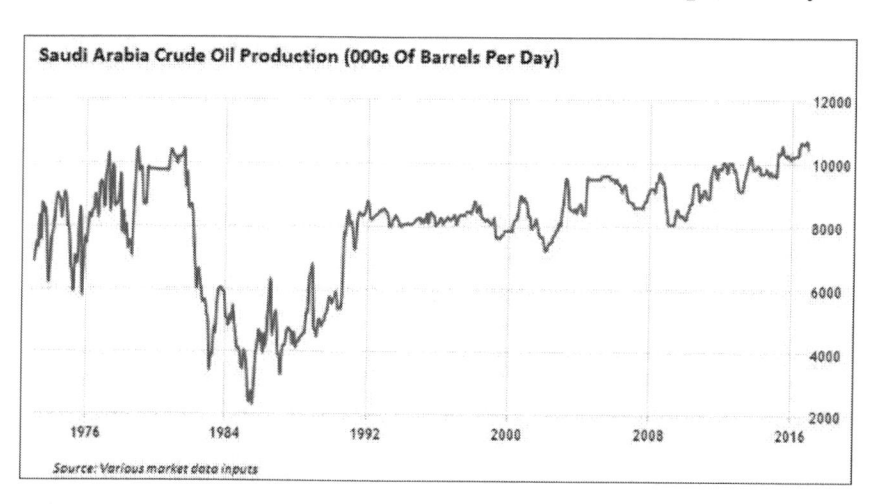

Saudi Arabia Crude Oil Production (000s Of Barrels Per Day)

Source: Various market data inputs

In this context of lying about resources – the product of Saudi Arabia's desire to remain the key hydrocarbons player in the world – the country has often stated that it has the ability to pump much more oil if required (called 'spare capacity' in the business); between

2-2.5 million barrels per day (mbpd) extra, it says, giving it the theoretical capability to ramp up its production to about 12.5 mbpd in the event of unexpected disruptions elsewhere. **However, it is very unlikely that it could pump at these levels for a sustained period of time,** and this idea has been supported by comments from Gulf officials at OPEC, who stated in the midst of Iraqi supply fears that Saudi Arabia could ramp-up output by another 1-1.3 mbpd in a best case scenario. Officials also mentioned that production of 11.5 mbpd is untested and could only be maintained for a very short period and that, in any event, higher production would be very difficult and would require producing heavy crudes. In addition, it has been noted that the country's rising domestic consumption, notably to power its growing electricity generation networks and transport sector, has been eating into its crude export potential. Despite Saudi Arabia's heavy focus on developing its gas resources to support its crude export growth, it is expected that the slow development will be insufficient to offset rampant growth in demand for electricity, leaving a heavy reliance on oil.

Combined with growing electricity demand, Saudi Aramco's aggressive expansion of its downstream sector (relating to the refining of crude oil and the processing and purifying of natural gas and the resulting products, including gasoline) will put further pressure on domestic consumption in the coming years. Indeed, there is likely to be average oil consumption growth of 7% per year across the next ten years, which compares to average oil production growth of just 1% (albeit from a higher base) over the same period. This has already reduced the country's spare oil production capacity and will continue to do so progressively, so reducing its ability to manipulate the global oil price and, as a corollary of this, its geopolitical power.

This power was utilised by the Saudis beginning in 2014 when it embarked on a strategy to destroy the nascent North American shale energy sector, which posed a massive economic and political threat to Saudi's position in the world. The strategy involved Saudi Arabia producing oil at a much higher

rate than usual, in order to drive oil prices down so that new shale energy operations would become unprofitable and would be forced to close down.

This did indeed result in a huge drop in oil prices around the globe and also in the suspension of many shale energy projects. For example, the US oil rig count in January/February 2015 saw its biggest period-on-period fall since 1991, and the gas rig count fell substantially as well.

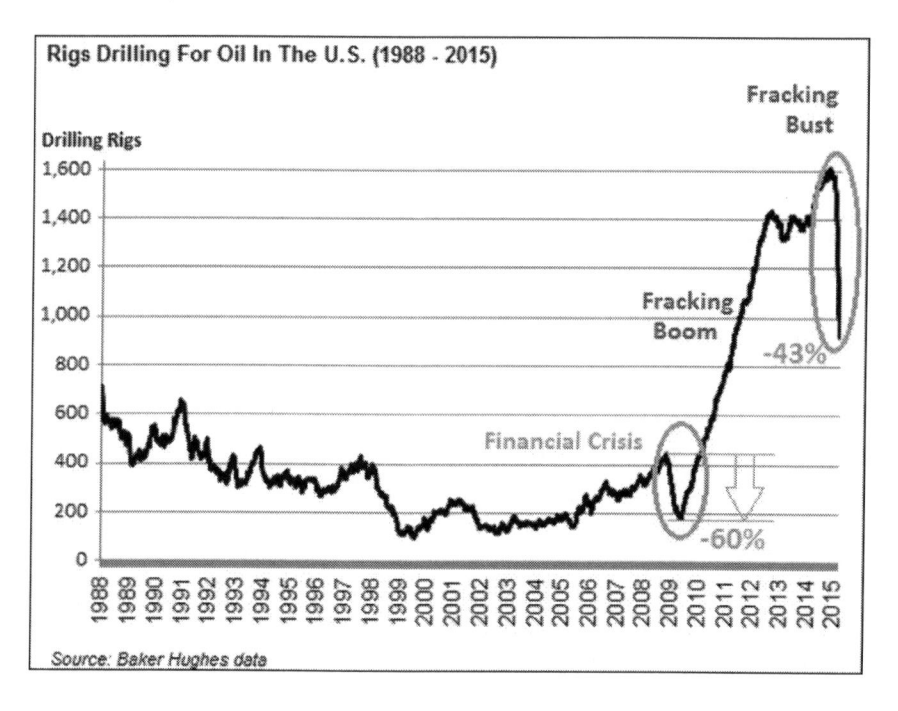

Rigs Drilling For Oil In The U.S. (1988 - 2015)

Source: Baker Hughes data

According to industry figures **as at the end of the first quarter of 2015, around one third of the 800 oil and gas projects (worth USD500 billion and totalling nearly 60 billion barrels of oil equivalent) scheduled for final investment decisions (FID) in 2016 were 'unconventional', meaning that around USD150 billion of shale projects were liable for cancellation or postponement.** Notable retrenchments included French energy giant Total recently deciding to postpone the FID on the Joslyn project in Alberta, Canada (estimated cost USD11 billion).

Additionally, Royal Dutch Shell's (RDS) liquefied natural gas (LNG) project in British Columbia required oil at USD80 pb to break even and RDS' Chief Financial Officer, Henry Simon, indicated in October 2014 that it was "less likely" to go ahead with unconventional projects in West Canada if oil fell below USD80 pb. Even in the US-centric Gulf of Mexico, one of the most attractive oil production areas in the world, projects were facing challenges. BP put on hold a decision on its 'Mad Dog Phase 2' deep water project in the Gulf after its development costs ballooned to USD20 billion.

Similarly, many Australian LNG firms require spot oil prices between USD75-90 pb in order to generate a 10% rate of return, so some of those projects were subject to delay. In this context, Woodside Petroleum's chief executive officer Peter Coleman said in a speech in November 2014 that a prolonged oil price slump would hurt returns at existing LNG projects and threaten future developments.

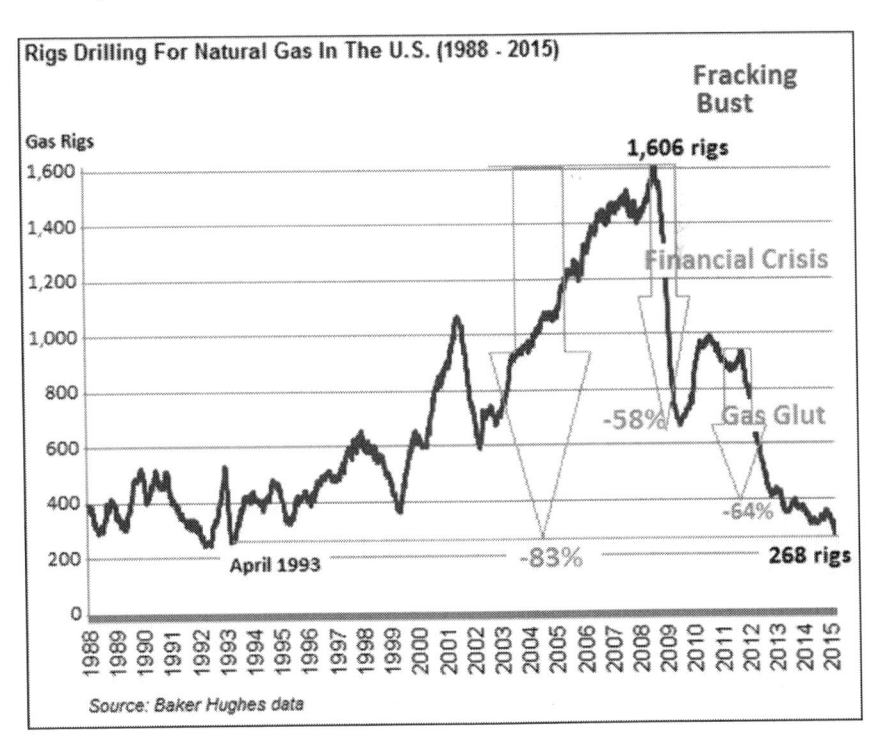

Rigs Drilling For Natural Gas In The U.S. (1988 - 2015)

Source: Baker Hughes data

However, over time, the Saudi strategy began to lose its punch. It is true that many of the larger, traditional oil companies in the US and elsewhere shelved big investment projects, which take years to realise. However, crucially it takes equally as long for lower investment to result in the lower supply required for the Saudi strategy to work. But it is also true that **the shale industry showed a remarkable, and completely unexpected, resilience in its operations.** Although over the course of 2015 production at these typically declined by around 50%, forcing them to cut investment to approximately USD60 billion over the year (compared to the USD100 billion or so spent in 2014), this adjustment was sufficient to keep shale production close to steady for the year after peaking in early 2015.

Allied to this were **remarkable productivity gains, for example in the Permian basin, for example – spanning western Texas and south-eastern New Mexico and currently the only major US region with growing production – where each rig now produces more than 400 bpd, compared to only 100 bpd in 2012.** Moreover, compared to the steep fall in horizontal rigs (two thirds have been discontinued since November 2014) US shale-oil production only fell modestly, from a peak 5.1 mbpd to around 4.8 mbpd by the end of the first quarter of 2016.

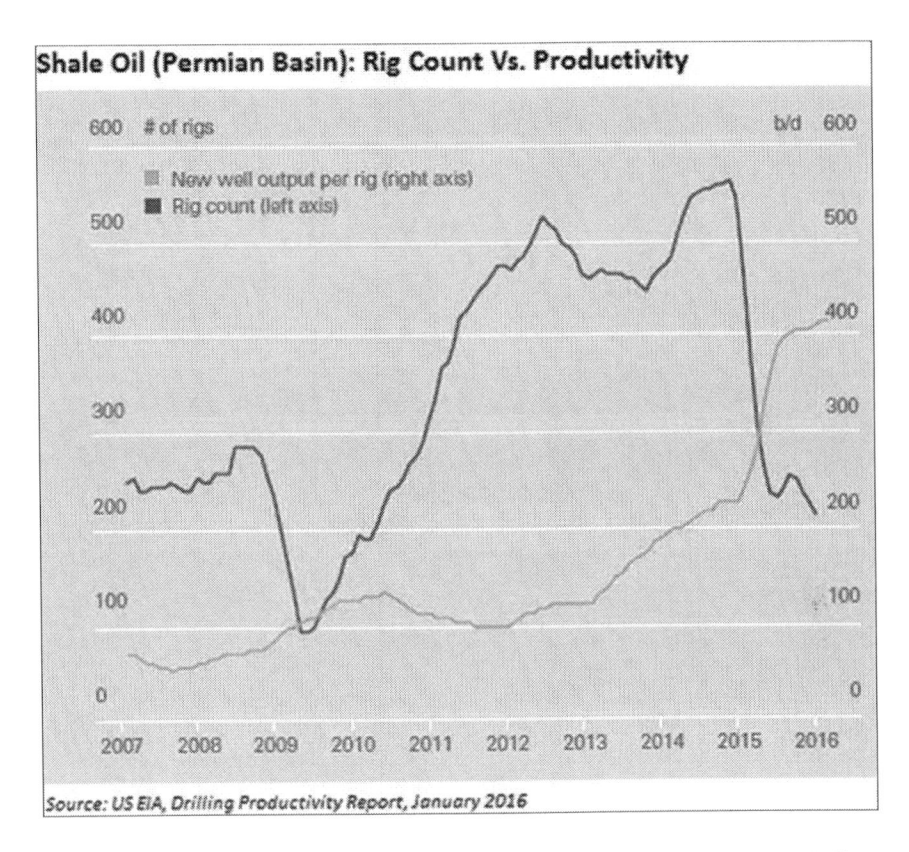

Shale Oil (Permian Basin): Rig Count Vs. Productivity

- New well output per rig (right axis)
- Rig count (left axis)

Source: US EIA, Drilling Productivity Report, January 2016

Before to the full extent of the gains through cost discipline, improved technology and efficiency by shale producers began to come to light, **it had been broadly assumed that US shale producers needed an oil price between USD60-90pb to invest in new projects.** But the situation has now changed markedly. **In the core areas of Bakken (in North Dakota), for example, increasing drilling even makes sense at USD50pb, whilst in the best fields of the Permian area break-even costs are now around the USD36pb level,** according to industry estimates. **Indeed, some of the very best shale oil firms have a break-even price of just USD20pb.**

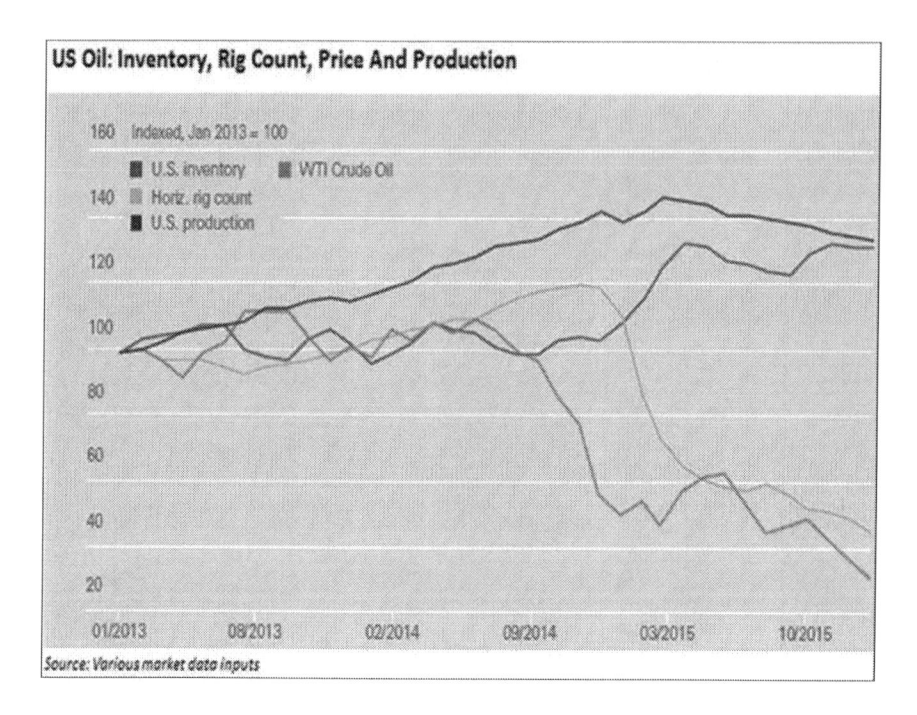

US Oil: Inventory, Rig Count, Price And Production

Indexed, Jan 2013 = 100
- U.S. inventory
- WTI Crude Oil
- Horiz. rig count
- U.S. production

Source: Various market data inputs

Ultimately, as at the end of the second half of 2017, total US production of 9.1 mbpd was roughly where it was a year ago when the price war began. In the meantime, according to the International Energy Agency, OPEC member states had collectively lost at least USD450 billion in revenues since Saudi embarked on its shale-stymieing strategy.

The fact that the Saudis then panicked and announced a freeze on production as the price actually started to plummet towards USD20 pb – and then announced that the cut would be sustained for another nine months until March 2018 – has made the situation worse, for five reasons. First, it showed weakness to the financial markets, which always seek to ruthlessly exploit such a trait; second, the 'freeze' was near record high production levels and thus was meaningless in absolute terms; third, it was not supported by the newly sanctions-free Iran, now one of the world's biggest oil producers; fourth, the shale producers continued to demonstrate a much greater flexibility in dealing with the lower oil pricing complex than had previously been imagined possible; and fifth, the resultant rally in the oil price up to the USD50 pb level allowed shale producers to hedge future production (essentially to lock in profits around this level) for 2017, 2018, 2019 and even as far out in some cases as ten years.

Indeed, flush with cash from the output cut-inspired US$50 pb oil price, US shale producers boosted drilling budgets ten times faster than the rest of the world to harvest fields that register large profits even at these price points and North American shale drillers made plans to lift their 2017 outlays by 32%, to USD84 billion, compared with just 3% percent for international projects, according to industry reports.

This prompted OPEC itself to revise up its estimate of oil supply growth from shale producers by 600,000 bpd in 2017. As a whole, in the same report, OPEC also revised up its estimate of oil supply growth from all oil producers outside the OPEC group during 2017 to 950,000 bpd, from a previous forecast of 580,000 bpd. Factoring this into the global supply/demand balance, together with other supply metrics, would make very grim reading for the Saudis and OPEC, whose 'production cut', incidentally, has still left oil stocks in industrialised nations at 276 million barrels above the five-year average, according to the EIA.

The EIA also estimates that US crude production will surpass the 10 million bpd (mbpd) mark by late 2018, breaching the record high set in 1970, with the sale boom propelling non-OPEC output up by some 1.3 mbpd in 2018, completely nullifying any OPEC cut and effectively filling up almost all the expected growth in demand. In this context, and factoring in rising oil output from Canada and Brazil in addition to the US shale figures, world oil production is projected to be 98.47 mbpd, whilst global demand will be 98.30 mbpd, according to the EIA.

Even more worrying for those looking for any meaningful sustained uptrend in the global oil price is that the much-vaunted 'deal' between Saudi Arabia and Russia to cut output is

meaningless in practical terms. In reality, the Saudis are utilising its strategic oil stockpile to sell up to 350,000 bpd into the spot market via investment banks, the so-called 'dark inventory', whilst the Russians are selling large quantities of oil directly to China without declaring it.

Also, China has made an offer to Venezuela that over the next three years it will invest USD25 billion in equipment and engineering that will lift its oil production by at least 55% over that period, which would bring it up to just over 3.4 million barrels per day. In addition, of course, the planned output cut deal – which is envisaged lasting until March 2018 – would once again not include Iran, whose aim is to increase output to 6 million barrels per day as soon as possible.

The real irony here is that the more the Saudis are actually able to hold up the oil price, the more the shale producers will be able to hedge their output at higher levels, meaning that their output will continue to increase, even while Saudi and its friends are losing all that money from the opportunity cost of lost production. If those production rises from shale push the oil price down again then the only ones whose finances will remain in a good state will be the shale producers.

The US

Given the huge economic and reputational damage done to the US as a result of the quadrupling of oil prices due to the Saudis' 1973 oil embargo, **the US Congress banned exports of oil to destinations outside the Americas from the country, despite its producing many millions of barrels of oil per day at that time, in order to make it more energy self-sufficient (or at least, not so dependent on the Saudis for energy).** Indeed, the US has been a significant petroleum product supplier to the Americas for the past decade: in 2003, it exported 0.6 mbpd of petroleum products to other countries in the Americas, primarily Mexico and Canada; and just ten years later US exports to the region totalled 2.0 mbpd, still primarily to Mexico and Canada but increasingly to other countries, most notably Brazil and Chile.

Global Crude Oil Quality, By Types

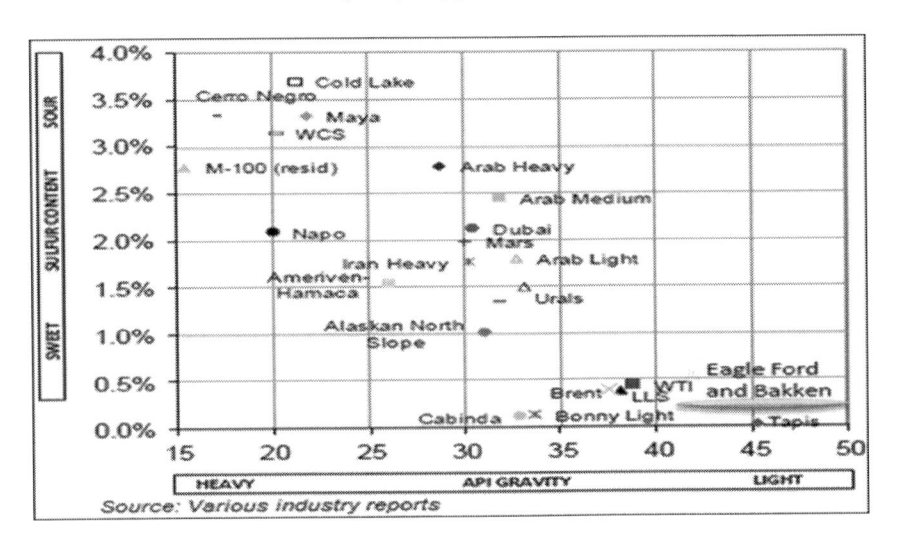

[Chart showing sulphur content (vertical axis, 0.0% to 4.0%, SOUR to SWEET) vs API Gravity (horizontal axis, 15 to 50, HEAVY to LIGHT) with various crude oil types plotted: Cold Lake, Cerro Negro, Maya, WCS, M-100 (resid), Arab Heavy, Arab Medium, Napo, Dubai, Mars, Iran Heavy, Arab Light, Ameriven-Hamaca, Urals, Alaskan North Slope, Brent, LLS, WTI, Eagle Ford and Bakken, Cabinda, Bonny Light, Tapis]

Source: Various industry reports

[Chart Key:
The petroleum industry classifies crude oil by three general parameters:
1. Its API (American Petroleum Institute) gravity (a measure of density) = horizontal axis label. Light crude has over 31.1 degrees API, medium has 22.3-31.1 degrees API, heavy has below 22.3 degrees API and extra heavy has under 10 degrees API, although definitions do vary slightly depending on the organisation involved. Light trades at a premium to the others as it produces a higher yield of petrol and is less difficult and costly to refine
2. Its sulphur content = vertical axis label. Sweet crude oil has less than 0.5% sulphur content and sour more than 0.5%. Sweet trades at a premium to sour, as it requires less refining to meet international sulphur emissions standards
3. Its broad geographic location = points plotted within the body of the chart. There are basically three global benchmarks for oil pricing, all of which are light and sweet: West Texas Intermediate (WTI), Brent and the average of the Dubai and Oman crudes]

US companies were allowed to export refined fuel, such as gasoline and diesel, to other regions but not oil itself, until **the US Commerce Department, which oversees the Bureau of Industry and Security, changed the definition of some ultra-light oil, clearing the way for two companies (Pioneer Natural Resources of Irving, Texas and Enterprise Products Partners of Houston, Texas) to sell abroad.** Additionally, and of a more game-changing nature, **the US Congress lifted the ban on crude oil exports to the rest of the world in December 2015** and, by the end of the first quarter of that year, a number of US majors were joining independent traders such as Vitol and Trafigura in exporting American crude. With American stockpiles at unprecedented levels, due to the re-emergence of a number of shelved shale energy projects, US oil initially made its way to France, Germany, the Netherlands, Israel, China and Panama and, since then, export destinations have increased markedly.

Since the ban was lifted, **the US has become an oil producer in the same league as Saudi Arabia, with EIA projections estimating production of around 9.6 mbpd between 2017 and 2020 (close to its historical high of 9.6 mbpd in 1970) and growth perhaps continuing through the 2020s and into the 2030s, with production reaching 13.3 mbpd in 2036.**

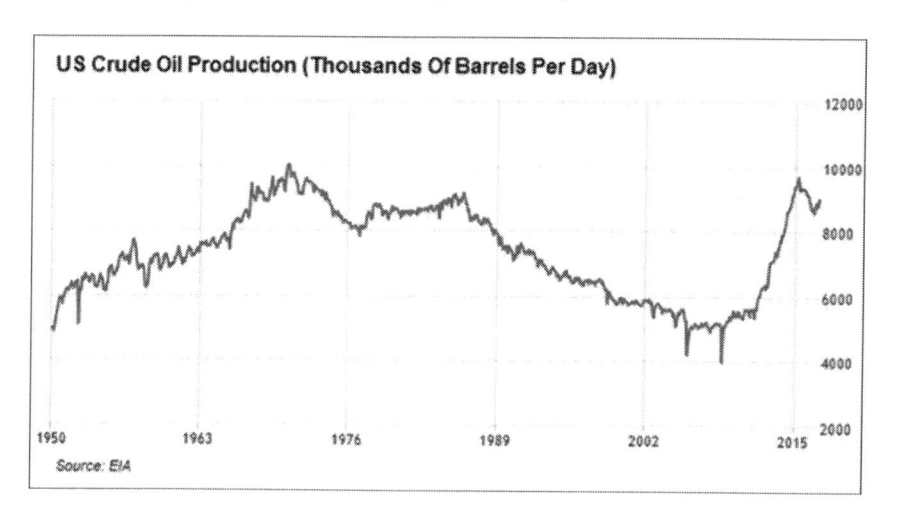

US Crude Oil Production (Thousands Of Barrels Per Day)
Source: EIA

Part of this has been a result of the US strategy of **reducing both its energy and economic dependence on oil and gas producers in the Middle East by developing its huge resources of shale oil (also referred to as 'tight' or 'light tight' oil) and gas,** which consist of light crude oil contained in petroleum-bearing formations of low permeability that are extracted via hydraulic fracturing and horizontal well drilling.

Technically Recoverable Shale Oil And Gas Resources Against Total World Resources

	Crude oil (billion barrels)	Wet natural gas (trillion cubic feet)
Outside the United States		
Shale oil and shale gas	287	6,634
Non-shale	2,847	13,817
Total	3,134	20,451
Increase in total resources due to inclusion of shale oil and shale gas	10%	48%
Shale as a percent of total	9%	32%
United States		
Shale / tight oil and shale gas	58	665
Non-shale	164	1,766
Total	223	2,431
Increase in total resources due to inclusion of shale oil and shale gas	35%	38%
Shale as a percent of total	26%	27%
Total World		
Shale / tight oil and shale gas	345	7,299
Non-shale	3,012	15,583
Total	3,357	22,882
Increase in total resources due to inclusion of shale oil and shale gas	11%	47%
Shale as a percent of total	10%	32%
Source: EIA		

In fact, drilling productivity in the seven major shale oil regions in the US has surged, as shown below.

US Shale Oil Production And Rigs (Jan. 2007 = 100)

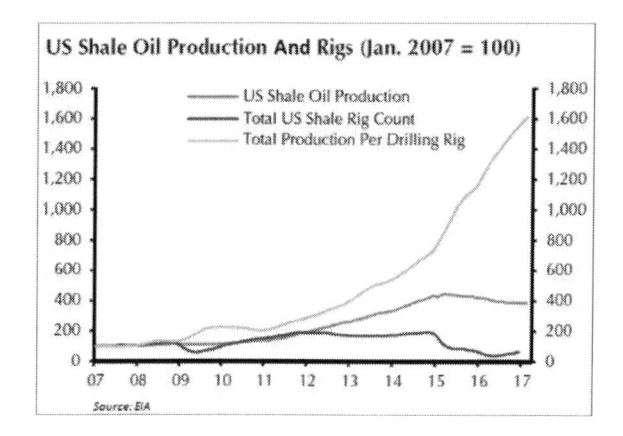

Source: EIA

As seen above, the total number of active drilling rigs fell by 64% from December 2014 to December 2016. However, over the same period, production per rig more than doubled to 4,411 bpd. As a result, total production fell by only 12%. Looking ahead, **if the current rate of productivity growth is sustained, we could see oil production reach or even surpass its previous peak within the next year.**

The **recent efficiency gains mean it could now take about half the oil rigs needed previously to replicate the production levels of 2015.** The rig count is already starting to edge up and on the basis of the relationship seen in the chart below an oil price of about USD65 per barrel would be consistent with a rig count of around 800.

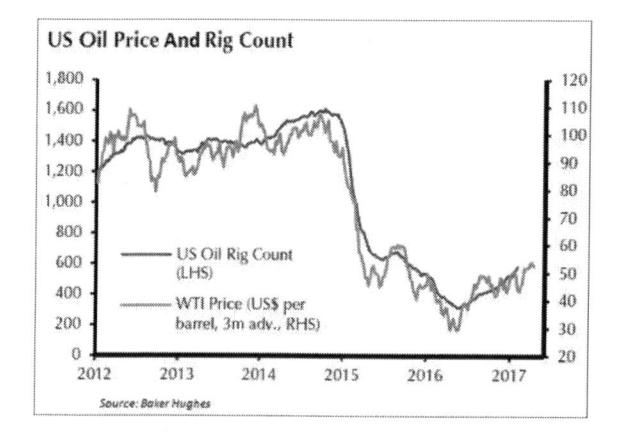

US Oil Price And Rig Count

Source: Baker Hughes

With the vast shale oil and gas reserves held by the US **and other non-Middle East (and non-OPEC) countries, this energy resource had been widely tipped as being a stunning game-changer for the global energy market, implying a corollary shift in geopolitical power.** This remains the case, albeit with two important caveats: there are wide discrepancies of shale oil resources recoverable both from different deposits and even within a single deposit itself, and the 'unconventional' extraction costs for shale oil are often significantly higher than for oil retrieved by 'conventional methods' in most of the key oil producing states.

Rank	Country	Shale oil (billion barrels)
1	Russia	75
2	U.S.	58
3	China	32
4	Argentina	27
5	Libya	26
6	Australia	18
7	Venezuela	13
8	Mexico	13
9	Pakistan	9
10	Canada	9
	World Total	345

Top 10 Countries For Technically Recoverable Shale Oil Resources

Rank	Country	Shale gas (trillion cubic feet)
1	China	1,115
2	Argentina	802
3	Algeria	707
4	U.S.	665
5	Canada	573
6	Mexico	545
7	Australia	437
8	South Africa	390
9	Russia	285
10	Brazil	245
	World Total	7,299

Top 10 Countries For Technically Recoverable Shale Gas Resources

Source: EIA

Iran

On **16 January 2016 the Joint Comprehensive Plan of Action (JCPOA) was implemented** in which the P5+1 group of nations (the US, Russia, China, France, the UK plus Germany) removed longstanding sanctions against Iran centred on its nuclear energy activities. Although some important financial sanctions remain on the US's part – focused on the use of the USD in transactions with Iran – **the implementation of the agreement was perhaps the most momentous event in the global oil and gas industry in a generation,** bringing back into the global markets one of the richest oil and gas plays in the world, one which offers international oil companies (IOCs) a vast and largely untapped opportunity to get in on the ground floor of exploration, development and expansion.

Monthly Iranian Exports Of Crude Oil (million barrels per day)

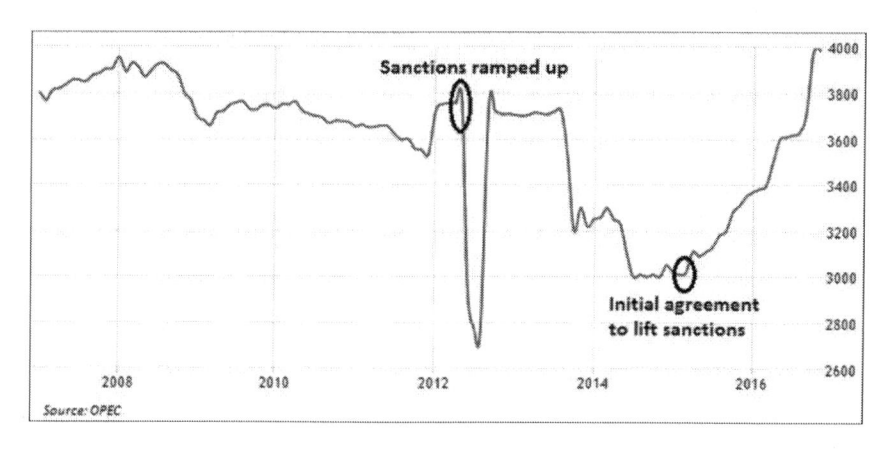

Iran has an estimated 157 billion barrels of proved crude oil reserves, representing nearly 10% of the world's crude oil reserves, 13% of reserves held by OPEC. It ranks as the world's fourth-largest reserve holder of oil and one of its top 10 oil producers. Its oil sector, though, was obviously enormously constrained by sanctions; only a year after the US and the European Union (EU) enacted increased sanctions measures at the end of 2011 and during the summer of 2012, Iran's net oil and natural gas export revenue dropped by 47% to USD63 billion, and the year after they fell another 11% to USD56 billion, despite gas exports numbers holding steady over the period.

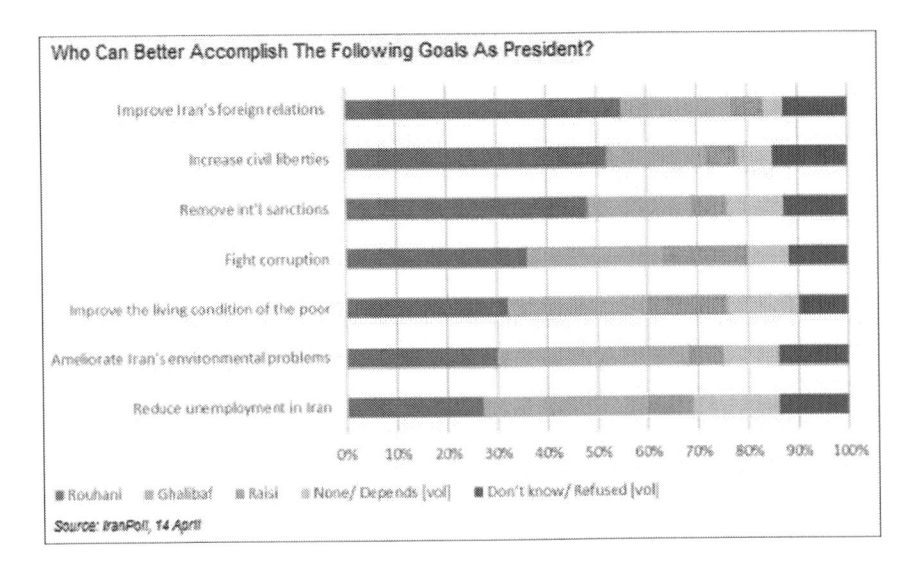

Who Can Better Accomplish The Following Goals As President?

[Bar chart showing responses for the goals: Improve Iran's foreign relations, Increase civil liberties, Remove int'l sanctions, Fight corruption, Improve the living condition of the poor, Ameliorate Iran's environmental problems, Reduce unemployment in Iran. Categories: Rouhani, Ghalibaf, Raisi, None/Depends (vol), Don't know/Refused (vol).]

Source: IranPoll, 14 April

Great as its oil reserves are, its gas reserves are even greater, with **Iran having estimated proved natural gas reserves of 1,193 trillion cubic feet (Tcf), second only to Russia, 17% of the world's total proved natural gas reserves and more than one-third of OPEC's reserves.** Additionally, Iran has a high success rate of natural gas exploration, in terms of wildcat drilling, which is estimated at around 80%, compared to the world average success rate of 30-35%. The country also holds a further estimated 2 Tcf of proved and probable natural gas reserves onshore and offshore in the Caspian basin. Its biggest field is its giant South Pars non-associated gas field – a 3,700 sqkm sector of the 9,700 sqkm basin shared with Qatar (in the form of the 6,000 sqkm North Field) – which accounts for around 40% of the country's natural gas reserves (mostly in the southern region in the Gulf) and around 60% of its gas production.

However, since sanctions have been lifted, crude oil production has bounced back to the level prior to this upping of sanctions in 2011/2012, and **the country's targets for oil, gas and petrochemicals output and exports have been increased dramatically, to game-changing proportions for the global hydrocarbons sector.** Specifically, the official target for oil output is

5.7 mpbd by the end of 2018, but the ultimate target is a minimum of 6.1 mbpd by the beginning of 2020, the official target for gas is 1 bcm by 2018 but the unofficial target is 1.25 bcm by 2020, and for petchems the official target is to increase production capacity to 130 million tonnes per year (mtpy) by 2020 and 180 mtpy by 2025 but the unofficial target is 180 mtpy by 2020 and 230 mtpy by 2025.

The situation since the inauguration of US President Donald Trump has complicated matters, however, although the resounding re-election of moderate and pro-West reformer, Hassan Rouhani as Iran's President on 19 May 2017 may help to untangle them again.

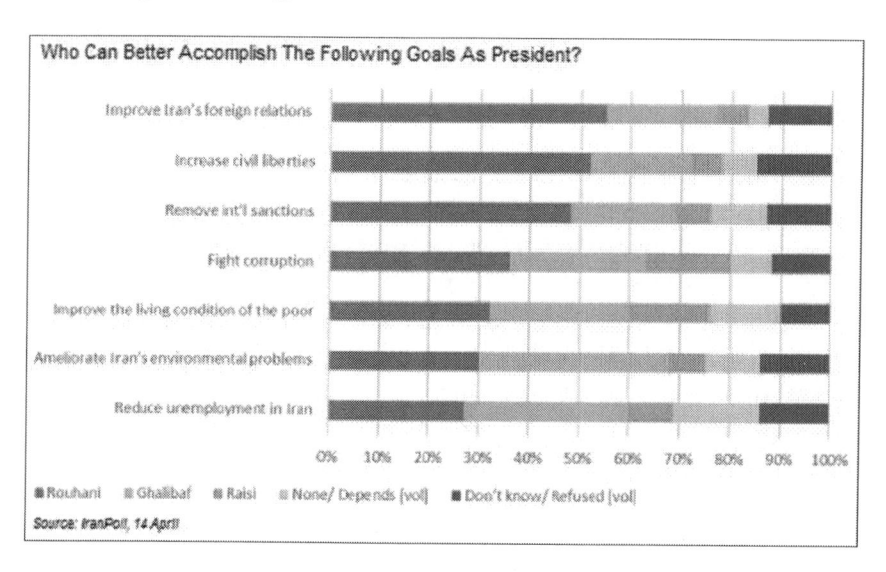

Source: IranPoll, 14 April

In the case of the former, March saw the US scale up its existing sanctions against Iran in response to Iran's ballistic missile test – adding 25 individuals and entities to the list of 'Specifically Designated Nationals' (SDNs) held by the US Treasury's Office of Foreign Assets Control (OFAC) – on top of ongoing financial sanctions, raising the question of what would happen next for US/Iran relations.

To begin with, despite the incendiary comments from President Donald Trump and then National Security Adviser Lieutenant

General (retired) Michael Flynn that "nothing's off the table" regarding a response to the missile test and that "we are officially putting Iran on notice," respectively, there is little prospect that the US is going to undermine or tear up the Joint Committee Plan of Action centred around Iran's nuclear activities. **Even Iran's staunchest opponents have expressed a view that ripping up the deal would be a bad idea,** with both Israel and Saudi Arabia having urged that the deal be rigorously enforced instead. In any event, for one thing, **ballistic missile tests are governed by a separate sanctions arrangement to the nuclear agreement, and for another, even if the US administration wished to scrap the nuclear deal, it would be very difficult to act alone on this,** with Washington presumably needing to get the agreement of the other five world powers that signed up to the deal (Great Britain, Germany, France, China and Russia).

That said, **there is plenty that the US can do itself outside the JCPOA that would re-introduce sanctions that would place Iran back in the same position regarding effective sanctions as it was before the JCPOA was agreed.** Trump is entirely prepared to invoke a laddered approach to scaling up sanctions, the end point of which would put Tehran back in a position similar to that of 2012.

As it is, Trump sees no upside for the US in the current arrangement with Iran and substantial downside, especially given the recent provocations of the missile test, the Iran-sponsored Houthi attack on the Saudi ship in Yemen, and the increasing influence of Iran in Iraq after all the US did there in terms of blood spilt and money spent. The ladder would involve: adding further people and firms to the SDN list, more rigorously implementing the financial sanctions against everybody, including firms in Europe that are testing them now, implementing new sanctions forbidding trade in oil and gas and petchems, and then implementing sanctions against the Iranian economy as a whole in terms of trading, investment, service provision and anything else Trump can think of.

For its part, **Iran currently has two key strategies to mitigate the possibility of the US further ramping up sanctions.** The first is to **convey to the Trump administration that Iran would welcome much more involvement from US firms in the Islamic Republic and to encourage Iraq to do the same.** Around 35 months ago, Iran decided that it was a beneficial idea to encourage more US firms – both IOCs and general industrial concerns – to become more involved in Iran, as it would be good for Iran and would also act as the basis for closer relations generally between the two countries, and this strategy is still on the table. The corollary encouraging of Iraq by Iran to do the same would also serve to mollify US concerns that Iran's influence with its neighbour is detrimental to US interests there, as was highlighted by Trump himself during his presidential campaign, when he Tweeted "Iran is rapidly taking over more and more of Iraq even after the US has squandered three trillion dollars there. Obvious long ago!' and then stated during the third debate with Hillary Clinton that 'Iran is taking over Iraq."

The second part of the strategy has been to **encourage deals with foreign firms to be done by Iranian firms that can be viewed as being of the 'private sector' – preferably listed in the Tehran Stock Exchange – rather than being more evidently state-controlled, with the inference of the involvement of the Islamic Revolutionary Guards Corps that this might entail.** In this context, prior to the implementation of the sanctions-removal deal, Emanuele Ottolenghi, a senior fellow with the foundation for Defense of Democracies, testified before a sub-committee of the US House Committee on Foreign Affairs that **the IRGC had significant ownership shares in 27 companies that are publicly traded on the TSE.** In support of his position he cited a pay-walled New York Times article that indicated that the IRGC had placed top commanders at the heart of more than 200 Iranian companies. Indeed, according to Ottolengthi, the IRGC is active in the Iranian oil, gas, petrochemical, automotive, transportation, telecommunications, construction, and metals and mining sectors

That said, though, aside from the difficulties arising from the ongoing financial sanctions, US oil firms have not lobbied as actively as might be expected. Clearly in the past, the IOCs have had a considerable interest and influence in American politics, but on the Iran issue the US IOCs appear currently conflicted. On the one hand, there is the view that the opportunities in Iran are enormous and that they should probably be more involved at the relatively early stages on field developments there but on the other Iran is regarded as being a very volatile political entity that could do something at some point that might undermine their reputation, so this has resulted in the oil and gas lobbyists placing minimal pressure on the previous or current administration or on congress.

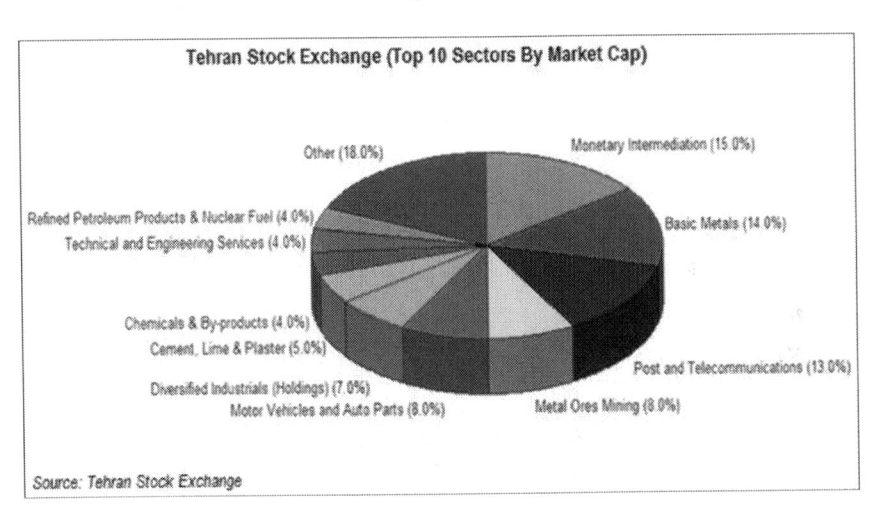

Tehran Stock Exchange (Top 10 Sectors By Market Cap)

- Monetary Intermediation (15.0%)
- Basic Metals (14.0%)
- Post and Telecommunications (13.0%)
- Metal Ores Mining (8.0%)
- Motor Vehicles and Auto Parts (8.0%)
- Diversified Industrials (Holdings) (7.0%)
- Cement, Lime & Plaster (5.0%)
- Chemicals & By-products (4.0%)
- Technical and Engineering Services (4.0%)
- Refined Petroleum Products & Nuclear Fuel (4.0%)
- Other (18.0%)

Source: Tehran Stock Exchange

One such bump in the road could appear shortly, with **the dumping of the US dollar by Iran as a currency of transactions and payments.** From Iran's perspective, the switch to either transactions based on a basket of currencies – like the IMF's Special Drawing Rights (SDR) asset or the euro – will pose few problems from the broader economic side as, due to the years of sanctions, it has very little trade with the US (its most important trading partner is the

UAE, which accounts for around 24% of all Iranian imports and exports. China is not far behind with 22%, followed by Turkey, India and the EU, all of which account for around 6% of Iran's trade). Having said that, the move (that triggered fury from the US when it was done in Libya and Iraq under Muammar Gaddafi and Saddam Hussein, respectively) may not be unwelcome to the US from Iran at this stage. It could be beneficial to the implementation of the current financial sanctions if the dollar was not allowed to be used in trade, further excluding US firms from getting involved with Iran.

An adjunct critical point is that **Iran is relying on support from its two key allies on the UN Security Council permanent members voting bloc – Russia and China.** In China's case, such support appears guaranteed, given its energy security needs and heavy involvement already in hydrocarbons fields in both Iran and Iraq, but in Russia's case, Tehran's confidence about unequivocal enduring support is, justifiably, measured. Iran's view is that it cannot 100% rely on Russia to back it up, with the reason being that although Russia will certainly veto in the UN any sanction for missile tests and increased sanctions, in reality Moscow would be very happy if further sanctions pushed Iranian oil exports down and the price of oil up, as Russia needs oil at USD86pb to take it into a neutral budget position rather than a deficit.

Additionally, the reduction of Iran's gas export plans into Europe is a top priority for Russia as it does not want Iranian supplies into Europe undermining its power there, which it regards as its own backyard. Added to this, Russia has high hopes of forging a very close relationship with new US Secretary of State Rex Tillerson who, as chairman and chief executive officer of US IOC giant Exxon, turned the desolate Sakhalin island into one of Russia's most lucrative oil provinces, affording the country a crucial entry into the fast-growing oil markets of Asia and generating nearly USD5 billion in tax dollars and other revenue for Moscow as of the end of 2016.

Ultimately, of course, as a self-proclaimed arch-dealmaker, **much of Trump's latest rhetoric may be simply geared towards** improving the business backdrop for the US in Iran (and Iraq); after all, he often spoke on the campaign trail of improving the JCPOA deal, rather than tearing it up (indeed, he added that: "We have a horrible contract, but we do have a contract"). Indeed, although he has frequently described the JCPOA deal as a 'disaster', ranking among the worst deals in US history, he has also stated that: "I would love to tell you that I'm going to rip up this contract, I'm going to be the toughest guy in the world but you know what life doesn't work that way." That said, the comment was made before the missile test, the attack on the Saudi ship and the threat from Iran of more tests, rendering the real Presidential viewpoint now as very fluid.

Iraq

Iraq's **master plan was to produce 4 mbpd by the end of 2015, which it achieved, and 9 mbpd by 2020,** with much of this being dependent on two long-term factors: a sustained deal with the Kurdistan Regional Government (KRG) and the ongoing and successful development of its giant West Qurna field, located 65 km northwest of the southern port city of Basra. With total estimated recoverable reserves of 43 billion barrels of oil in place, this makes it the second biggest field in the world after Saudi Arabia's Ghawar.

However, unlike Ghawar's numbers and those of many neighbouring countries, **Iraq's reserves figures look solid – in fact if anything an under-estimate – with much verification work done by the Americans when they were on the ground in Iraq, as well as the numbers produced by the international oil companies before, during and after the occupation,** and the Iraqi administration itself. With the current development programme comprising Phase 1 (operated by ExxonMobil, Royal Dutch Shell, Petro China and Iraq's own South Oil Company) holding around 9 bbbl reserves and Phase 2 (operated by Lukoil) with about 14 bbl reserves, in theory West Qurna could be a game changer for the global oil market. In practice, though, there remain questions over the degree to which Iraq's ambitious output plans will be realised on schedule, particularly with regard to West Qurna-1 and relations with the KRG.

In the case of the former, **disagreements between the US energy giant and the Iraqi government in Baghdad over the former's dealings with the KRG have served to slow development progress on the field ever since the original contract was signed in 2009.** Ultimately this led to ExxonMobil selling 35% of the 60% stake that it held with RDS to the Chinese (25%) and Indonesia's Pertamina (10%) in November 2013, but prior to this Russian oil giant Rosneft was very close to buying out almost the entire stake from Exxon, and it was only when the US government vetoed the idea with Exxon that the company started to look elsewhere. However, given the rapidly changing political dynamics between Russia, Iran and Iraq, there are likely to be opportunities in West Qurna-1 for Russian firms in the near future.

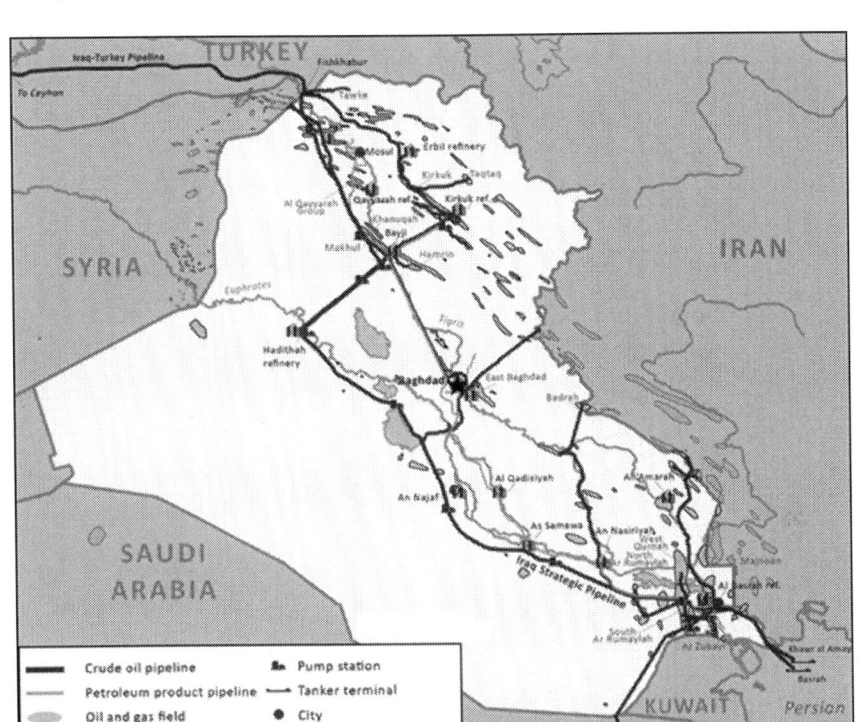

Iraq: Selected Oil And Gas Infrastructure

Source: EIA

For ExxonMobil, the decision to sell the rest of its stake in West Qurna-1 is being made all the more palatable by continued delays in the Common Seawater Supply Facility (CSSF), which would treat seawater from the Gulf and pump it more than 100 km inland for the water-injection purposes required to boost reservoir pressure in both West Qurna phases, but more urgently in the first, more mature, field. In this respect, industry reports stated that the lack of water for injection led to a decline in production at West Qurna-1 in the first half of 2014 of 40% to 300 kbpd from the same period in 2013, and it is unlikely that the CSSF will become fully operational until mid-2018.

Similar delays are apparent as well in the matter of exporting oil from the south. For some time now, the available pumping and storage capacity at the main export depot of Fao has been constrained, both by lower than required storage capacity and by its pumps not being powerful enough. Indeed, the delay in building the 24 new storage tanks envisaged has necessitated the construction, for the new single point mooring systems, of interim pipelines bypassing the terminal. As a consequence, oil is pumped onto tankers directly from more than 100 km onshore and any halt to offshore loading – which can often be weather-related – can force a reduction in production at the West Qurna fields. Until the problems at Fao are addressed, expanded or new pipelines linking the existing offshore terminals at Khor al-Amaya and Al-Basra to onshore facilities will be irrelevant in bringing seaborne export capacity up to the 8 mbpd sufficient to support Iraq's top-end production and export targets for 2020.

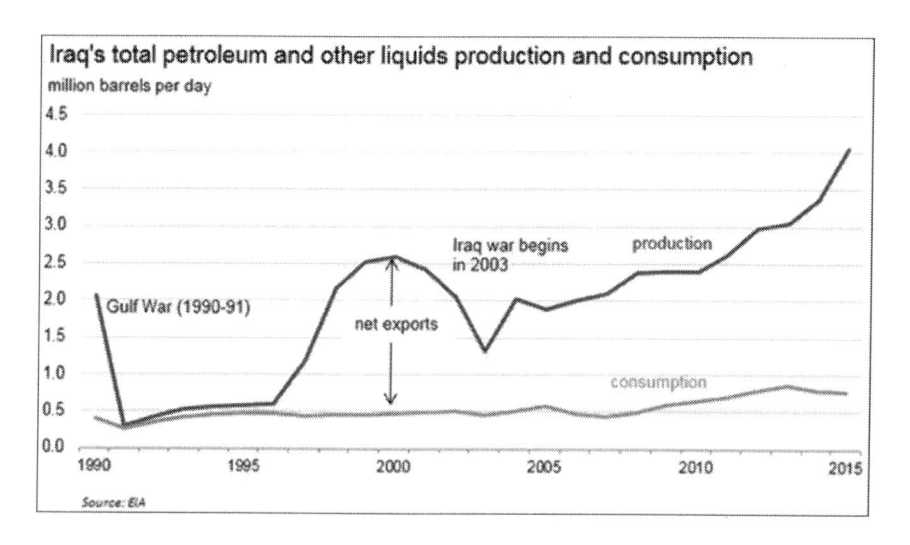

Iraq's total petroleum and other liquids production and consumption
million barrels per day

Chart showing production and consumption from 1990 to 2015, with annotations: Gulf War (1990-91), Iraq war begins in 2003, net exports, production, consumption. Source: EIA

In the latter's case, meanwhile, **the KRG's Prime Minister, Nechirvan Barzani, has repeatedly warned that if Baghdad does not honour its part of the budget cash for oil deal struck in December 2014 then nor will the Kurds.** This deal involved the KRG having agreed to export up to 550,000 bbl/d of oil from its own fields and Kirkuk via Iraq's State Oil Marketing Organisation

(SOMO), in return for which Baghdad was to have re-instated all budget payments to the Kurds that it had stopped in 2014 as punishment for the semi-autonomous region's moves to export oil independently.

It is not just the money in which the KRG is interested but rather what it signifies in terms of an acknowledgement of the Kurds' wider involvement in the Iraqi state, especially its role as the West's 'boots on the ground fighting' proxy – the Peshmerga – against Islamic State (IS). **The understanding between the US and the Kurds was that if the Kurds held the north then the KRG's claims to have a completely autonomous state for the Kurds would be expedited. This, though, was not a notion that was necessarily fully shared by Baghdad.** The Shiite-dominated Iraqi government and its backers in Iran have sought to prevent the Kurds from consolidating control over the oil-rich province of Kirkuk, and they continued to do so by operating through Shiite militias that were battling alongside the Peshmerga against the Islamic State and playing off the personal ambitions of the Kirkuk governor.

The Metals Market

There are two basic types of metal for the purposes of trading:

1. Those **precious metals** used predominantly as a **store of value** (the main one here being gold, but also silver), used as a hedge against inflation by investors and as a **safe haven** during times of market stress, despite giving no actual investor return (i.e. interest rate or dividend).

2. Those **base metals** whose value comes from their **practical applications** (like copper, aluminium and zinc, in housing and industry), again offering no actual investor return.

In terms of the influence of the supply and demand balance mentioned as a cornerstone of commodities pricing earlier, the first group, especially gold, **is less subject to what is found in terms of new supplies or rises in demand than the second group.** On the supply side there are two elements that conspire to ensure that supplies remain relatively steady at levels able to meet any sudden surges in demand. The first is that **vast quantities of them, especially gold, are held around the world as a store of value,** with most major central banks around the world having very large stores of physical gold in their vaults, along with some trading houses and banks. Consequently (all other factors remaining equal) if the price of gold rises markedly some of this retained gold is likely to be sold in order to make profits by those holding it, which will push the price back down again, and when the price then falls markedly buyers will step in to replenish or add to their reserves, so the price of gold in usual circumstances remains range-bound.

This vast amount of stored gold offsets the second factor pertinent to steady supply, which is **the constraint on bringing new mines online, with the latter taking 5- ten years to bring into production.** The same dynamic, although less definitively, applies to silver and platinum whilst for base metals, price movements tend to be much longer-lasting and uni-directional.

The trading correlations – both positive and negative – between metals and other asset classes are gone into in great depth later on in this book.

Gold

Historically, as briefly touched on already, gold has been a **principal beneficiary of heightened risk across the globe,** because, unlike currencies, more cannot simply be produced at the drop of a central bank's printing presses, as in quantitative easing (QE) programs. Indeed, between 1998 and 2008, as the US dollar weakened first on poor economic data and then on extended QE programs, the price of gold tripled. Risk-related changes to the capital requirement rules around the globe have also acted in very recent years to underpin the gold price. In particular, the Basel III directive introduced on 1 January 2013 (in conjunction with various other changes to the global regulatory investment framework) changed the rules on what can be used as collateral in investments and how much collateral any item can be used as. Crucially, in this respect, gold can now be used as collateral on a 1:1 basis (called Tier 1 capital) and not on a 1:2 basis (Tier 3 capital as it was before). In addition, in some cultures in Asia – notably India – gold is given as part of wedding celebrations, producing a significant spike in demand in the key month of October.

Gold has also been regarded as the archetypal **'safe-haven' commodities asset in times of political uncertainty** (troubles in the Middle East, for example, sparking buying not just in that area but around the globe) **and economic uncertainty** (ongoing anaemic growth in some key global economies) in the same way that the Swiss franc is seen as such in currency terms. This is why when stocks are generally performing badly – a product of bad prevailing economic conditions – gold does well. In recent years, for example, stocks did poorly but gold did well, in the booming 1980s and 1990s stocks did well but gold did poorly, and during the Great Financial Crisis, when stocks plummeted, gold shot up.

Gold Price (USD Per Troy Ounce) — Source: ADVFN

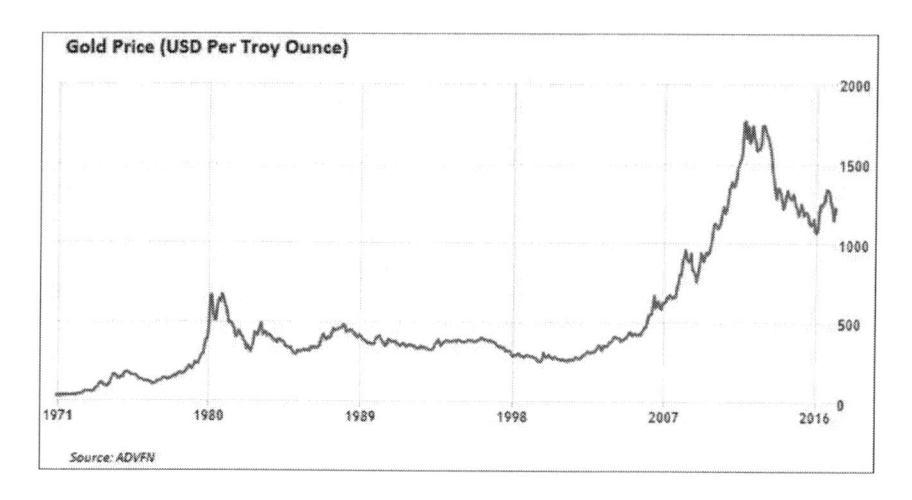

Additionally, it has been seen as a hedge against inflation concerns that have risen sharply on the basis of the QE policies adopted by the Fed, the BOJ, the ECB – the long-term refinancing operations (LTRO) was QE by another name – and until recently the BOE as well.

Recently, as well, gold is seen as a good buy in the unusual interest rates scenario that we are seeing playing out around the world (very low or negative rates). One factor in this context is that, although the economic uncertainty and distress associated with low or negative rates would tend to increase interest in gold anyway, the more pronounced shift of monetary policy in this direction by central banks is encouraging even greater flows into bullion, as the opportunity cost of holding gold (which offers no yield to investors, either in terms of interest rate or dividend) has narrowed markedly compared to other assets (which now in the developed markets hold very low interest rates).

Silver

Slightly down the pure investment scale from gold, **the price of silver comprises two factors: first, the investment rationale, as delineated for gold above, and second its practical applications,** which most notably include use in cell phones, computers, televisions and batteries. Each part of this equation forms around 50% of the total demand profile for silver, although relatively small changes in this balance can produce much bigger changes in price. For example, during the booming years of emerging markets, in which demand for the above-mentioned items rocketed, the silver price moved sharply upwards at the same time as its demand as an investment vehicle remained fairly static.

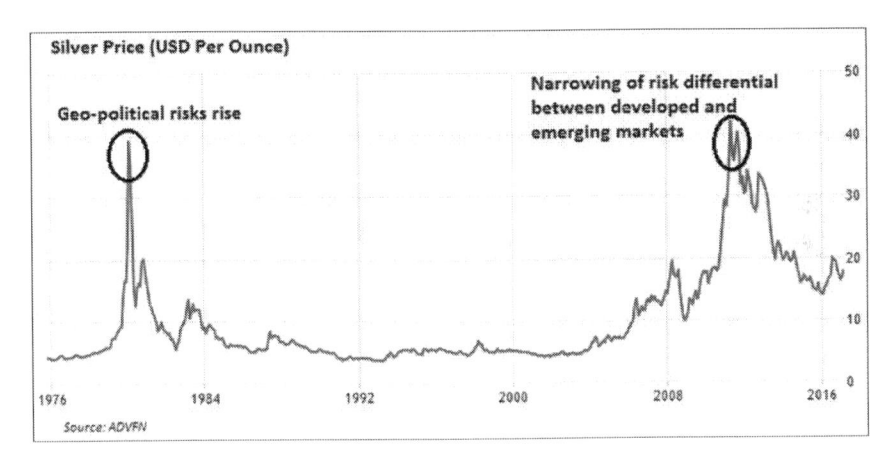

Silver Price (USD Per Ounce)

Geo-political risks rise

Narrowing of risk differential between developed and emerging markets

Source: ADVFN

However, it is also apposite to note that pure investment flows are critical to both gold and silver trading, as for every 100 ounces of gold and or silver traded on paper there is only one actual ounce of gold or silver to back up these trades. Highlighting this is the often-observed incongruity between the physical supplies of silver (and, indeed, gold) and the metals' prices. For example, the price of silver rose from around USD4/oz during a period of supply deficits to around USD32/oz during a period of surplus supply, as shown below.

Silver Deficit-Surplus vs. Price

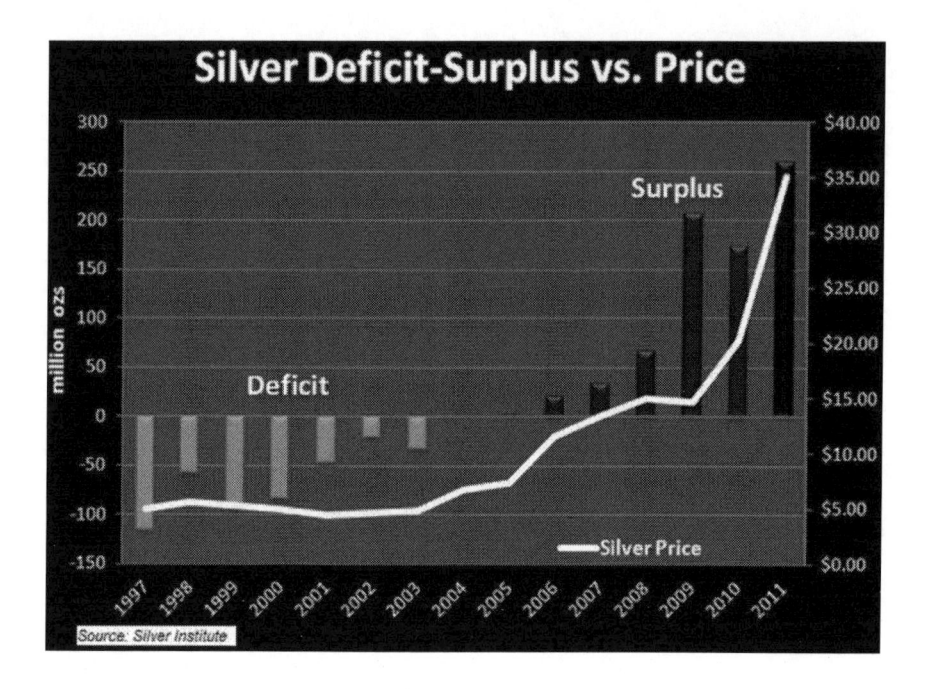

Source: Silver Institute

Other Metals

Unlike gold and silver, other metals are subject less to the straightforward 'investment' arguments – and thus the same dramatic whipsawing in price that we saw with gold in the past few years or so – than to a combination of 'investment and/or industrial utility' rationales.

For the platinum group metals (PGMs), **platinum itself is barely viewed as an investment asset at all, principally because there is so little of it physically that it makes electronic trading in the metal a much more difficult prospect than gold or silver.** Indeed, of the 245 tonnes or so of platinum sold on average per year, around 113 tonnes are used for vehicle emissions control devices (46%), 76 tonnes for jewellery (31%) and the remainder being utilised in various other minor applications, such as investment, electrodes, anti-cancer drugs, oxygen sensors, spark plugs and turbine engines. Meanwhile, its PGM counterpart, palladium, is 60% utilised in the automotive industry (in catalytic converters).

For the major base metals – copper, iron ore, aluminium, zinc – **the argument for future investment trajectories becomes less directly about expectations for inflation, interest rates and FX levels and more about growth prospects in key markets, especially China, and then about supply projections to meet that growth** (more of this later).

In this context, **China has accounted for around 50% of the world's total demand for all base metals and around 20% of its energy demand in the past twenty years, but over that period the country's growth was heavily skewed towards manufacturing and infrastructure development, whereas in the most recent five year economic plan it has shifted its growth strategy towards being more consumer-led.**

The Basics Of Bond Trading

A Key Part Of Any Investment Portfolio

In its simplest terms, **a bond is simply a loan – to a government, corporation or other entity – and anyone buying a bond becomes a creditor of that borrower. Like any loan, the lender needs to assess the balance between the reward (in this case, the interest rate being offered) and the risk (the likelihood that the loan will be repaid in full at the designated time).**

As highlighted in the earlier sections, the likelihood of a loan being repaid as it should be can be gleaned from the credit rating of the borrower, with the basic demarcation being between those classed as 'investment grade' (the most likely to repay in full on time) and 'junk' (at the opposite end of the scale), with the full listing of the grades available below. Obviously, the greater the perceived chance that the borrower will repay in full on time then the less risk involved and the lower the compensation (interest rate) that the borrower needs to pay the creditor in order to entice his money from him (clearly the reverse of this equation also holds good).

At A Glance Credit Risk Assessment Grid

Quality	Grade	Moody's	S&P	Fitch
Strongest	Investment	Aaa	AAA	AAA
Very Strong	Investment	Aa1, Aa2, Aa3	AA+, AA, AA-	AA+, AA, AA-
Above Average	Investment	A1, A2, A3	A+, A, A-	A+, A, A-
Average	Investment	Baa1, Baa2, Baa3	BBB+, BBB, BBB-	BBB+, BBB, BBB-
Below Average	Junk	Ba1, Ba2, Ba3	BB+, BB, BB-	BB+, BB, BB-
Weak	Junk	B1, B2, B3	B+, B, B-	B+, B, B-
Very Weak	Junk	Caa1, Caa2, Caa3	CCC+, CCC, CCC-	CCC
Extremely Weak	Junk	Ca	CC, C	CCC
Weakest or In Default	Junk	C	D	DDD, DD, D

Source: Credit ratings agencies

In the broadest sense, **bonds can be viewed as less inherently risky investments than FX, equities and commodities, although there are significant exceptions to this rule, as was shown in the disastrous bond plays that blew up during the Great Financial Crisis.** Nonetheless, the longer-term bonds (ten years plus duration) of major developed market countries can legitimately be seen as 100% likely to repay in full on time, which is why they offer low interest rates in comparison to even major corporations in those same countries.

This is why, in times that risk is regarded as being generally high across the globe, investors tend to move their money into bonds rather than hold it in stocks, and **this broad-based inverse relationship is essential for the trader to understand in order to capitalise on these major shifts in sentiment in all asset markets.** From the perspective of readers of this book, then, there are two ways in which bonds can be viewed: first, actually holding (buying) bonds as part of an overall investment portfolio to provide longer-term safe returns; and, second, trading (buying or selling them at any given moment) for shorter-term gains.

One way to reduce risk in your portfolio is to use the method of asset allocation. A good rule of thumb is the "Rule of 100". Simply subtract your age from 100 – that's the percentage you should consider investing in stocks, with the remainder in bonds, which reflects a lower risk taken as one grows older.

For the trader, **the absolute basic concept to understand is that bonds fall in market price if the interest rate of the country in which they are issued goes up and they rise in market price if the interest rate of the country in which they are issued goes down.** The reason for this basically is the opportunity cost of holding a bond giving a certain amount of interest against the interest rate of new bonds coming out.

In simple terms, if an investor is holding a US bond that is giving him a 5% annual rate of return and the interest rate in the US is 4% then the difference in interest rate on the bond is favourable for the investor, but if the US interest rate moves up to 6% then that difference becomes unfavourable and the amount that investors are willing to pay to hold it will go down (and vice-versa, of course). As with all trading, it is not just the actual current interest rate that influences the price of a bond but the perceived future interest rate as well (in addition to not just the issuer's current credit rating but also the perceived future rating).

Another absolutely critical point to understand is the straight mathematical relationship between price and yield: that is, for reasons outlined below, when the price of a bond goes up the yield goes down and vice-versa.

Finally, all bonds have three basic characteristics: face value, coupon and maturity date, with a fourth characteristic, duration, being a calculation that allows the investor to assess relative interest rate risk.

Basic Terminology

Face Value ('Par')

This is the amount of money the bond holder will receive from the issuer when a bond reaches its maturity date. This is usually in units of 1,000 of the currency of the country in which the bond is issued (so, in the US, the biggest bond market in the world, the face value of most bonds is USD1,000), although multiples of this are also seen.

Bonds that trade at more than face value are said to be trading at a 'premium', while those trading for less than face value are said to be trading at a 'discount' and one bond can trade alternately at a premium and a discount at different periods during their lifespan.

It is important to note that the price of a bond is always expressed in units of 100 of the currency of the country in which the bond is issued (so, in the US, bond prices are always expressed in terms of USD100).

The 'principal' amount that a buyer of a bond will pay is the calculation between the price and the face value.

Coupon

This is the amount of interest paid on the bond, which can be 'fixed' at a certain rate for the lifetime of the bond, or can change over that lifetime ('floating') or can pay no coupon at all ('zero coupon' bond, from which the investor receives a return instead from the deep discount to the face value that he can buy the bond when it is issued).

Obviously, then, if a bond has a face value of USD10,000 and a coupon of 10% then the bond holder will receive USD1,000 interest every year for the lifetime of the bond and, if he holds the bond until maturity then he will also receive the USD10,000 face value.

Maturity Date

This is the day when the issuer has promised to repay the bond holder the full face value of the bond.

It is important to note that generally the bond from an issuer with a longer maturity date than a shorter one will attract a higher coupon, as the risks (of default, changes in interest rates, credit ratings and so on) on the longer-dated bond are deemed to be greater the more time goes by.

Yield

This is not to be confused with the 'coupon', as both show a return of sorts, but rather the yield is a figure that shows the return gained on a bond at a particular point in time, incorporating the bond's current price.

The most basic version of yield is calculated using the following formula: Yield = Coupon amount/Price.

When you buy a bond at par, yield is equal to the coupon but when the price changes, so does the yield. So, for example, when you buy a new bond with a 10% coupon at its USD1,000 face value then the yield is 10% (USD100/USD1,000). However, if the price goes down to USD600, then the yield goes up to 16.66% because you are receiving the same guaranteed USD100 on an asset that is now worth only USD600 (USD100/USD600). Conversely, if the bond goes up in price to USD1,400, then the yield falls to 7.14% (USD100/USD1,400).

Yield To Maturity

In the markets, when bond players refer to yield, they are usually referring to 'yield to maturity', and this is a calculation that reflects the total return that you will receive if you hold the bond to maturity.

It equals all the interest payments you will receive (and assumes that you will reinvest the interest payment at the same rate as the current yield on the bond) plus any gain (if you purchased at a discount) or loss (if you purchased at a premium).

Duration

This is used to estimate how sensitive a particular bond's price is to interest rate movements. More specifically, it is a weighted average of the present value of a bond's cash flows, which include a series of regular coupon payments followed by a much larger payment at the end when the bond matures and the face value is repaid.

Duration is expressed in years – usually less than maturity – and is affected by the size of the regular coupon payments and the bond's face value. For a zero-coupon bond, as there are no regular coupon payments and all cash flows occur at maturity, maturity and duration are equal. Because of this feature, zero-coupon bonds tend to provide the most price movement for a given change in interest rates, which can make zero-coupon bonds attractive to investors expecting a decline in rates.

The key use of the duration calculation, which differs for every bond issue, is that it allows investors to compare all bonds (with differing maturities, coupons, face value and so on) on a like-for-like basis. By extension, it also gives an idea of the price change that will occur to each bond issue in the event of a 1% change in interest rates.

Different Types Of Bonds

Government Bonds

This includes 'sovereign' debt, which is issued and usually backed by a central government. A number of governments also issue sovereign bonds that are linked to inflation, known as inflation-linked bonds. On an inflation-linked bond, the interest and/or principal is adjusted on a regular basis to reflect changes in the rate of inflation, providing a 'real' return. It is important to note that inflation-linked bonds, unlike other bond types, are liable to experience greater losses when real interest rates are moving faster than nominal interest rates.

In addition to sovereign bonds, the government bond sector includes sub-components, such as *Agency and 'quasi-government' bonds,* issued by various government agencies and sometimes (but not always) guaranteed by the central government, and by supranational organisations, like the World Bank and the European Investment Bank); and *Local government bonds,* issued by local governments to finance various projects.

Corporate Bonds

These are issued by companies to finance operational expansion or new business ventures.

Emerging Market Bonds

Sovereign and corporate bonds issued by developing countries are also known as emerging market (EM) bonds. Since the 1990s, the emerging market asset class has developed and matured to include a wide variety of government and corporate bonds, issued in major external currencies, including the US dollar and the euro, and local currencies (often referred to as emerging local market bonds).

Mortgage-backed Securities (MBS) And Asset-Backed Securities (ABS)

In these, the cash flows from various types of loans (mortgage payments, car payments or credit card payments, for example) are bundled together and resold to investors as bonds.

Non-Government Bonds

These tend to be priced relative to government bond yields; for example, US Treasuries (UST) or the London Interbank Offered Rate (Libor), with the difference being referred to as the 'credit spread' (e.g. UST+50 bps or Libor+50 bps), with a basis point (bp) being one hundredth of 1% (or 0.01%).

Basic Bond Trading Strategies

To recap, there are three key points to bear in mind when looking at investing in bonds – that there is an inverse relationship to stocks (i.e. when stocks are in demand bonds are not), that when interest rates are rising bond prices fall, and that when a bond's yield increases its price decreases. **There are also a number of basic bond trading strategies that investors should know, whether trading them for their own account or looking to identify bond market trends in order to trade other assets.** These are briefly outlined below.

Passive ('Buy And Hold')

As the name suggests, this involves **buying individual bonds, holding them to maturity and using the interest gained on them** to either fund general income needs or, better from the overall investment perspective, reinvesting these interest payments in more bond purchases or in investing in other asset classes. High credit quality bonds are typically the mainstay of this strategy.

A slightly more proactive approach to the passive strategy is **'bond laddering'**. In this as one set of bonds reach maturity, the capital sum redeemed is invested into another group of bonds with a new maturity. The investor would decide on the overall length of the ladder; for example, he decides to invest up to a maximum of ten years, so buys bonds that have a maturity of one year from the initial investment and then one year after that and so on. Once the initial one year matures, then the two year bond becomes the one year run of the ladder and the money redeemed from the initial one year investment is reinvested in 10 year bonds.

A variant of this is the **'barbell'**, in which money is invested in a combination of short-term and long-term bonds; as the short-term bonds mature, investors can reinvest to take advantage of market opportunities while the long-term bonds provide attractive coupon rates.

Indexing

This is a step up from straight passive investing and involves **attempting to provide the risk and return characteristics of a pre-selected bond index** (such as, for global bonds, the Barclays Capital Aggregate Bond Index or the Citi World Broad Investment-Grade Bond Index, and for emerging market bonds, the J.P. Morgan Emerging Markets Bond Index), with high credit quality bonds again being the foundation stone of this approach.

The upside is that if the bond index selected does well then so does the investor's own bond portfolio, with the reverse being true as a downside, plus when the index being tracked is re-balanced the investor has to do the same, incurring greater transaction costs than the basic buy-and-hold strategy.

Immunisation

Here, a portfolio is geared towards **producing a defined return for a specific period of time regardless of any extraneous factors** (like interest rates, inflation, credit changes and so on). The classic form of this approach is investment in zero-coupon bonds, matching maturities to the dates on which interest rate payouts are required.

Active

There is a wide variety of tactics that feed into this overall strategy but its **basic aim is to produce greater returns (income and/or capital appreciation) than can be achieved by any of the above passive strategies, including indexing.**

Many of these trading edges – including bottom up, top down, sectoral rotation, supply and demand shifts and macroeconomic variances – have already been touched on and will be gone into in more depth throughout this book.

There are, though, nuances that apply to bond investment of this type, as below:

Duration management

This reflects the shortening or lengthening of a bond portfolio's overall maturity profile to anticipate expected changes in interest rates. So, if a rise in rates is expected then the duration can be shortened (as bond prices will fall) by selling some longer-term bonds and buying short-term bonds. The reverse, of course, applies, if a fall in interest rates is expected.

Yield curve positioning

Although yields normally rise the closer they get to their maturity date, the relationship of different bonds with different maturities changes all the time, and portfolios can be adjusted to reflect either actual or anticipated changes.

Roll down

Generally speaking, given the 'time value of money' – that is, money available immediately is worth more than the same amount in the future due to its potential earning capacity – short-term interest rates are lower than longer-term rates.

Consequently, bonds are valued at successively lower yields (because less compensation is required to make up for time value lost) and higher prices (mathematically, prices rise as yields fall) as it approaches maturity or 'rolls down the yield curve'.

Therefore, the trick here is to hold a bond as it appreciates in price and sell it before maturity in order to realise the gain.

Developed Market Debt Versus Emerging Market Debt

Another key principle when looking at the bond markets, aside from those mentioned above (when stocks are in demand bonds are not, when interest rates rise bond prices fall, when a bond's yield increases its price decreases) is that **when developed market (DM) bonds do well then emerging market (EM) bonds do not and vice-versa.** Doing well in this context means that the total pool of global investment money moves in favour of one market at the expense of the other, with the corollary effects on prices and yields.

Basic Convergence Premise

In broad terms, **all emerging markets can be regarded as the ultimate convergence trade,** as most palpably evidenced perhaps in the way that the valuations of eastern European countries' assets in line for EU-accession gradually began to align with those of EU countries' assets (equities up, bond yields down, currencies strengthening) the nearer to accession they drew. **How far off an EM is from having converged into being a DM can be seen from its credit rating, most palpably, aside from other economic and political factors that have been discussed above, and often the broad-based shift in global investment flows can be seen in the first instance in the relative demand of DM and EM bonds.**

Prior to the onset of the Great Financial crisis in 2007/2008, the more immediately investable of this EM sector was probably best symbolised by the **BRIC** countries, comprised of Brazil, Russia, India and China, which led the way on EM valuations by dint principally of their projected economic growth paths. These were followed by the **Next-11** (Mexico, Indonesia, South Korea, Turkey, Bangladesh, Egypt, Nigeria, Pakistan, the Philippines, Vietnam and Iran), of which the first four of the grouping had consistently outperformed the remainder, earning the sobriquet of the **MIST** countries along the way.

As with all elements in the global financial markets, there has been an ebb and flow of money into and out of EM markets, relative to DM markets. **As the relative risk perception between DM countries and EM ones began to narrow from around the 1980s, investment flows into emerging markets increased from USD25 billion in 1980 to USD1.2 trillion in 2013, and over the past ten years alone these flows averaged 5-6% of GDP of the recipient countries, up from around 2% in the '80s and 4% in the '90s.** After that there was a broad-based weakness in EM as a product of the fallout from the lower growth in China which permeated into the EM asset class as a whole and money shifted back to select DM markets.

Even as it stands, though, any gaps in the developed markets' landscape is likely to be filled increasingly over time by the assets of those emerging economies that meet **the basic criteria of an investment destination:**

1. A sustainable fiscal policy.
2. A sound balance of payments profile.
3. A solid financial and political system.

The **additional benefits of EM investment destinations is that more often than not they benefit both from momentum trading and carry trading strategies, given their relatively high interest rates in a broadly zero (or negative) interest rate policy developed markets world.** In this context, it is highly likely that incrementally value-added returns will be accrued from investment in the BRICs, MIST and N-11 countries over time simply as they converge towards developed markets status.

Emerging To Developed Market Progress Is Rarer Than Thought

Having said that, the assumption that is still prevalent amongst global investors of all degrees of talent and experience – that an emerging market will eventually converge into a developed market – has not in fact been borne out historically, although from the pragmatic trading standpoint it is important to know the fact that the global investment community largely believes the idea. Additionally, simply moving towards DM standards of economic, political and institutional transparency reassures investors that risk in a particular EM is declining, so shifting the risk/reward balance favourably towards it.

Nonetheless, from a purely empirical perspective, **it is worth noting that it remains the case that just five of the 38 countries with stock markets – a litmus test in determining EM to DM transfer status – in 1900 have moved from emerging to developed market status to date.** Of the rest, 17 were and are developed, 14 were and are classified as middle-income emerging and those with developed markets in 1900 still dominate the equity landscape, comprising 84% of the MSCI All World Index.

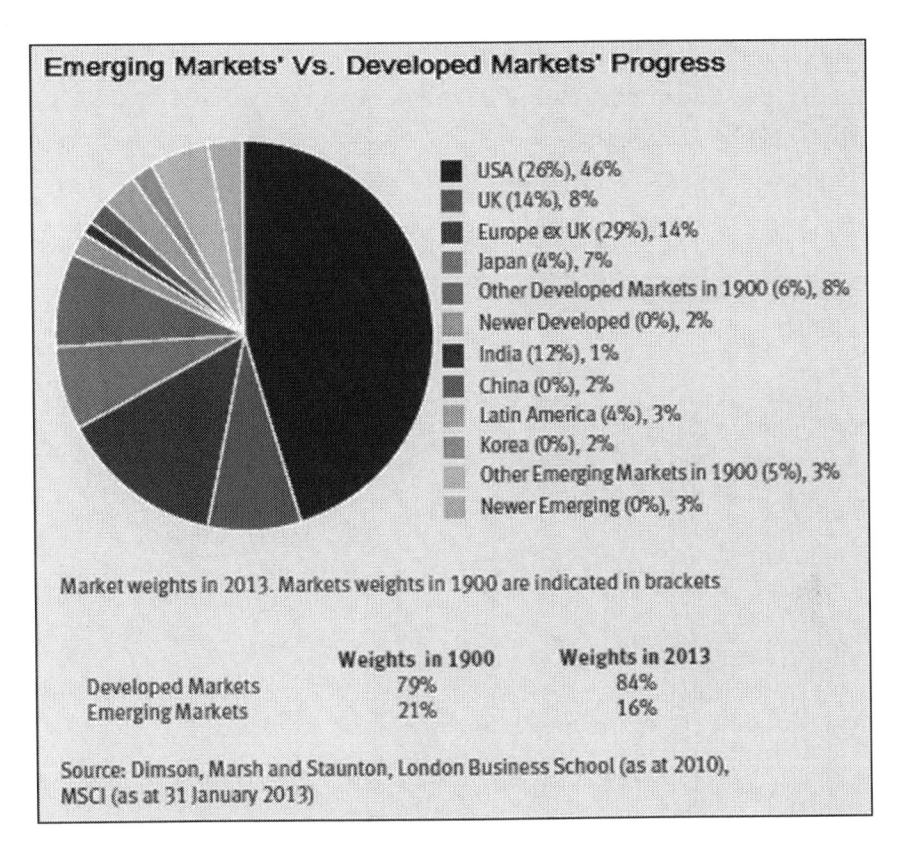

Emerging Markets' Vs. Developed Markets' Progress

- USA (26%), 46%
- UK (14%), 8%
- Europe ex UK (29%), 14%
- Japan (4%), 7%
- Other Developed Markets in 1900 (6%), 8%
- Newer Developed (0%), 2%
- India (12%), 1%
- China (0%), 2%
- Latin America (4%), 3%
- Korea (0%), 2%
- Other Emerging Markets in 1900 (5%), 3%
- Newer Emerging (0%), 3%

Market weights in 2013. Markets weights in 1900 are indicated in brackets

	Weights in 1900	Weights in 2013
Developed Markets	79%	84%
Emerging Markets	21%	16%

Source: Dimson, Marsh and Staunton, London Business School (as at 2010), MSCI (as at 31 January 2013)

Moreover, academic research into the 'middle income trap', which assesses the likelihood of an EM economy progressing to DM status, suggests that the distribution of income also matters. **In this respect, the studies suggest that the more equal the distribution is (that is, the lower the GINI coefficient), the more likely a country is to move up from one level to another.** Other factors that influence development outcomes include the soundness of a country's institutions, progress on structural reforms and sustaining superior growth rates over the decades it would take for income levels to converge with those of developed markets. Indeed, according to the World Bank, only 13 countries have moved from upper middle to high income since 1960. Of those, five are the Asian tigers; others include Greece, Ireland and Spain in Europe and Israel.

In aggregate, **the emerging markets did particularly well during the boom years of 2003-2007, rising from 20% to 34% of global GDP and from 4% to 10% of global equity markets but subsequently, after an initial bounce in 2009, there has been little progress overall.**

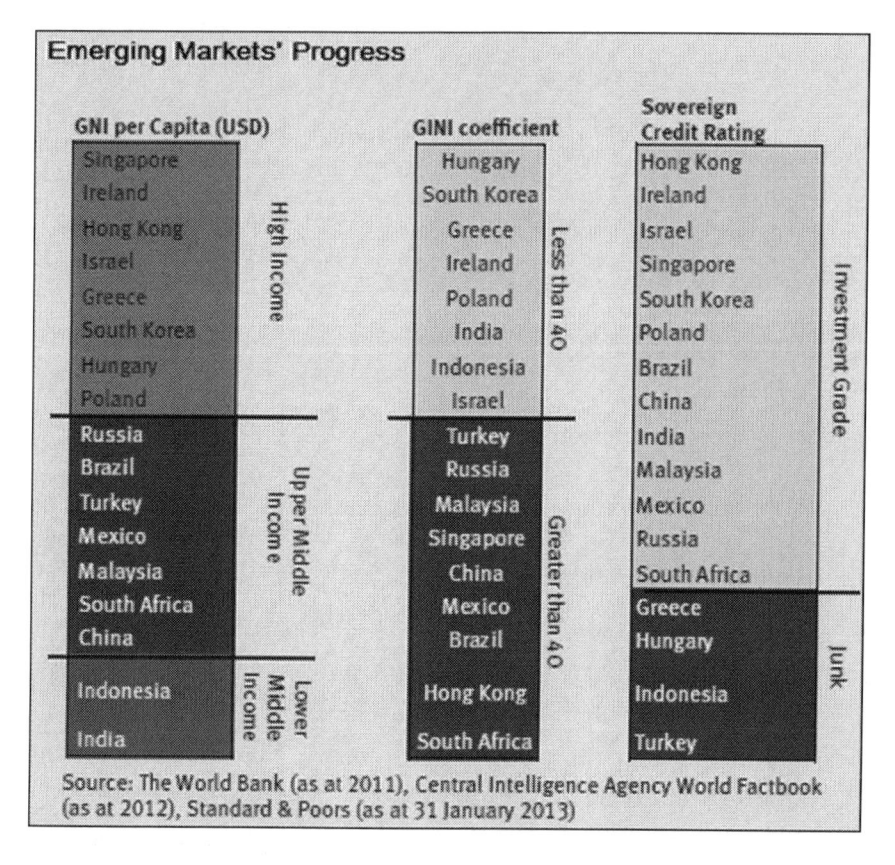

Emerging Markets' Progress

GNI per Capita (USD)		GINI coefficient		Sovereign Credit Rating	
Singapore	High Income	Hungary	Less than 40	Hong Kong	Investment Grade
Ireland		South Korea		Ireland	
Hong Kong		Greece		Israel	
Israel		Ireland		Singapore	
Greece		Poland		South Korea	
South Korea		India		Poland	
Hungary		Indonesia		Brazil	
Poland		Israel		China	
Russia	Upper Middle Income	Turkey	Greater than 40	India	
Brazil		Russia		Malaysia	
Turkey		Malaysia		Mexico	
Mexico		Singapore		Russia	
Malaysia		China		South Africa	
South Africa		Mexico		Greece	Junk
China		Brazil		Hungary	
Indonesia	Lower Middle Income	Hong Kong		Indonesia	
India		South Africa		Turkey	

Source: The World Bank (as at 2011), Central Intelligence Agency World Factbook (as at 2012), Standard & Poors (as at 31 January 2013)

For a country to continue to enjoy enduring appeal to international investors – which creates a push effect on it achieving DM status over time (historically, markets tend to underperform the EM benchmark in the 12 months after an upgrade) – there needs to be a sea-change in the type of assets available in which to invest, both in terms of stocks and of building out a bond curve (different types of bonds at different maturities from short-dated to long-dated). Nonetheless, as mentioned earlier, **the truth does not actually** matter that much in investment terms: it is the perception of reality that counts.

The Current General Environment For Bonds

From the first quarter of 2014 in particular, the global economy slowed due to the rapid rise in the US dollar (which precipitated a broad-based tightening in global liquidity), the collapse in energy prices (due to the aforementioned Saudi strategy) and policy tightening in China amid a broader structural slowdown and rebalancing (from manufacturing-led growth to consumer-led growth). Against this backdrop, long-term bond yields moved consistently net down.

However, as it stands, **there are tentative signs that an improvement in the environment might be on the cards for the global bond market.** For a start, global interest rates have risen due to the changing outlook for fiscal easing and growth, exacerbated by the recent victory of Donald Trump in the US and the end of QE in that country (although it remains in place in the Eurozone and Japan). Trump and the Republican-led Congress are likely to push through with a fiscal stimulus package that could provide a further temporary growth boost starting in mid-2017.

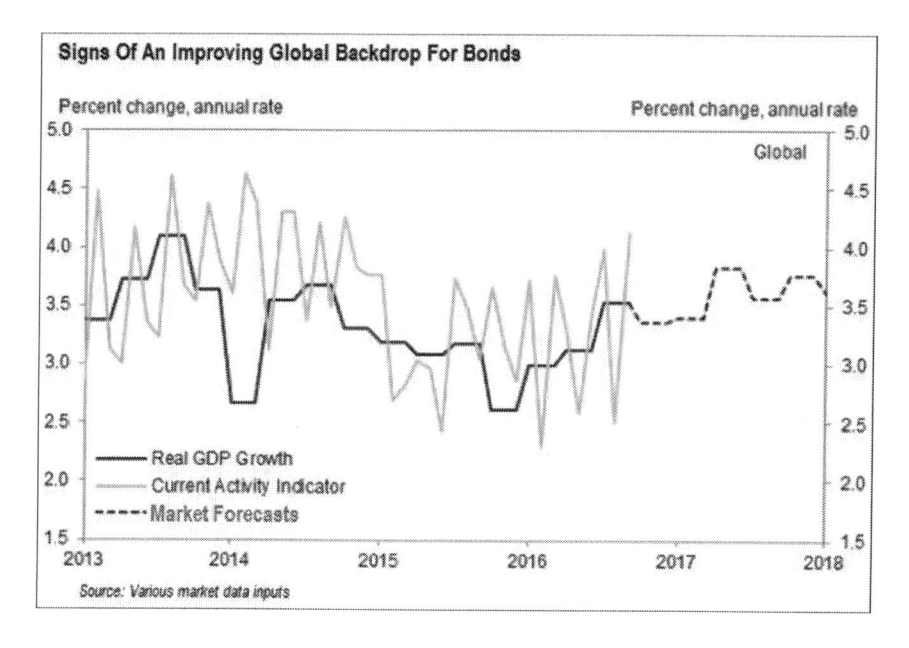

Signs Of An Improving Global Backdrop For Bonds

Figure: Percent change, annual rate — Real GDP Growth, Current Activity Indicator, Market Forecasts (2013–2018). Source: Various market data inputs.

Trump's proposed policies are also **likely to reinforce the gradual upward move in inflation that is already underway, as output and employment are now close to potential, leading the Federal Reserve to raise interest rates substantially more than implied by current market pricing and at a faster pace.** This, in turn, will force similar rates rises around the world, lifting overall yield curves up and, as an adjunct meaning money will move from stocks to bonds in the overall global investment portfolio.

There are **two important caveats** to this: given low growth and low inflation levels, the **European Central Bank** (ECB) is likely to attempt to insulate itself from the resulting tightening in financial conditions by extending its asset purchase (QE) programme. The **Bank of Japan,** in the meantime, is likely to do the same and to continue to try to weaken the yen and to more tightly implement its yield control policy.

The Current Investment Balance Between DM And EM Bonds

Much of the improved outlook has already been priced into DM government bonds and investment-grade non-government bonds have also seen their spreads tighten markedly. As such, although the prospects for further increases in yields remain, on the basis that Trump-led growth and adjunct interest rate rises will be greater than expected even now by most, it is likely that investments in EM bonds will increase.

Absolute yields on EM debt are 6-7% and spreads remain attractive, with hard-currency EM debt looking especially biddable on the back of continued balance of payments improvements, more stable commodities prices and more global growth.

Emerging Markets Aggregate Financial Conditions Indicators

Emerging Markets FCI

Uptrend

Source: Goldman Sachs

Technical Analysis

In its simplest terms, Technical Analysis is a methodology by which past trading patterns – primarily prices and volumes of trade at those prices – can be used to predict future trading patterns. The basics of Technical Analysis – support and resistance levels – are absolutely essential to being able to maximise profits and minimise risks, allowing as they do the clear identification of key price points at which other traders look to buy or sell a given asset. **Without understanding the basics of Technical Analysis, any meaningful risk management cannot be achieved and this is the fundamental reason why retail traders go bust.**

Many traders believe that, in and of itself, Technical Analysis reveals certain key truths about how the markets have worked in the past, work currently and will work in the future. More specifically, these traders believe that by looking at how markets have performed in the past their future performance can be predicted, in that key patterns from the past will recur and inform market movements going forward. Whether or not there is a genuine mathematical basis for this belief is irrelevant for practical trading purposes; the fact that the vast majority of traders believe it is sufficient to make Technical Analysis a key driver of trading patterns – along with fundamental factors – in the future. **The belief that Technical Analysis predicts future trading patterns is, in fact, a self-fulfilling prophecy and every trader – retail or otherwise – needs to know at least the basics.**

This is even truer now in the age of automated and algorithmic trading when the programs involved use key support and resistance levels to execute massive sell or buy orders, thus triggering other stop loss orders centred around these levels. So, whilst economic fundamentals, political shocks, moves in bonds, equities and commodities, general trading tricks, psychology and plain old rumours are essential to predicting market movements, it is also essential now to know everything one can about Technical Analysis, simply because everyone else looks at it too.

Candlesticks

Key to Technical Analysis is the **candlestick method of charting. This is particularly useful as it not only shows simply whether the market has largely bought the asset (typically shown in green or white) or sold it (typically shown in red or black) but also how strong these buys or sells were (indicated by the length of the lines above each candle, 'wick', for buying or below, 'shadow', for selling).**

Candlestick Structure

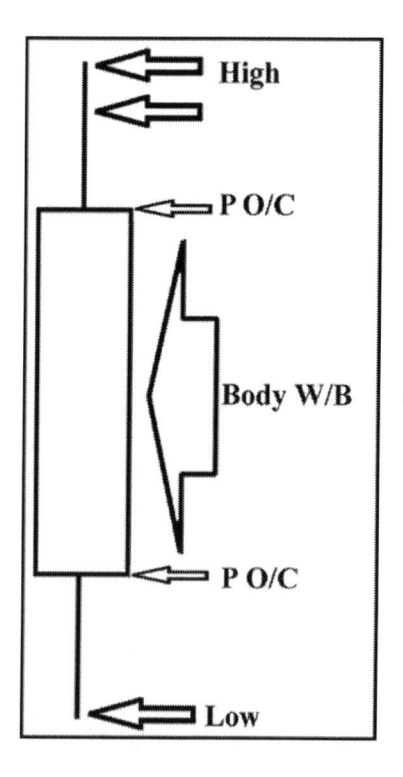

[Chart Key:
High = Highest price during trading time period
P O/C = Trading time period open or close price
Body W/B = Real body is white (or green) if asset closed higher over the trading period or black (or red) if it closed lower
P O/C = Trading time period open or close price
Low = Lowest price during trading time period]

If a market is undecided as to where it views the direction of an asset then the candlestick will have no substantial body, wick or shadow **('doji'),** reflecting that the price closed the day where it opened and that neither buyers ('bulls') nor sellers ('bears') prevailed in moving the asset their way over the course of the trading hours.

A similar inference can be taken from the **'Spinning Top'** pattern, although not to quite the same degree, as some intra-day movement will have taken place. In either event, both can be viewed as **marking possibly the end of the previous trend,** as it has run out of steam. These patterns make ideal places to enter new trades or exit existing ones.

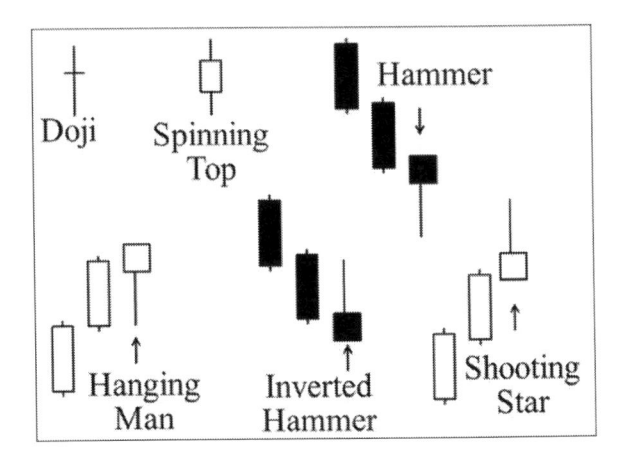

The **'Hammer'** pattern appears after a previous move to the downside and indicates that a move to the upside is on the cards. The long shadow shows that, despite it trading substantially lower during the day, the weight of selling was not sufficient for it to stay at depressed trading levels. Consequently, the inference is that major buyers have stepped in at these levels and may well continue buying overnight or as the new Western trading period properly commences.

The same can be said for the **'Inverted Hammer'**, although to a lesser degree, as although buyers have stepped into the market, they have failed on this occasion to reverse the downtrend entirely.

Conversely, the **'Shooting Star'** should be read as a sign that a move to the downside is on the cards, after a previous move to the upside, with bulls having failed to continue to push the pair higher and substantial bears having now entered the market.

The same can be said for the **'Hanging Man'** although to a lesser degree, as although sellers have stepped into the market, they have failed on this occasion to reverse the uptrend entirely.

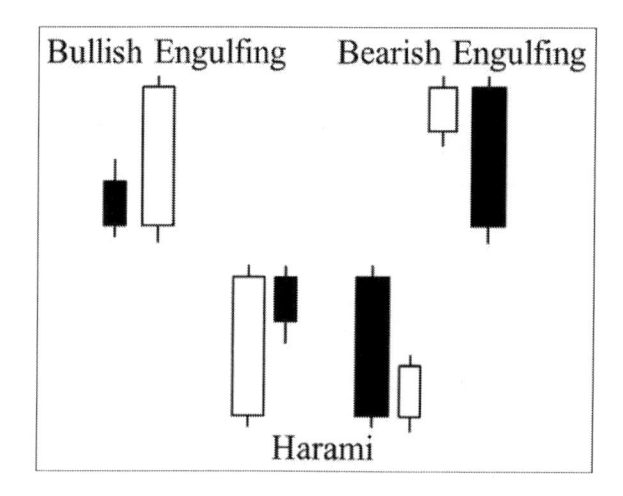

Bullish Engulfing   Bearish Engulfing

Harami

A **'Bullish Engulfing'** pattern is a clear indication that the signs of reversal of a previous trend (either through a Shooting Star or Hanging Man) have gained momentum, and the reverse is true of the **'Bearish Engulfing'** pattern (either through the Hammer or Inverted Hammer).

The **'Harami'** pattern, though, which can occur after a move either up or down, can be taken again as a sign of uncertain price follow-through and may mark the beginning of a change of trend direction.

USDCAD (Historical)

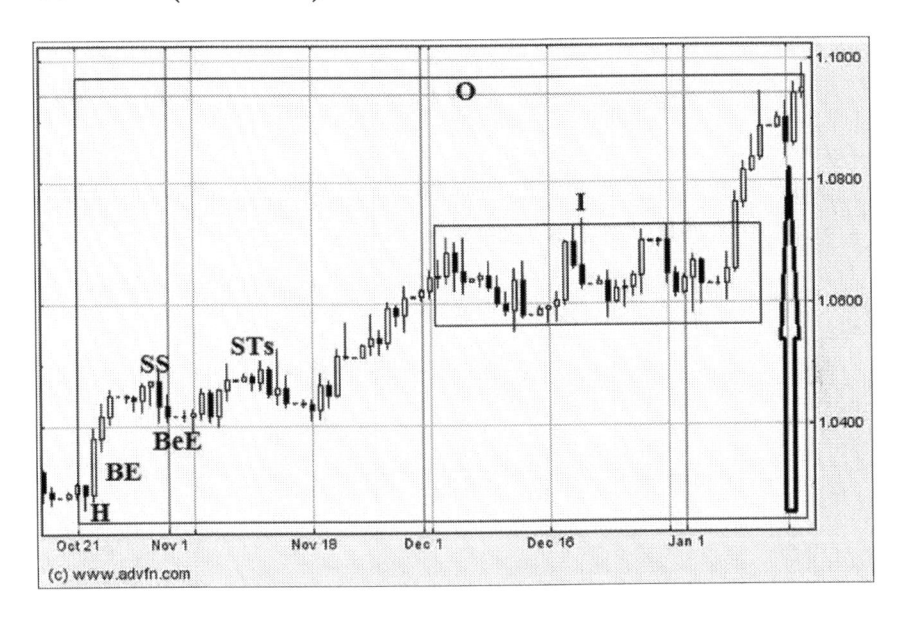

[Chart Key:
H = Hammer
BE = Bullish engulfing
SS = Shooting star
BeE = Bearish engulfing
STs = Spinning tops
O = Overall uptrend
I = Indecision of the market]

In all of the above cases, the **weight that should be attached to these patterns should be increased when additional confirmations are found.**

These can be where they occur at **major resistance and support levels, Fibonacci levels** (key mathematical ratios of an original number, representing a move up or down: 23.6%, 38.2%, 50% and 61.8%) or **Moving Average levels** (simply, each day's price added together and then divided by a certain number of days: 20, 50 and 100 are the most used), including selected oscillators.

In the above chart, for instance, aside from a few moves down (which fail to gather momentum, as indicated by the Spinning Top patterns) all of the significant moves have been to the upside (as indicated by the rolling Hammer patterns).

Resistance And Support Levels

Support levels (where the market has overwhelmingly bought the asset in the past, once it has been in decline) will invariably be found **below the current market price,** whilst **resistance levels** (where the market has overwhelmingly sold the asset in the past, once it has been on the rise) will be found **above the current market price.**

In other words, in chart terms, support levels can be found where selling turns to buying (denoted on candlestick charts, see below, as a red bar turning to green, or a black bar turning to white), whilst resistance levels can be found where buying turns to selling (denoted on candlestick stick charts as a green bar turning to red, or a white bar turning to black). R1 is the first resistance level and so on, whilst S1 is the first support level, with the current market price indicated in the black box.

EURUSD (Historical)

[Chart Key:
S1 = First support level
S2 = Second support level
R1 = First resistance level
R2 = Second resistance level]

These levels should be the cornerstones of all serious trading activity, as they act as signals to buy or sell into a new position or to exit existing ones (together with other confirmations, discussed below).

To reiterate, though, **it is essential to note that resistance and support levels do not always coincide with any/all of these additional confirmation signals.** For example, if the asset is a currency, it may be that a particular level has been **targeted by a country's central bank** as being essential for the advancement of its economic or monetary policy and that it will act decisively to ensure either that its currency weakens at a certain level (to encourage exports and boost economic growth, for instance) or strengthens (to discourage demand-led inflation, for instance).

The chart below, for example, shows the **extraordinary actions of the Swiss National Bank (SNB) over its implementation of a policy to ensure that the Swiss franc (CHF) did not appreciate to a degree that it hurt the country's economy.** Originally, the floor was at 1.2000 against the euro but one day, out of the blue, the SND stopped supporting the floor (i.e. buying euros and selling CHF). Consequently, the CHF appreciated like a rocket and a lot of traders and institutions went bankrupt in an instant.

When the CHF appreciated beyond the parity (1 to 1) level with the euro – very damaging to Switzerland's economy – the SNB decided to intervene again.

EURCHF (Historical)

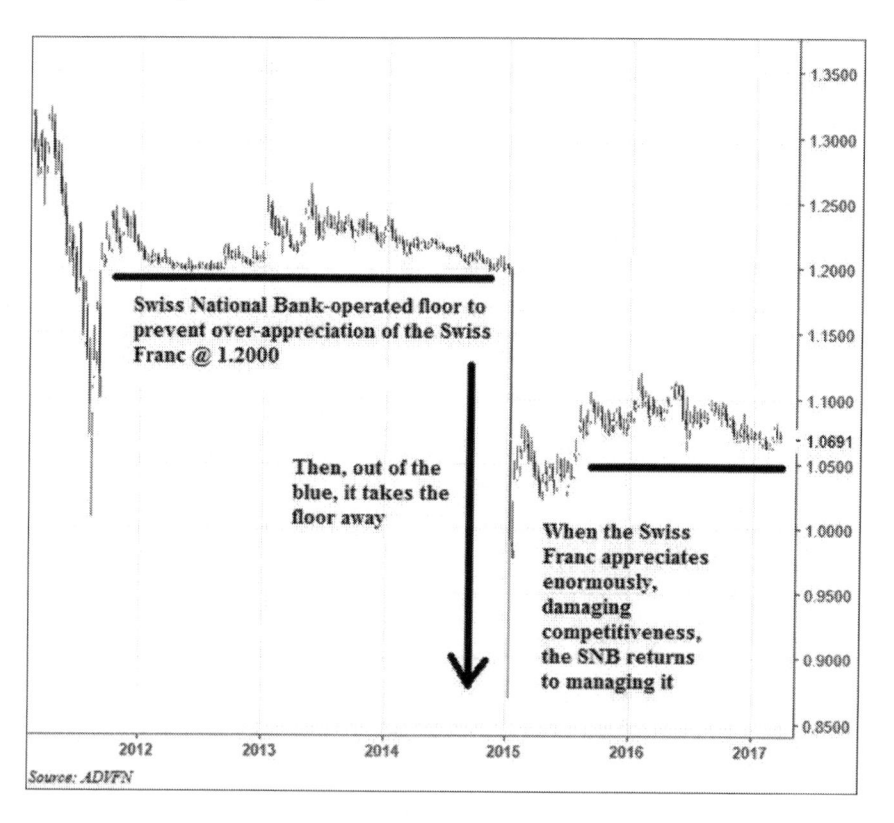

Similarly, it may be that there are enormous options contracts that would be triggered if an asset reached a certain level. In this case, whoever held the option would do everything cost-effective that they could to prevent it reaching the strike price for the option.

Often, one will see levels that apparently have little or no other obvious significance being resolutely defended up to a certain date (the expiration date for the option) and then dramatically going through that level once the option has lapsed.

Fibonacci Levels

These are key mathematical ratios of an original number (price), representing a move up or down: **23.6%, 38.2%, 50% (not actually a Fibonacci ratio, but most Fibonacci users include it anyhow), 61.8% and 100%.**

These can be overlaid on a chart, from the bottom of a trend to the top in a bullish market or from the top of a trend to the bottom in a bearish one.

As mentioned earlier, they can often mark resistance and support levels, as shown below.

US DJIA (Historical)

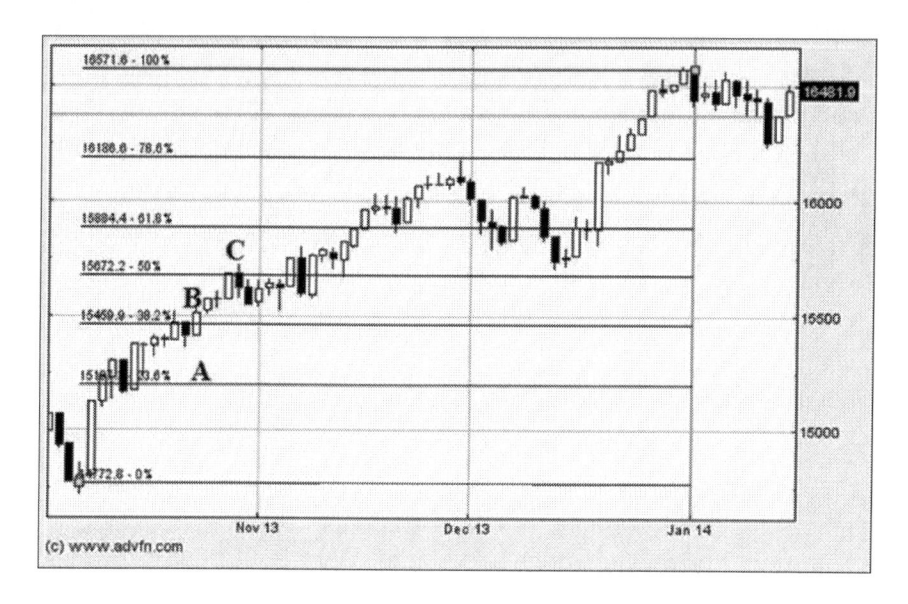

[Chart Key:
A = 23.6% Fib level acts as support
B = 38.2% Fib level acts as resistance
C = 50% Fib level acts first as support and then as resistance]

In the above chart, we see clearly the **correlation between Fibonacci levels and those of support and resistance.** Interestingly here we also see that at the 50% level, initially this starts out as a resistance but then, as the cycle progresses, it acts as a support.

Moving Averages

These are particularly useful in determining short-term indications as to whether a market is set to continue in its current trend, reverse that trend or trade in a range. As mentioned earlier, MAs are simply each day's price added together and then divided by a certain number of days: 20, 50 and 100 are the most used.

As an additional confirmation (to established support and resistance levels, for instance) they offer a good idea of **whether an asset is likely to break to the topside or the downside, when different time-period MAs cross over each other,** as illustrated below.

USDJPY (Historical)

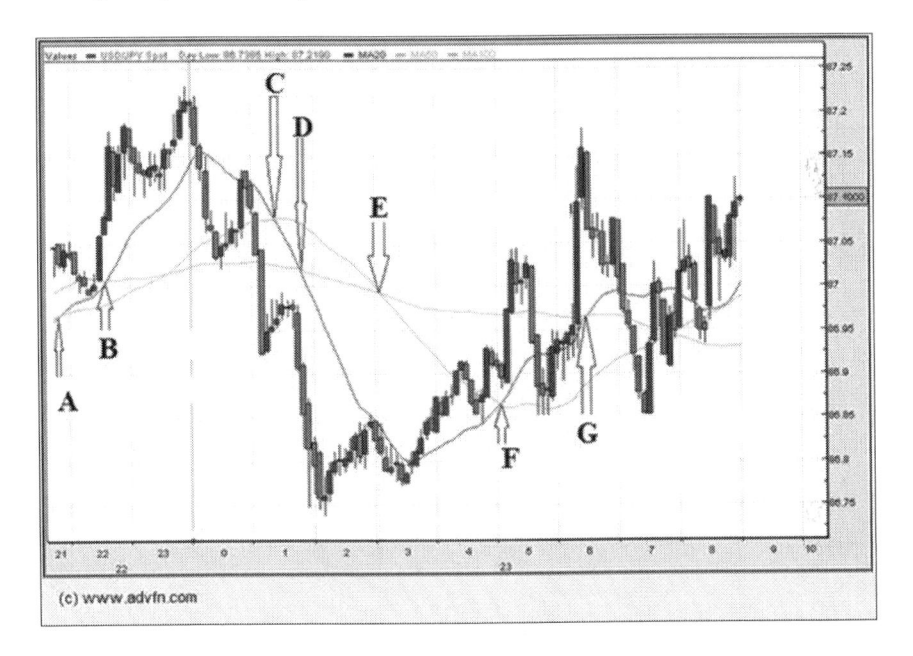

[Chart Key =
A = MA20 up through MA50 = BUY
B = MA20 through MA100 = BUY
C = MA20 down through MA50 = SELL
D = MA20 down through MA 100 = SELL
E = MA50 down through MA100 = OVERSOLD
F = MA20 up through MA100 = BUY
G = MA20 through MA50 = BUY]

Broadly speaking, as shown above, if the short-term MA20 breaks through a longer-term MA then one might expect the currency pair to trade in whichever direction that break has occurred. More helpfully still, MAs can be used for earlier trading indications, using the **Moving Average Convergence-Divergence (MACD)** indicator, as shown below.

USDJPY (Historical)

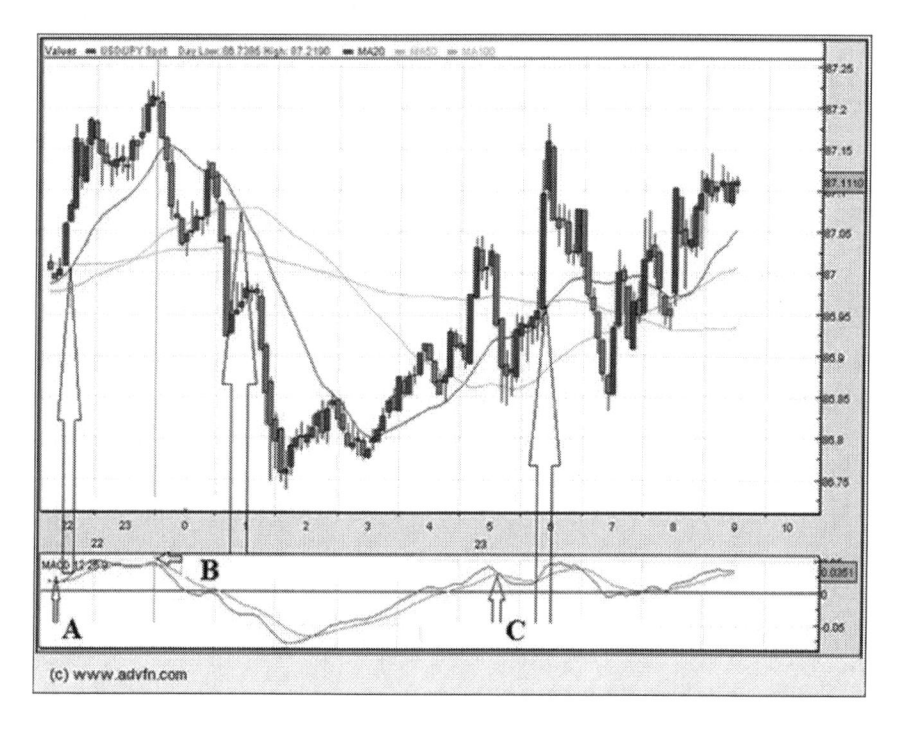

[Chart Key:
A = Early signal for crossover = BUY
B = Early signal for crossover = SELL
C = Early warning for crossover = BUY]

MAs are also a vital part of determining the momentum of a price movement, in its application with the 3/10 Oscillator. This is a simple indicator constructed by subtracting the 10 day period

Exponential Moving Average from the 3 day period Exponential Moving Average (but do not fret, virtually all charting packages allow one to replicate this with the MACD by setting the short term parameter to 3, the long term parameter to 10 and the smoothing parameter to 1.)

Dow Jones Price/Oscillator Convergence/Divergence Signals

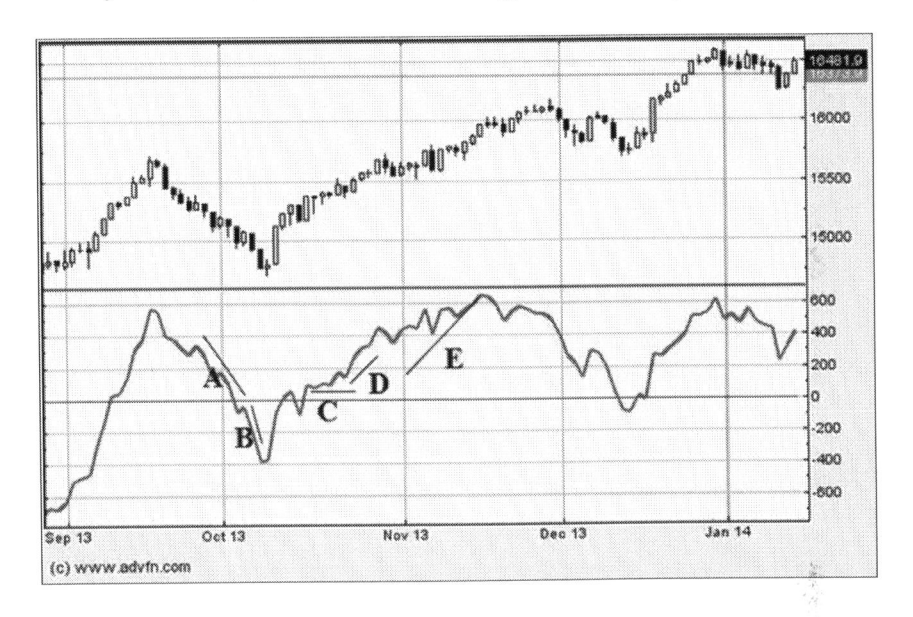

[Chart Key:
A = Selling momentum gathers force
B = Selling momentum diverges = change of direction due
C = Range trading momentum
D = Buying momentum kicks in
E = Buying momentum gathers force]

Anyhow, the concept underlying this indicator (similar in theory to the RSI) is that if a price moves up or down and is expected to be sustained then one would anticipate that, along with a range of higher highs (for an upmove) or lower lows (for a downmove), the momentum (or force) behind each of these would also be sustained. If not, one would have to question whether the move can have the strength (more buyers than sellers or the other way around) to continue.

Dow Jones Bearish Regular Divergence Of Price/Oscillator

= *Although the price is rising, momentum is going down* = *bearish divergence*

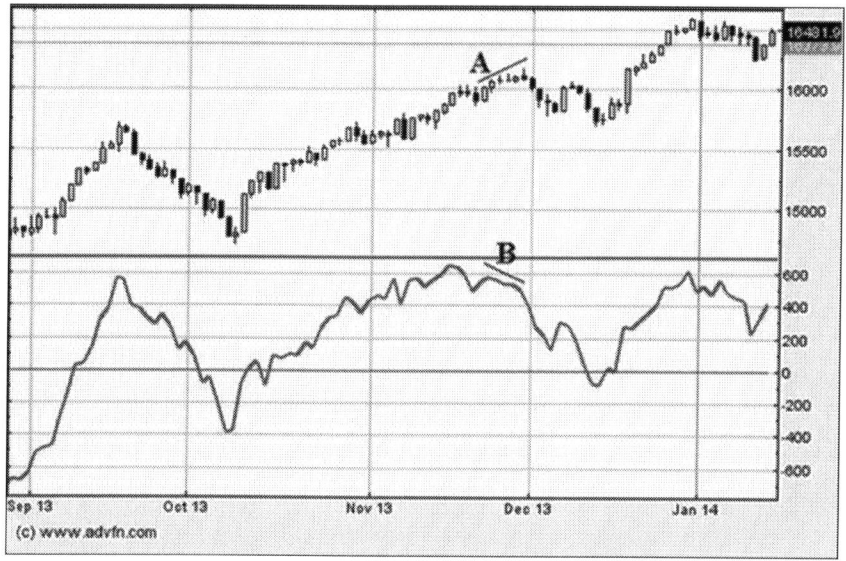

[Chart Key:
A = Higher high
B= Lower high]

Dow Jones Bearish Hidden Divergence Of Price/Oscillator

= The price is still bid, but at a lower level, and momentum is gaining at lower prices

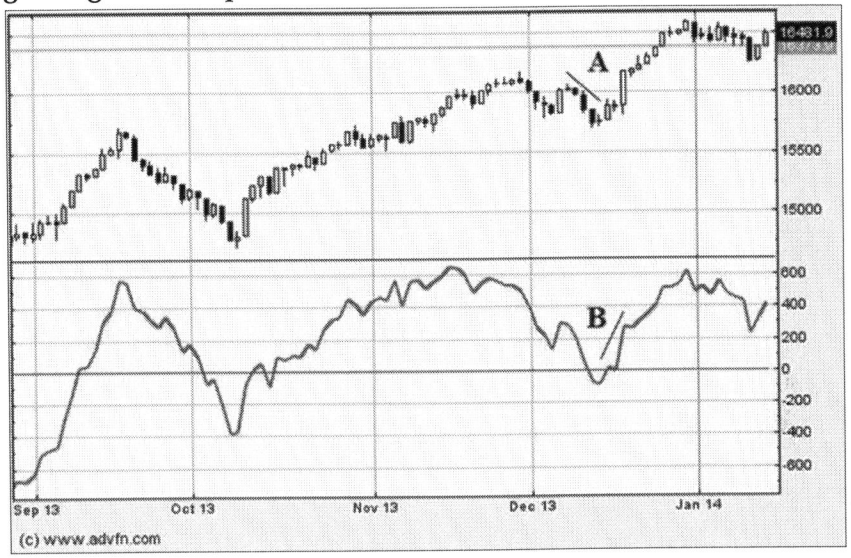

[Chart Key:
A = Lower high
B = Higher high]

Dow Jones Bullish Regular Divergence Of Price/Oscillator

= *Although the price is falling, there is less momentum pushing it down*

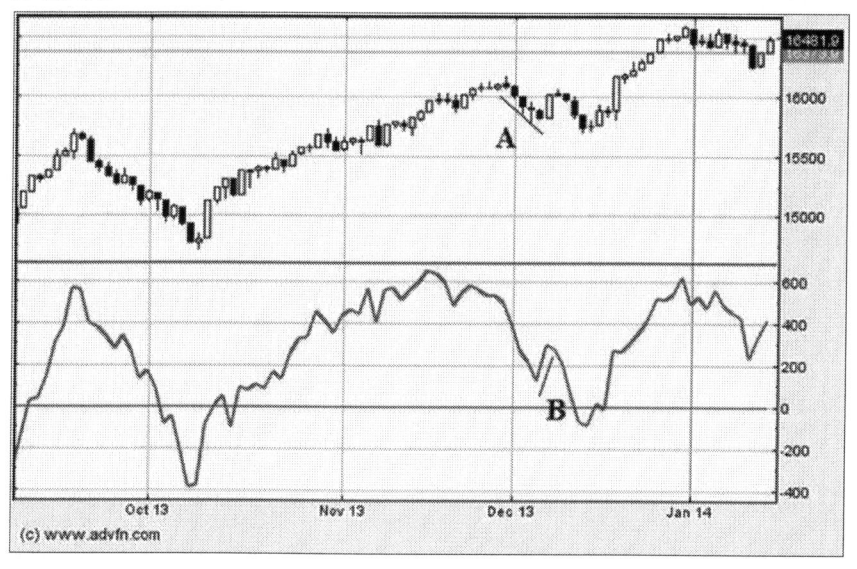

[Chart Key:
A = Lower low
B = Higher low]

Dow Jones Bullish Hidden Divergence Of Price/Oscillator

= *Although it is still offered, the momentum gains as the price rises relatively*

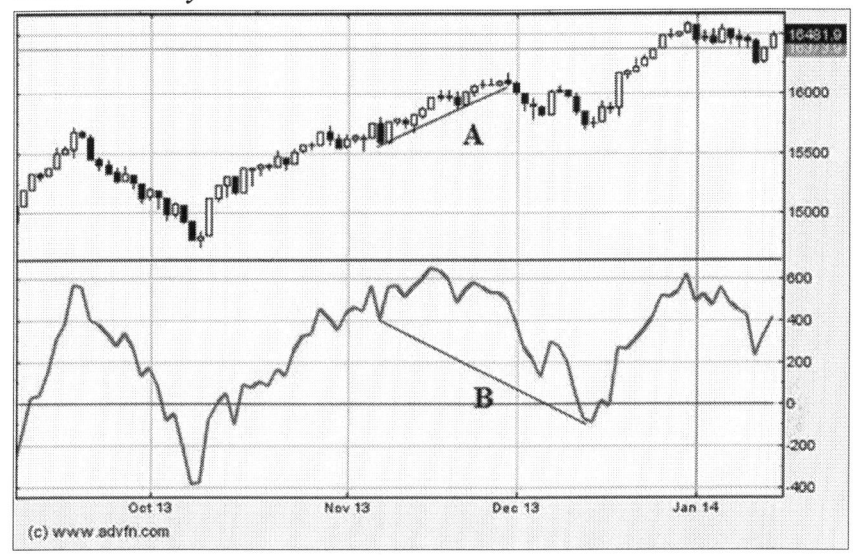

[Chart Key:
A = Higher low
B = Lower low]

Relative Strength Index

The Relative Strength Index (RSI) is another extremely useful oscillator indicator. **In general terms, the RSI shows the momentum of a pair's trading – in effect, the degree of market participation in its current price movement – and can act as a valuable pre-emptive indicator showing a potential reversal of trend.**

For example, even if a pair appears to be rising quickly, if the RSI is showing that negative momentum is occurring then it might be time to look at the other indicators that signalled a long position and look to either exit an existing long or establish a new short.

Conversely, as shown in the chart below, there is a very notable shift upwards in RSI higher before the actual market price follows it.

EURUSD (Historical)

= RSI confirms upward trend before actual price turns higher

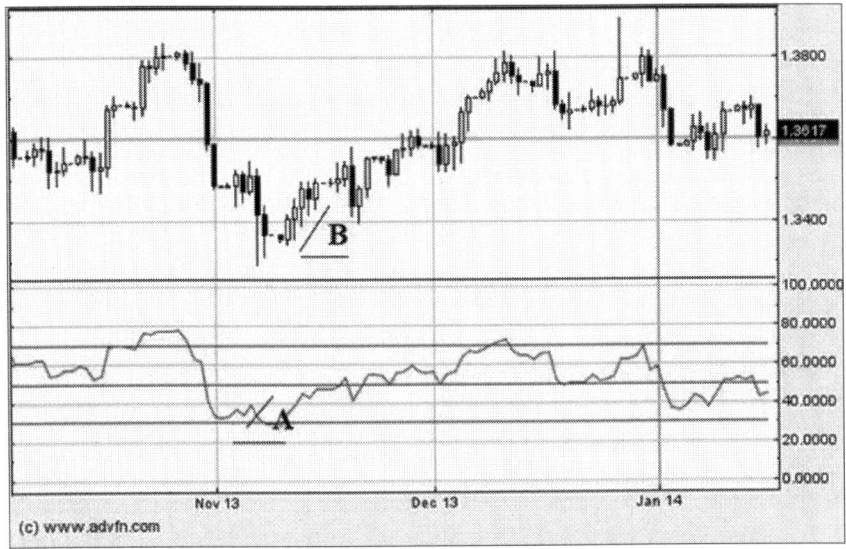

[Chart Key:
A = RSI rises sharply higher, in advance of the price movement
B = Actual market price catches up with bullish momentum on RSI]

More specifically, the RSI moves between a scale of 0 to 100, with 100 showing that every participant in the market is buying the base currency of a pair and 0 showing the opposite. **As a rule of thumb, any reading of 70 and above indicates that the pair is overbought, with a possible reversal on the cards, and any reading under 30 shows it is oversold and that the opposite is true.** This, together with the formations of usual double top/bottom patterns, can show up even before they do in the actual price movement ('Divergence').

Similarly, areas of support and resistance show up very clearly on RSI patterns, as shown below.

EURUSD (Historical)

= RSI confirms strong resistance before actual price turns lower

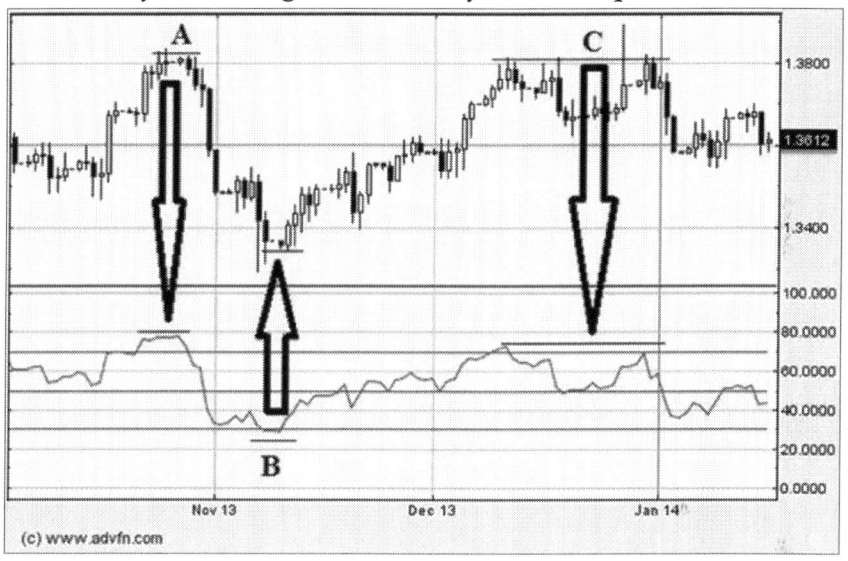

[Chart Key:
A = RSI shows genuine resistance level in the price, in advance
B = RSI shows genuine support level in the price, in advance
C = RSI shows genuine rolling resistance level]

As is evident from the above, RSI's principal use is not in already trending markets, in which it can be used as a confirmation of direction or as an early warning indicator of a change of direction (if above 70 or below 30) but rather in range-bound markets looking for direction.

Here, as shown above, it can act as a proxy for volume interest in particular positions, so that, for example, a sharp spike up in RSI in a market trading around the mid-level could be taken as an early signal of a bullish move and vice-versa.

Bollinger Bands

Bollinger bands are plotted an equal distance either side of a simple moving average. The default settings on trading programmes use a 20 period simple moving average with the upper band (UB) plotted 2 standard deviations above the moving average and the lower band (LB) plotted 2 standard deviations below it.

In periods of low price volatility, these standard deviations become smaller (this process is called a 'squeeze' in Bollinger parlance) than in periods of high volatility and vice-versa (a 'bubble').

Given this, there is undoubtedly money to be made from anticipating/participating in such a breakout/breakdown to the existing bands.

EURUSD (Historical)

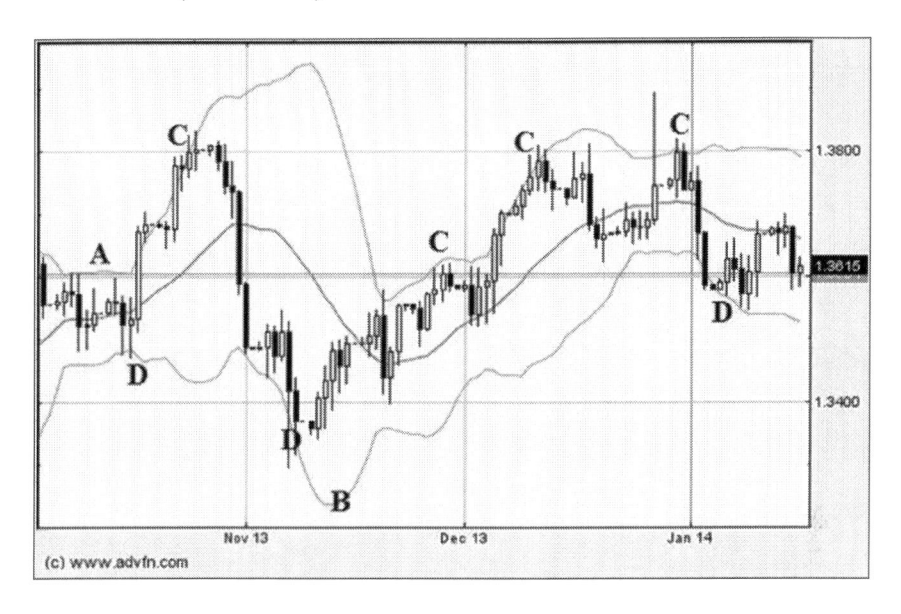

[Chart Key:
A = Squeeze
B = Bubble
C = Upper band acts as resistance level
D = Lower band acts as support level]

More appositely, it is better to use Bollinger bands together with other firmer indicators such as support and resistance levels, Fibonacci levels and so forth, and to use them in such a way as to modify the results with what the Bollinger bands tell you about the probability of a move continuing/reversing.

If the price is moving towards the top of a band then beware longs, and if it is moving towards the bottom of a band then beware shorts. But do not get too hung up on what Bollinger Bands say in and of themselves.

Elliott Wave Theory

Elliot Wave Theory is particularly useful as it shows major moves and minor ones, with **the major moves likely to be caused by institutional investors (and well worth following, if they are not spoofs) and the minor moves likely to be caused by retail investors playing catch-up (normally a good time to start thinking about exiting a trade)**.

In its most basic form, Elliott Waves show that the market does not move in a completely chaotic fashion but rather is a product of patterns that repeat themselves over time. These patterns ('waves') define a trend, which can be the basis for predictive trading.

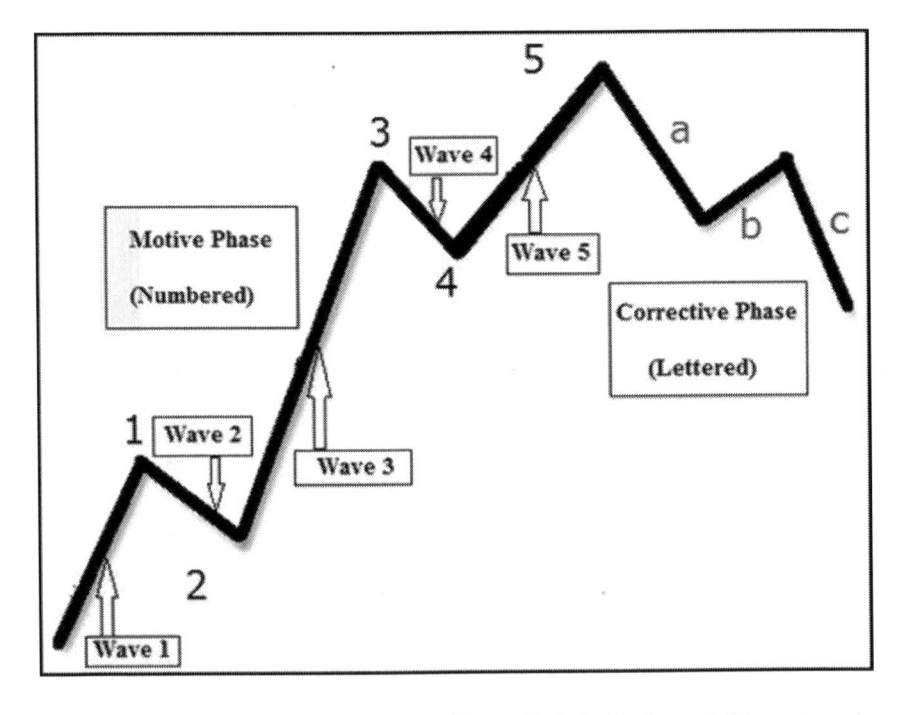

More specifically, according to Elliott (Ralph Nelson Elliott, just in case you were wondering, who posited his theory in around 1934), a trending market moves in a **five-three wave pattern**, where the first five waves ('motive waves') move in the direction of the larger trend.

Following the completion of the five waves in one direction, a larger corrective move takes place in three consecutive waves ('corrective waves'), as illustrated in the above chart.

Interestingly, **the patterns identified by Elliott occur across multiple time frames:** that is, a completed five wave sequence on a small time frame (5 minutes, for instance) may well be just the first wave of a longer temporal sequence (in a daily chart, for example) and so on and so forth.

Elliott Waves On EURUSD (Historical)

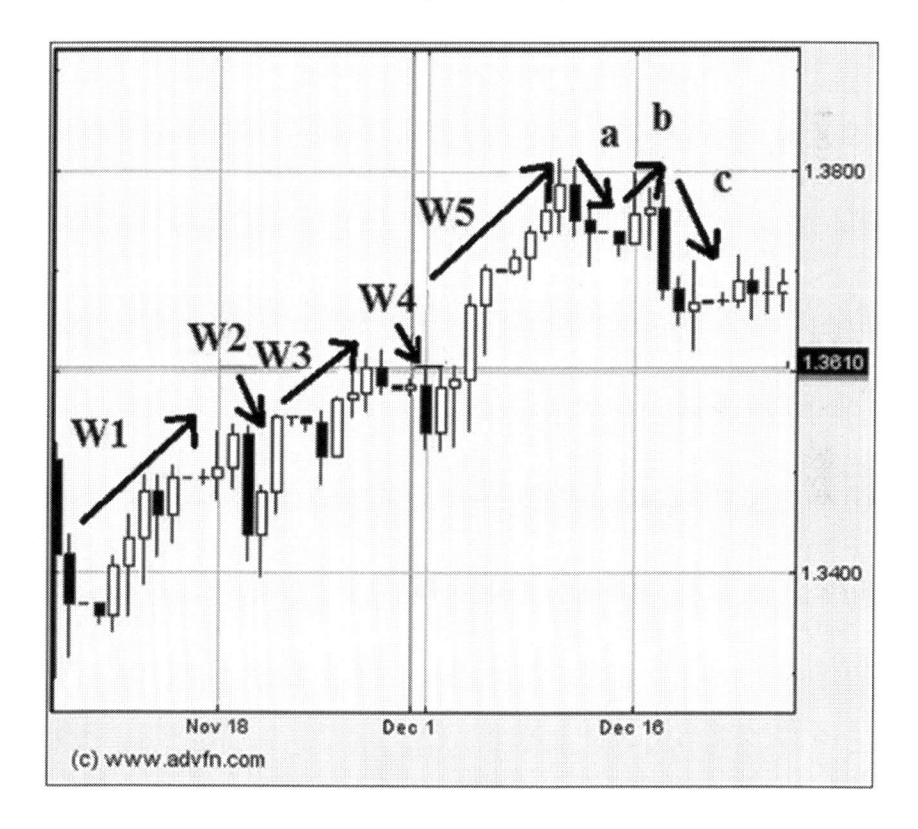

[Chart Key:
W1 to W5 = Motive phase waves
a to c = Corrective phase waves]

The **combination of Elliott Waves and Fibonacci ratios is particularly useful in trading into new positions or trading out of existing ones,** as they are usually also important levels of support and resistance.

The motive and corrective levels are often measured by percentages of the previous wave length, with the most common levels being the Fibonacci ones of 38%, 50%, 61.8% and 100%; timings with a distance of 13, 21, 34, 55, 89 and 144 periods should be particularly monitored (e.g., if you find a crucial reversal or an unfolding of a pattern on a daily chart then expect another crucial unfolding at the above daily points thereafter); a corrective move that follows a motive move from a significant low or high usually retraces 50% to 61.8% of the preceding impulse; wave 4 usually corrects as far as 38.2% of wave 3; given that wave 2 generally does not overlap the start of wave 1 (i.e., the 100% of it), the start of wave 1 is an ideal level to place stops; and the target of wave 5 can be calculated by multiplying the length of wave 1 by 3.236 (2 X 1.618).

It is also interesting to note that long-term economic patterns (see sub-section earlier) can be seen in terms of Elliot Waves. That is, that at the onset of a long-term economic cycle there is likely to be a lack of confidence and a fear of falling back into slump or depression, before inflation, interest rates and credit slowly start to rise as confidence in the new age increases (you might say, Elliot Wave 1).

As the economy expands (indicated in this instance by inflation) and interest rates increase as an adjunct to this, then so business and consumer confidence grows further and credit is extended more (Elliot Wave 3 correlation).

As we enter into the final up-phase of the move, confidence levels morph into over-exuberance and extraordinary loose 'bubble-like' credit conditions, with interest rates also declining (Elliot Wave 5 correlation).

Finally, rising concerns over loose credit, inflationary upward spiral and bad debt causes business and consumer reticence to embark on new projects (in business terms, expansion and in consumer terms, new purchases), default rates increase, credit is squeezed, the economic outlook turns negative, unemployment rises, disinflation turns into deflation and we have a negative world view.

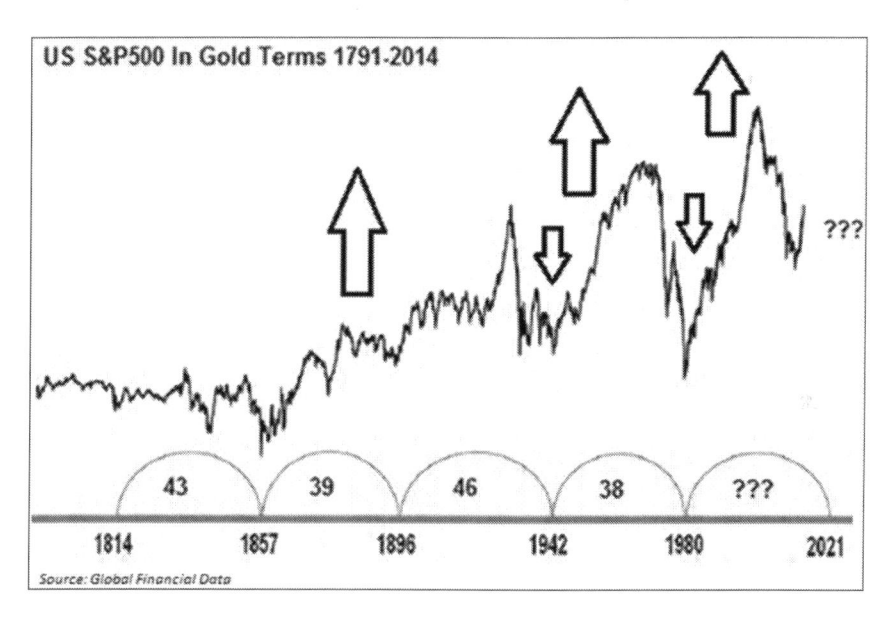

US S&P500 In Gold Terms 1791-2014

1814	1857	1896	1942	1980	2021
	43	39	46	38	???

Source: Global Financial Data

Consequently, it would be fair to say that based on this time set, the **US stock market, and for that matter the UK one and those of the major northern European countries, are currently in an overall cyclical upturn and that, for the time being, the overall trend – economically and in terms of asset prices, interest rates and volatility – may be net up over the next few years.**

Continuation Patterns

These patterns allow the trader not only to understand from where the price action and momentum has come but also to anticipate where and to what degree it is headed. Thus, as these patterns are also watched by thousands of other traders around the globe, they allow a retail trader to obtain an ongoing record of the sentiment surrounding an asset at any given time and consequently allow the trader to manage his order placing better as well.

Ascending And Descending Triangles

Triangles allow the trader to gauge which of the myriad support and resistance levels on a chart are the ones he should be watching most carefully in determining false or genuine breakouts.

An **ascending triangle** is formed by a combination of diagonal support and horizontal resistance, implying that the bulls are gaining the upper hand in the ongoing trading dynamic of the pair and buying at higher and higher levels, while the bears are merely trying to defend an established level of resistance.

EURGBP (Historical) Ascending Triangle

[Chart Key:
A = Horizontal resistance level

B = *Inclining support]*

Clearly, in the above example, the trader has advance warning that the pair is more likely to break up through the resistance level than down through the support one. Also, of course, by anticipating the formation of the triangle the trader can gain/not lose further points, depending on his position, as currency pairs often trend, consolidate and then re-trend.

In the case of a **descending triangle,** the bears are gaining strength and selling at lower and lower levels, while the bulls are merely trying to defend an established level of support.

AUDUSD (Historical) Descending Triangle

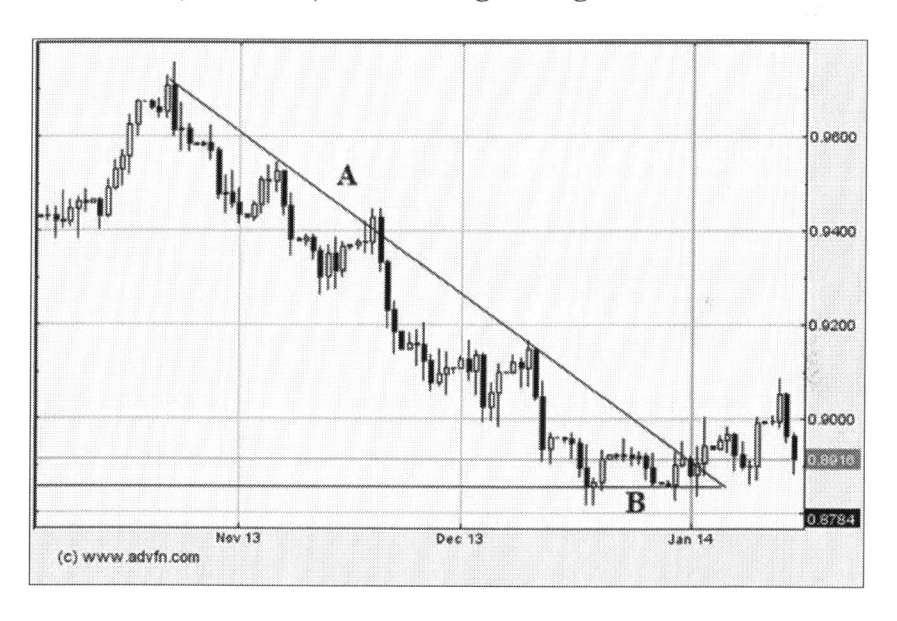

[Chart Key:
A = Declining resistance
B = Horizontal support]

Given these two scenarios, it is easy to see that one can make money riding the principal wave up or down, respectively, and

also to see that triangles make the placement of stop loss orders relatively simple as well; in the ascending triangle example, they would be placed just under the inclining support line at a level that accorded with one's own risk/reward ratio for a rolling long position.

Conversely, in the descending triangle example, they would be placed at a point above the declining resistance level that accorded with one's own risk/reward ratio for a rolling short.

In the cases of both ascending and descending triangles, **any true break (more than one spoof break-out) of its direction (up for descending triangles, down for ascending ones) should be taken seriously by traders to consider exiting trades made on the trend until that point (taking profit) and reversing positions.**

Flags

Flags generally represent a pause in trend and can be used either to take profits on a position going with that trend or to add to that trending position, if the trader is feeling particularly aggressive (and, preferably, has confidence bolstered by other factors meriting an increase in position size – for example, more favourable than expected fundamental or political developments).

The example below is of a downward trending USDJPY, which pauses for consolidation in a flag pattern before resuming its downward trajectory. Often a trader can expect pretty much the same number of pips in the second part of the downtrend (labelled 'B' on the chart) as in the first part of the downtrend ('A' on the chart), but in the chart below, it seems on cursory glance that this is not the case.

However, looking further into the distance and going on the basis of a longer-term trade, it becomes apparent that, in fact, the real second wave makes up the entire pips expected as a result of the first downtrend.

USDJPY (Historical) Flag In A Downtrend

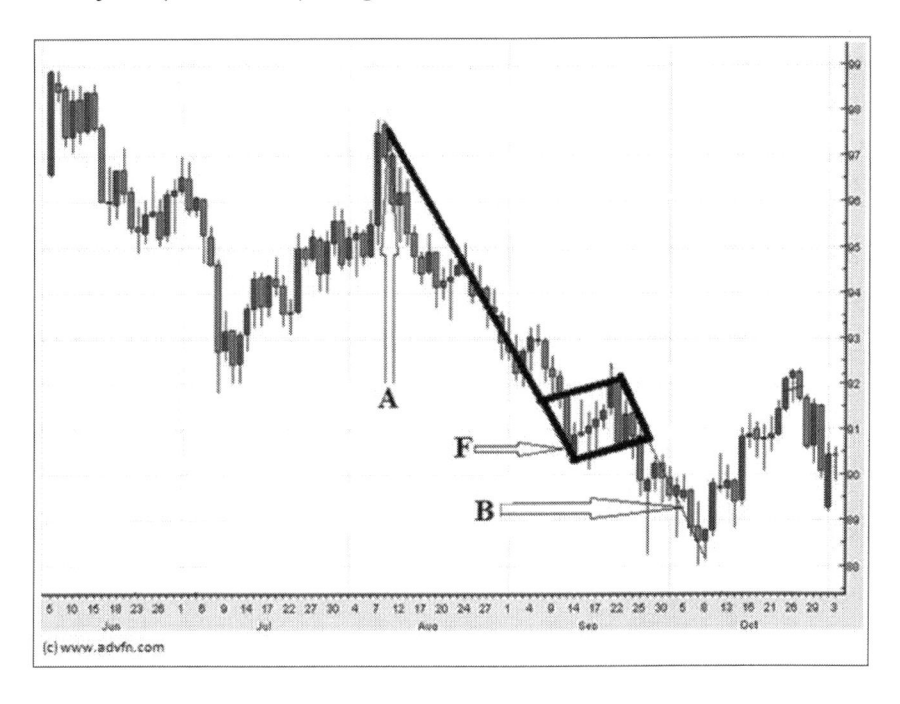

[Chart Key:
A = Downtrend 1 = 723 pips
F = Flag
B = Downtrend 2 = 348 pips, OR DOES IT? See below]

In fact, this flag and many similar presage a much sharper move down, as can be seen below.

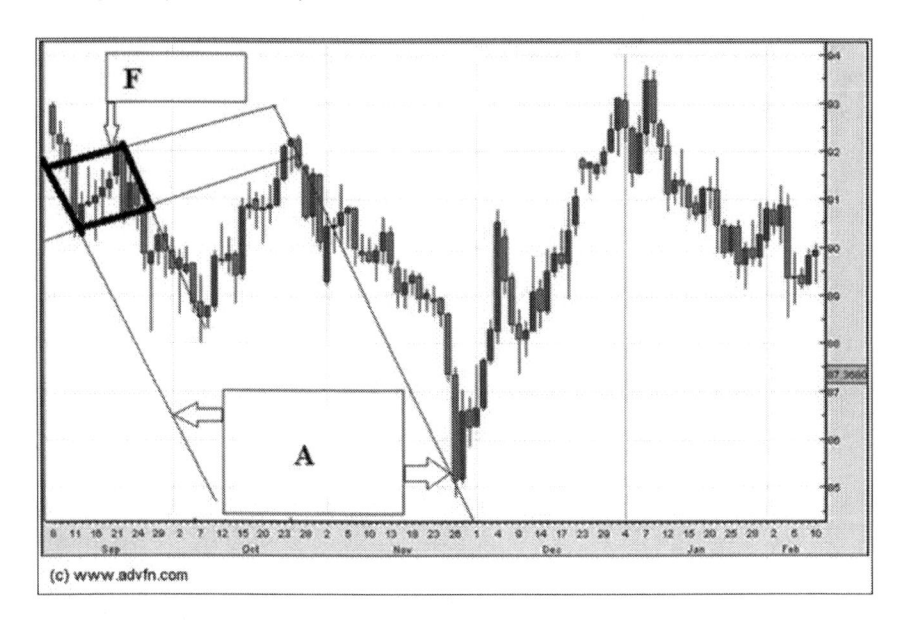

USDJPY (Historical) Continuation In A Downtrend

[Chart Key:
F = Flag from previous chart
A = Logical conclusion of the original downtrend 1 = 700 pips had the trade been stuck with]

Trend Reversals

Given that the market has a way of generally correcting any untoward excessive movements one way or another in asset prices over time, spotting a real reversal in a trend from just a shimmering mirage is key to making money on a long-term basis.

In this respect, there are a couple of other, more basic, patterns that a trader should look out for.

Double Top And Double Bottom

A Double Top is when prices stop rising at the same point twice in a short sequence of time, as shown below. In order for a real reversal of trend to be indicated, the pair must break down through the key support level as indicated on the chart.

GBPUSD (Historical) Double Top

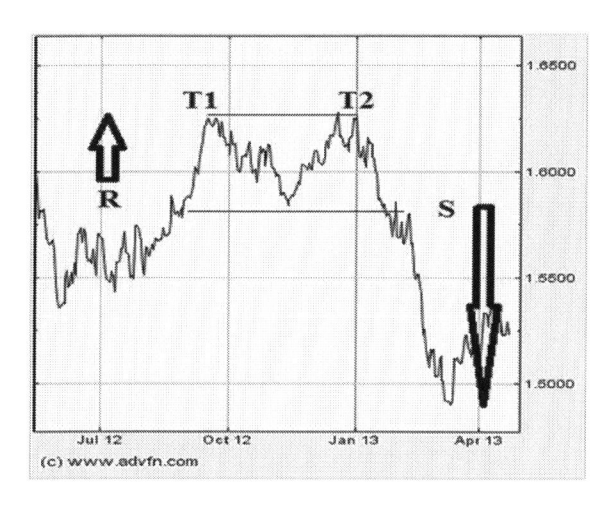

[Chart Key:
R = Rising trend
T1 = First top
T2 = Second (double) top
S = Break below this double support level here implies downtrend]

A double bottom is the same principle, only reversed.

Head And Shoulders Patterns

A head and shoulders pattern, as illustrated below, develops with the asset price trending up and forming the left shoulder on a reversal. Then the market trends higher to form the head and falls back to the same support of the first shoulder to form the right shoulder. The neckline is thus the line connecting the troughs between the peaks. If it is broken, expect a downside move to occur.

AUDUSD (Historical) Head And Shoulders Trend Reversal Pattern

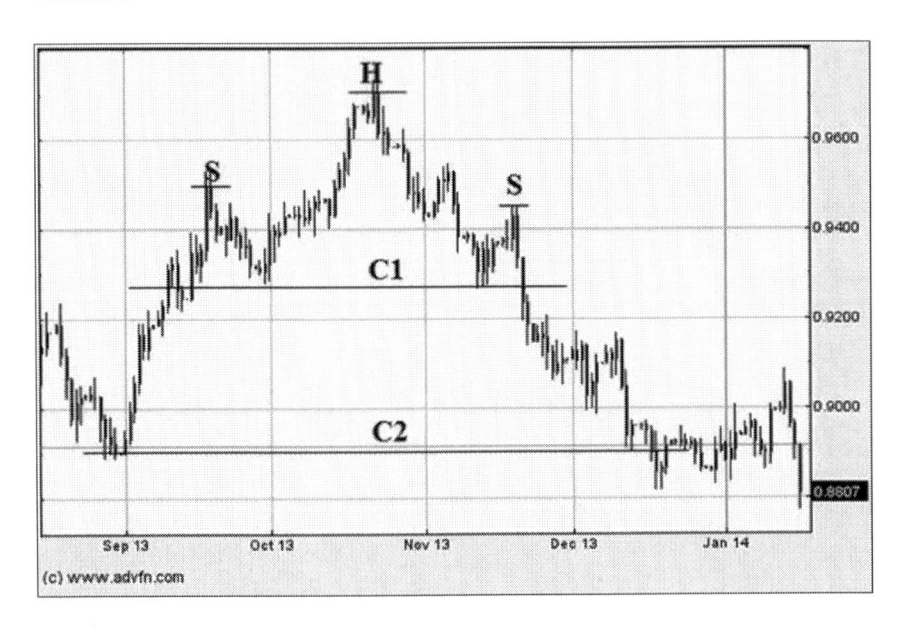

[Chart Key:
S = Shoulder
H = Head
C1 = Confirmation of breakdown 1
C2 = Confirmation of further breakdown 2]

Ichimoku Kinko Hyo

Technical Analysis can appear daunting enough without introducing Japanese into the mix as well, but Ichimoku Kinko Hyo ('Ichimoku' for short) is – like Technical Analysis itself – **actually extremely straightforward, providing that the trader focuses on its fundamentals: primarily support and resistance levels and price momentum.**

In Ichimoku all three of these key elements are combined in one chart pattern, which makes determining where and when to enter trades easy to see at a glance. In fact, this is what the name of this system implies: 'ichimoku' translates to 'a glance', 'kinko' means 'equilibrium' and 'hyo' is Japanese for 'chart'.

Ichimoku, created by Japanese journalist and trader Goichi Hosada, is a technical indicator that is also a trend trading system in and of itself in both rising and falling markets, across all time frames and for any liquid asset, with **the caveat that it is not much use when no clear trend is present.**

The Cloud

At its most basic level, the cloud ('Kumo') allows the trader to see at a glance what the current trend is and its momentum.

Dow Jones Industrial Average (Historical) – Uptrend

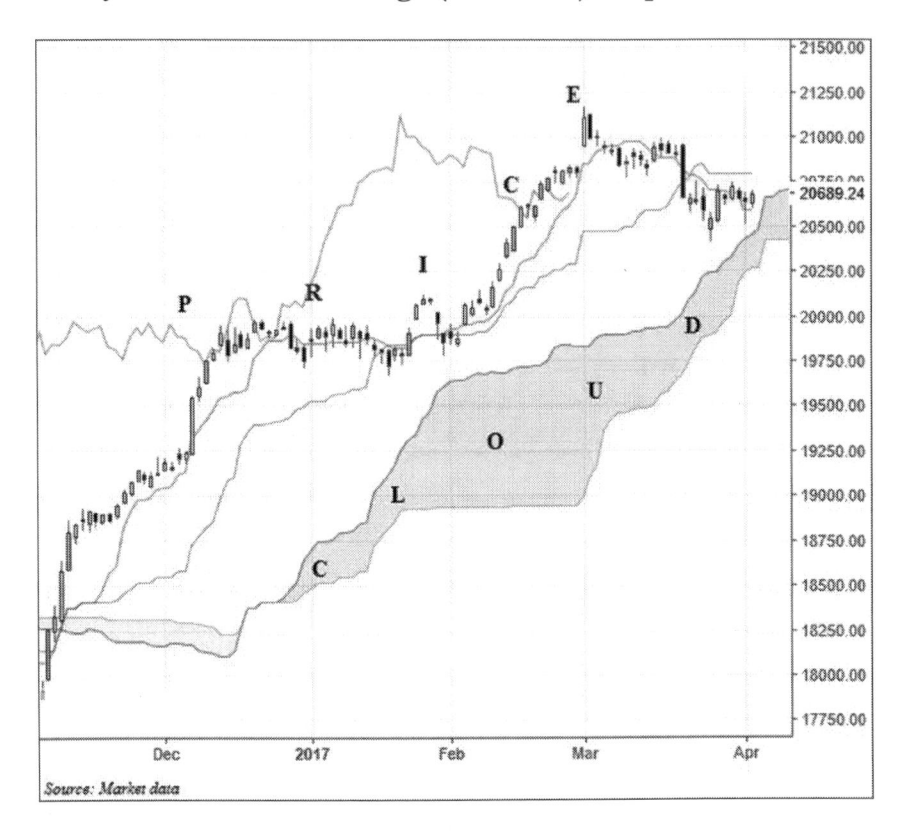

[Chart Key:
Cloud – shaded area – under Price = UPTREND]

EURUSD (Historical) – Downtrend

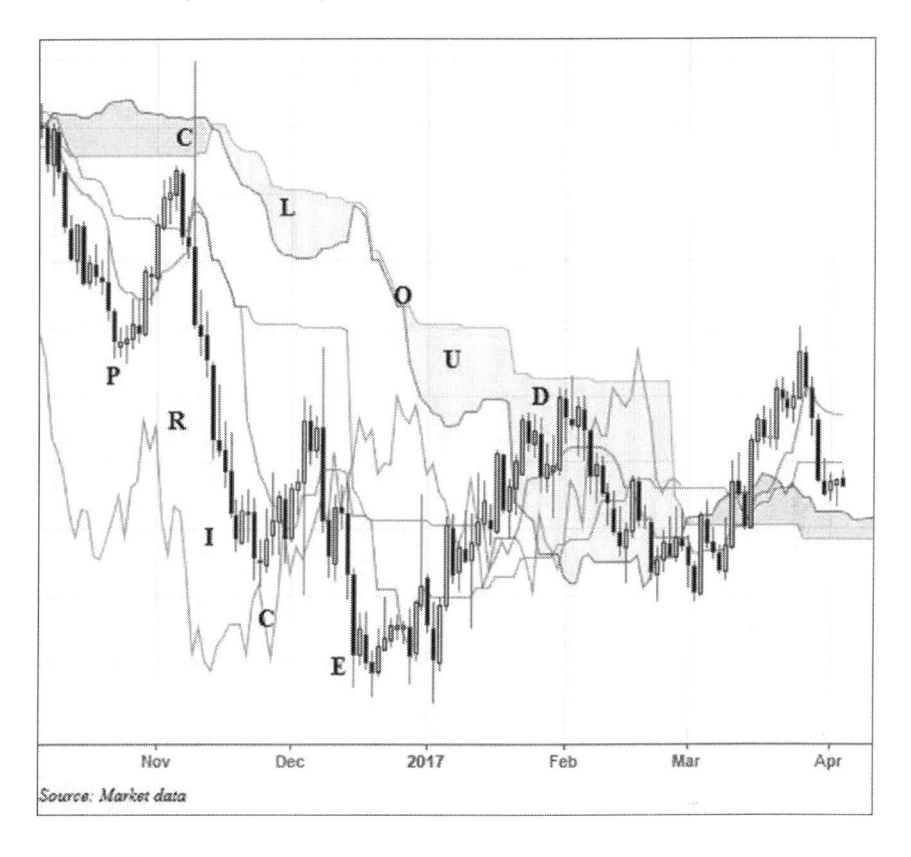

[Chart Key:
Cloud – shaded area – above Price = DOWNTREND]

The Basic Components Of Ichimoku

The **'Kijun Sen'** (the blue line), also called the base line, is a calculation averaging the highest high and lowest low (see *Moving Averages* sub-section earlier) over the past 26 periods of a determined timeframe. The **'Tenkan Sen'** (the red line), also called the turning line, is derived by averaging the highest high and the lowest low for the past nine periods.

There are three other key lines to monitor. The **'Chikou Span'** (the green line), also called the lagging line, is the current closing price plotted 26 periods behind. Then there are two lines that comprise the **'Senkou Span'** (the orange lines): the first Senkou line is calculated by averaging the Tenkan Sen and the Kijun Sen and plotted 26 periods ahead, whilst the second Senkou line is a calculation averaging the highest high and the lowest low for the past 52 periods and plotted 26 periods ahead.

Key Ichimoku Terms

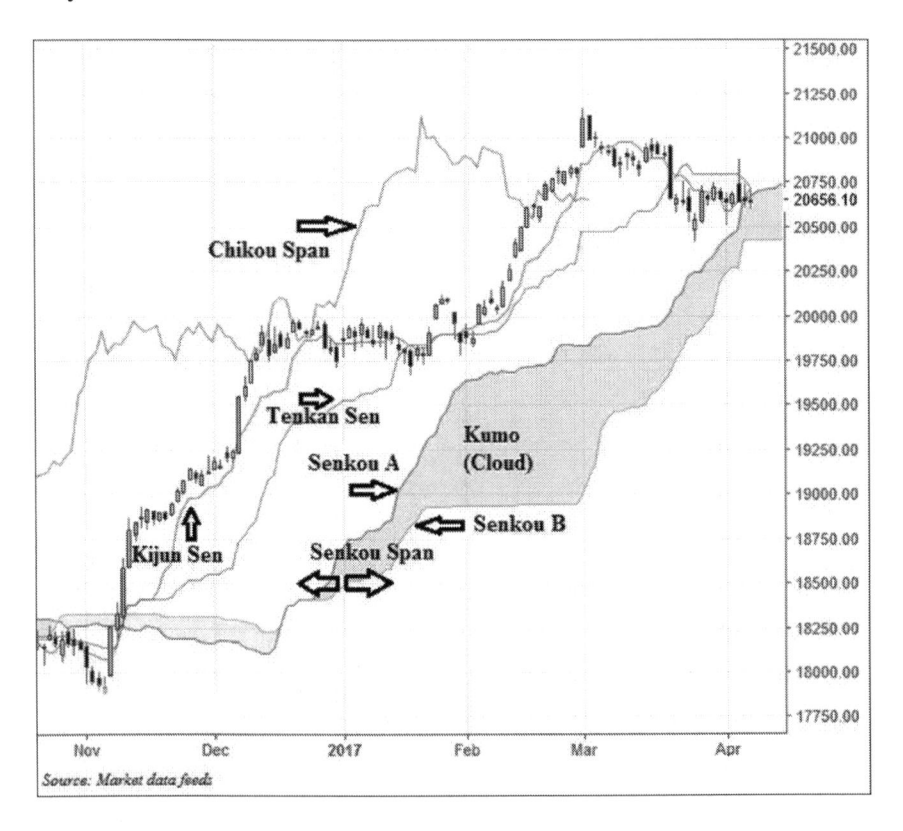

Traders do not need to know the ins and outs of how these lines are calculated, of course, they just need to know what signals they give off, which are as follows.

Key Trading Signals

Tenkan-Sen: The key indicator of market trend. If this line is going up or down then a trend is in place but if it is horizontal then no trend is apparent.

Kijun-Sen: The key indicator of future price movement direction. If the price is higher than the Kijun-Sen then the price will most likely rise but if the price is lower then the price will most likely fall. When the price intersects this line, changes in the trend are likely to occur.

Buy = Tenkan-Sen crosses the Kijun-sen from below ('strong' if above Kumo, 'normal' if within Kumo, 'weak' if below Kumo), known as the 'Bullish TK Cross'

Sell = Tenkan-Sen crosses the Kijun-sen from above (strong if below Kumo, normal if within Kumo, weak if above Kumo), known as the 'Bearish TK Cross'

Chikou Span: It **indicates the *strength of a buy or sell signal.*** If the Chikou Span is below the current price then the momentum lies with the sellers, and when it is above the current price then the momentum is with the buyers.

Kumo Support And Resistance Levels: If the **price is trading up towards the Kumo from below, then the Kumo is acting as resistance levels (Senkou A and then Senkou B)** but if the price is falling down towards the Kumo then the Kumo is acting as support levels (Senkou A and then Senkou B).

Additionally, if the *price is above the Kumo then the trend remains bullish* but if the price is below the Kumo then the trend remains bearish.

Finally, the volatility of the market for the asset being looked at is shown by the thickness of the Kumo: ***the thicker the Kumo then the more volatile the market is*** (and the greater the support or resistance encountered within the two lines of the Kumo).

Risk/Reward Management And Hedging

The Nature Of Risk

Ultimately, money goes to where it is best rewarded (yielded in the first instance from interest rates or dividends but later additionally from capital gains) for the concomitant risks involved (indicated broadly by credit ratings but also from more specific geopolitical, market and systemic risks) and this is, broadly speaking, the definition of the 'risk curve'. **Traders, in order to be successful over time, need to be constantly aware of this risk curve and also to manage the risk/reward ratio of their own investment portfolio in a logical, sensible and emotionless fashion, otherwise they will go broke; it is as simple as that.**

In the case of **in-the-money (ITM) positions (those that are running in the profit zone),** bad traders (i.e. those not managing their risk properly) exit at the wrong time, either getting out once the peak profit-taking opportunity has passed (through misplaced greed) or getting nervous and taking profit way before they should (through misplaced fear). In the case of **out-of-the-money (OTM) positions (those that are losing money),** they hang on to bad positions hoping that they will turn around. The key guiding principle here is: **do not run losses past a comfortable stop-loss point (with the order having gone in at the same time as the entry trade), only run profits.**

Greed And Fear

These two emotions are the two to which all traders at all levels of experience are innately prone and which are **responsible for the vast bulk of all losses that they make throughout their careers.** As human beings it is not possible to eradicate emotion completely from trading actions but it is vital for a trader to be able to take a step back out of himself to recognise whether or not he is being guided by either of these twin damaging emotions. Ninety nine times out of a hundred, one of them will be responsible for a trading loss, so minimising their influence on daily trading activity will result in a major increase in reward to risk trading results.

Greed manifests itself when the trader is positioned correctly in an overall market trend and the less experience and self-discipline a trader has, the more he will succumb to its ill-effects on trading strategy. The problem for the trader comes when he gets greedy for further profits and decides to hold his position for that bit longer, just to capitalise on his good fortune. The logical outcome of this is that he will hold on to his position until such a point that the trade starts to reverse. Unfortunately, this turnaround can happen extremely quickly.

At this point, the prevailing emotion is still greed, as the trader begins to fret that he has not taken all the profit he could and waits for his position to go back more into profit again, the same sort of levels that prevailed just seconds before. In this event, of course, the position may well continue to go against the trader at which point his prevailing emotion starts to change to **fear;** fear that he cannot get out of his position except at levels that are less profitable than they were a few seconds ago – and counting – and greater fear as all his profit is wiped out and his position starts to go into the red.

The negative effects of both of these emotions are compounded by the fact that trading is essentially a truly lonely occupation. The markets are an unforgiving and potentially hostile place in which no one cares about any one at all, no matter who they are, and people only wish someone well if they know they are terminally ill. In practical terms, this has two ramifications: first, that there are very few people that a trader can talk to about his positions, as other traders are concentrating on their own trades; and, second, even if a trader finds someone else to talk to the other trader is extremely unlikely to be helpful because either they are also positioned wrongly, in which case they are likely simple to talk up the erroneous merits of their own trades or, if they are not, do not want to jinx their own trades (despite the reputation many have as 'icemen', virtually all traders have the superstition that discussing their positions, particularly winning ones, is 'unlucky').

Orders Are The Cornerstone Of Risk Management

The optimal way to avoid this 'greed and fear' trading paradigm is by using orders properly on a daily basis, as described in depth earlier. The very best traders over time get up very early (5 a.m. is a good time for a trading day to start), analyse all of the markets in which they have an interest – and those tangential to them – and either take out entry trades on the spot (together with stop losses) or leave orders to enter positions (plus stop losses). Then they do something else entirely, whilst keeping an ear out for any developments.

This is one factor that benefits those who are trading whilst also doing another day job, rather than those who simply stick themselves in front of their computer for hour after hour every day. If a trader has worked through the news in the markets first thing in the morning, then done the technical analysis on each of his targeted markets and then decided on how much he is prepared to lose on a particular trade (the risk/reward management through orders), then there is no reason why any of this should change within a normal trading day (in which there are no major economic figures or political or economic announcements due).

The Risk Curve

The more risk involved in an asset, the more reward is required. Hence, the worse an economy is perceived to be doing, the more reward investors will want as compensation for holding an asset in that country. By extension, if that interest rate does not increase then that asset will be unpopular and thus weak.

Having said that, there is a major difference between probability and a risk/reward profile, in trading terms. The law of probability (more accurately, the *Law of Large Numbers*) is:

> "If the probability of a given outcome to an event is P and the event is repeated N times then the larger N becomes, so the likelihood increases that the closer, in proportion, will be the occurrence of the given outcome to N*P."

In practical terms, this means that if a two-sided coin is tossed a sufficient number of times then the distribution of the results between heads coming up and tails coming up will be exactly the same.

There is an evident problem here for the trader: there is a 50/50 chance on the first toss that heads will come up and, therefore, according to the logical extension of what many 'trader training companies' say, it would be perfectly reasonably to put half your money on heads but – having put money on this outcome – it instead comes up tails. Nonetheless, according to the aforementioned rationale, the trader then puts everything on heads coming up, as given that tails came up first time and the probability of heads coming up was 50% (1 in 2) heads is bound to come up next time but it does not and, continuing to pursue this rationale, the trader will go broke. **The fact is that probability only goes a part of the way to explaining sequences of numbers.**

There is also the random walk theory, in which followers believe that market prices follow a completely random path up and down, without any influence being exerted on them by past price action, making it impossible to predict with any accuracy which direction the market will move at any point or indeed to what degree. However, as has been proven repeatedly, this is incorrect, as patterns of all sorts manifest themselves daily, indeed hourly, and all that is required is to know what to look for: risk/reward ratios are what a trader needs to know.

Net Margin/Trading Requirement (NMR/NTR)

When trading on any platform, a **retail trader will find that his room for manoeuvre in trading is not only limited by the total amount of capital that he has in his trading account but also by the NMR/NTR of that particular platform,** according to the platform's judgement of the risk involved in any particular asset that he is trading.

For example, even if not trading on any leverage at all (instead, trading GBP1 per pip meaning GBP1 gained/lost for each pip gained/lost), a trader will find that for each GBP1 traded the platform will reduce his available account balance by anywhere from GBP100 to GBP200 or more, depending upon the type of contract that he has entered into (depending on how risky/volatile the platform assesses each contract to be).

Not only will this eat into available capital but additionally any losses that a trade incurs as it is ongoing will also be deducted from available capital. So, let us say that a trader sold EURUSD at 1.1400 at GBP4 per pip. Even before the pair has moved the retail trader's platform capital account will be showing that he is down on available capital by, perhaps, GBP800. If he had available capital before trading of GBP1,000 then he could only afford to have the position go 200 pips against him before he is automatically closed out of the position by the trading platform (and thus wiped out entirely).

Moreover, it affords no opportunity for hedging positions as they run (see below). Conversely, of course, if the position makes money from the beginning then the trader's available capital will increase (although this will not affect the amount that the platform has set aside for his risk margin).

Account Size And Setting Targets

In order to have any peace of mind, **it is necessary for a trader to have an account with sufficient capital for his trading ambitions. Or, conversely, a trader needs to have trading ambitions that are cut according to his capital.** There cannot be an imbalance here.

It is true, theoretically, that with a GBP500 initial stake in an account, a trader can become a millionaire within just over five years, if he doubles his money every six months, as the table below illustrates:

Capital Accumulation Over Six Years From An Initial £500 Investment	
Months	Capital
0	500
6	1000
12	2000
18	4000
24	8000
30	16000
36	32000
42	64000
48	128000
54	256000
60	512000
66	1024000
72	2048000

This, though, requires a high degree of self-discipline, rigorous order management, excellent market knowledge and contacts, and highly developed skills of technical analysis.

In terms of self-discipline first, the trader must cut his profit target according to his account balance. **At minimum, a risk/reward ratio of 4:1 in the first few years of trading should be set – that is, for every GBP1 a trader might lose he could make GBP4, based on where the key support and resistance levels are.**

Second, if trying to double funds over the 0-6 month period then a trader must make GBP500 during that first half year period. This amount split down into weeks implies a weekly profit target of GBP19 per week.

Concomitant with this, a trader will need to work out how much is the maximum that he can place on any one trade. Professional bank and fund management traders will typically risk anywhere between 1-5% of their capital on any single trade but, to begin with for the relatively inexperienced retail trader, no more than 1% of total capital should be risked on any one trade. Therefore, on any single trade, a trader could risk no more than GBP5 in total.

This is clearly not much, if doing GBP1 per pip, which is why this becoming a millionaire with just GBP500 in just over five years is unlikely, as it allows no real room for error, as the spread alone (the difference between a trading platform's bid and offer prices for the base currency in a currency pair) is often at least 3 pips.

Therefore, a sensible **minimum amount to have in a trading account to begin with is at least GBP10,000.** This allows flexibility in hedging ongoing positions that are not performing well in the very short-term but that a trader believes (based on empirical evidence) will come good in the slightly longer term. Of course, the doubling process outlined in the earlier chart is still the same.

In order to make GBP10,000 within the first six months, a trader must make a weekly profit of GBP385 per week over six months: 1% of GBP10,000 is obviously GBP100, which means that this amount should be the stop-loss level on every single order, and these should be placed at exactly the same time as the entry trade. At GBP1 per pip that is a 100 pip movement against a trader, which is relatively reasonable in a market of average volatility. Indeed, it may be that, under these conditions, a trader might consider putting GBP2 per pip on the trade, whilst simultaneously cutting his stop-loss to 50 pips from the point of trade entry. As such, it is fairly straightforward and realistic to make the required sum in the target period and even more quickly if using weightings across different asset classes, given proper risk management.

Straight Averaging Up

Given the premise that the aim of trading is to minimise any losses and to maximise any wins, averaging up – if done well – is a good way of achieving the latter.

The basic averaging technique is pretty self-explanatory: it involves **adding to a winning position as the trade continues into profitable territory.** So, for example, in the chart below, a position had been entered by buying EUR against the USD (selling USD) at 1.3000 (this is an historical example, but the point is the same for any time period). After completing the technical analysis, it was clear that a break of this key resistance level would indicate a move higher, and it had been decided to add GBP1 per pip at every 50 pip upwards increment. Having done this three times, there was an average long position of GBP3 per pip at EURUSD1.3050.

EURUSD (Historical)

[Chart Key:
A = Buy EURUSD at 1.3000, GBP1 per pip
B = Buy again at 1.3050, GBP 1 per pip
C = Buy again at 1.3100, GBP 1 per pip
D = Therefore, average long price at GBP 3 per pip is 1.3050]

On GBP1 per pip at 1.3000, a trader would have made GBP250 as the EURUSD hit 1.3250. Another GBP1 per pip at 1.3050 would have netted a further GBP200 and the final GBP1 per pip at 1.3100 a further GBP150. The total, therefore, would have been GBP600. Of course, had the trader put on GBP3 per pip in the first trade, the profit would have been GBP750. Additionally the break-even on the trade has now moved up to 1.3050 rather than 1.3000.

If the trader had not sold at the top of that particular move and the pair had traded down to 1.3100 then he might have lost the third leg profit of GBP150, which would have resulted in a net profit of just GBP150. Also, if the pair had traded back down through the 1.3050 area then the trader would have incurred a loss on the third long, together with no profit on the second, which would have resulted in a net profit of nothing at all.

Layered Averaging Up

Another way of averaging up that tends against the above phenomenon of being averaged out of any profit is to **add to a long position on pullbacks to the preferred entry level, or the other way around if a net seller.** So, if a trader decides to go long as above then he simply adds GBP1 per pip on any move back towards the 1.3000 level, if he is expecting a sustained move upwards over time.

Such tactics are particularly useful if there is an ongoing struggle between a central bank and a fund on two sides of the trade. For example in USDJPY, after the new Prime Minister Shinzo Abe came to power at the end of 2012, the Bank of Japan was buying USD and selling JPY very aggressively in order to support its export market (and thus aid broader economic recovery) from around the USD85.50 level, whilst certain funds – especially hedge funds – were selling USD and buying JPY anywhere above 87.00.

Once Abe was more firmly ensconced as PM, this battle moved up the values on USDJPY, as the Bank of Japan was given a much broader policy mandate than before. This was in line with those given to the US Fed and the Bank of England at the time, which included looking at employment rates, interest rates and inflation. In this vein, the banks used quantitative easing where necessary, together with direct currency intervention and forward guidance as a means of manipulating their respective currencies.

It was only when, in fact, the Bank of Japan was tasked with ensuring a broad-based policy strategy – engineering sustained nominal annual economic growth of 3% (there had been no average annual nominal GDP growth for 15 years) and at least a 2% annual inflation rate every year from 2015, as well as commencing a massive domestic bond-buying QE programme (Fed-style) – that the JPY managed sustained depreciation of the sort wanted by Abe and moved through the key USDJPY100 resistance level.

Alternately, **adding smaller amounts to the initial position is also a better way to take advantage of further moves** (in the aforementioned case) whilst also limiting the potential – as shown above – for all profits to be eradicated (or even to start making a loss). The converse of this, of course, is averaging down, in which a trader adds to losing positions in the hopes of making money back quicker as the original position reverses.

Value Averaging

As a natural corollary of the above, value averaging is another added value way of managing positions, this time by **constantly readjusting the risk/reward exposure to a pre-determined level.** Therefore, in practical terms, a trader sets an amount that falls within his risk/reward parameters.

For example, he may decide that he wishes to have a total exposure per day of GBP100 in EURUSD, at GBP1 per pip. In this event, if the position makes GBP10 in one day then next day he takes the GBP10 out and still has GBP100 riding on the position (at the original price). Conversely, if the position loses GBP10 in one day then the following day he would add another GBP10 at whatever the new price is to compensate. Thus, he has now spent GBP110 on the long, albeit at a more favourable average, given a down-trading market.

Trailing Stop Loss Orders

As a position turns into profit, the available amount of Net Margin Requirement (NMR)/Net Trading Requirement (NTR) that a trader has in his account increases, which can be used either for reinvestment in one of the methods detailed above or can be left where it is, depending on the nature of the market at the time. Nonetheless, depending upon how he manages his position, **there is no point in keeping the stop loss exit order at its original point, but rather it should move up as the profit margin increases.** This is the notion of trailing stops.

So, basically, if a position increases profit by 10 pips the stop loss should be moved up by 10 pips and so on.

Hedging

A perfect hedge means one in which no risk whatsoever is taken. As a corollary of this, it means that there will also be no reward. The perfect hedge would be, for instance, buying EURUSD 1 million and simultaneously selling EURUSD 1 million. Thus, perfect hedging is a pointless exercise.

Instead, broader hedging can either help to reduce overall net losses in a bad position (by making offsetting gains in other related areas) or help to add to overall net profits (whilst not actually proportionately increasing the risk involved). In this sense, then, hedging is a method of dynamically managing the risk/reward profile for the trader, and knowing how to do it properly and quickly in any situation is vital.

Cross-Currency Hedging

Beginning with the obvious, as mentioned earlier, all currency trades involve buying one currency and selling another and, because of this duality, hedging currency exposures is actually fairly straightforward.

For example, a trader is long the EUR, which means he is also short USD: in market code +EURUSD. The position should always be marked in terms of the base currency first, then the amount (EUR1 million for bank dealers or, for spread traders, 1 per pip for example, be it GBP, USD, or EUR, most commonly) and then the price (here, 1.5063). Therefore, in market terms, it should be written: +EURUSD1 @1.5063. In this example, we will use the EUR1 million example but the points are the same for whatever amount the spread trader is using.

EURUSD (Historical)

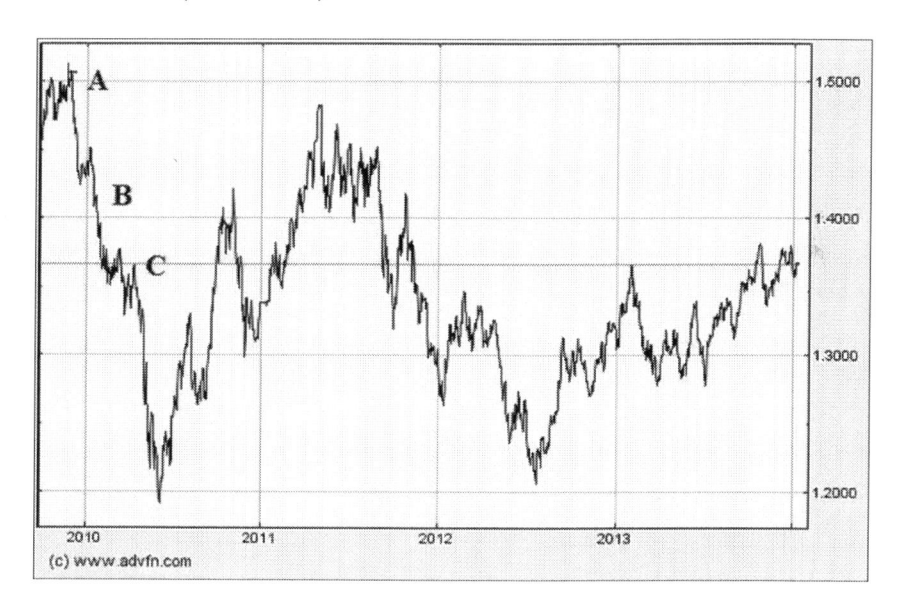

[Chart Key:
A = Trader buys euros, 1 million and sell US dollars at 1.5063

B = Getting nervous about the euro story, he buys US dollars, 1.5 million and sells Swiss francs at 1.0262

C = The trader now has options – he is long EURUSD, long USDCHF; making money on the latter going up as the former goes down. Additionally, he can re-weight positions, depending on how each pairing performs (he can, for example, add to his long USDCHF position or reduce his long EURUSD position) or simply sell EURCHF, as he is effectively net long of that, or he can do counter-balancing stock indices trades]

The market is going against the trader but he believes that the EUR will go up soon. However, he is not exactly sure when and how much the swing against him might be. He knows that, by definition, if the EUR element of this pair is going down then the USD element of it is going up. Therefore, he can go long the USD against something else to attempt to make money on the rising USD as the EUR goes down, so he goes long USDCHF1.5 million as EURUSD breaks through the 1.4750 level.

USDCHF (Historical)

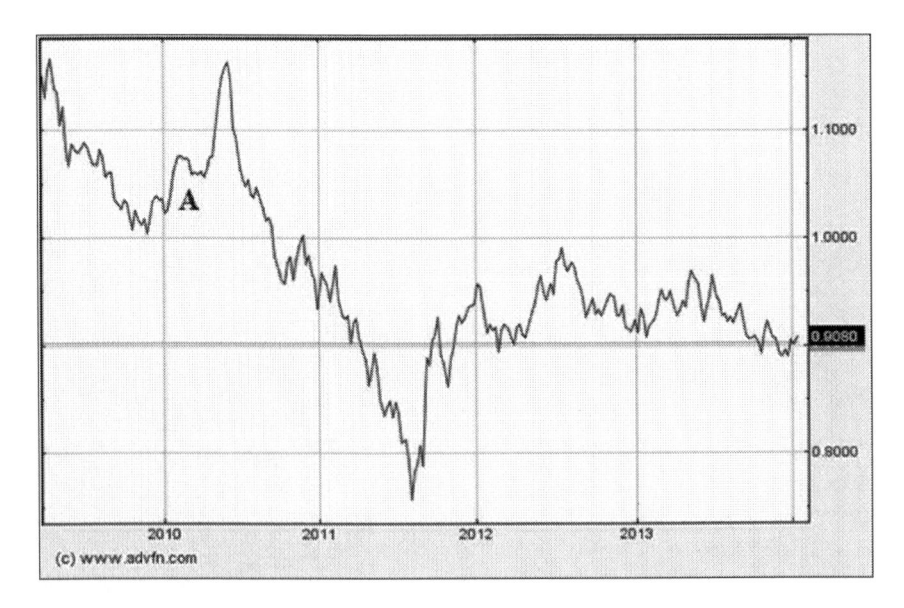

[Chart Key:
A = Buy USD/sell CHF1.5 million at 1.0262]

Now things are looking up, as one trade is counterbalancing the other almost perfectly, as can be seen from the chart below, given that **he is essentially long EURCHF.**

As the EUR continues in its downward trend, the trader can use some of the averaging techniques described above to help loss turn into profit. This is simply a question of re-weighting each trade. As it stands, he has the same overall capital involved in each trade (EUR1 million, or around USD1.5 million) but as the EURUSD continues to trade down, he can add to his long USDCHF position. Let us say that he doubles it, at 1.0400, to USD3 million for the entire duration of the downtrend in EURUSD.

Looking at these trades in profit and loss (P&L) terms then:

+EURUSD1 million @ 1.5063, liquidate at 1.1800 = total loss of EUR326,300 (= USD at the new rate = USD385,034).

+USDCHF1 million @ 1.0262, liquidate at 1.1700 = USD143,800

and +USDCHF2 million @ 1.0400, liquidate at 1.1700 = USD260,000.

Therefore, the **total profit for the venture (which did not start out well) was USD77,500.**

EURCHF (Historical)

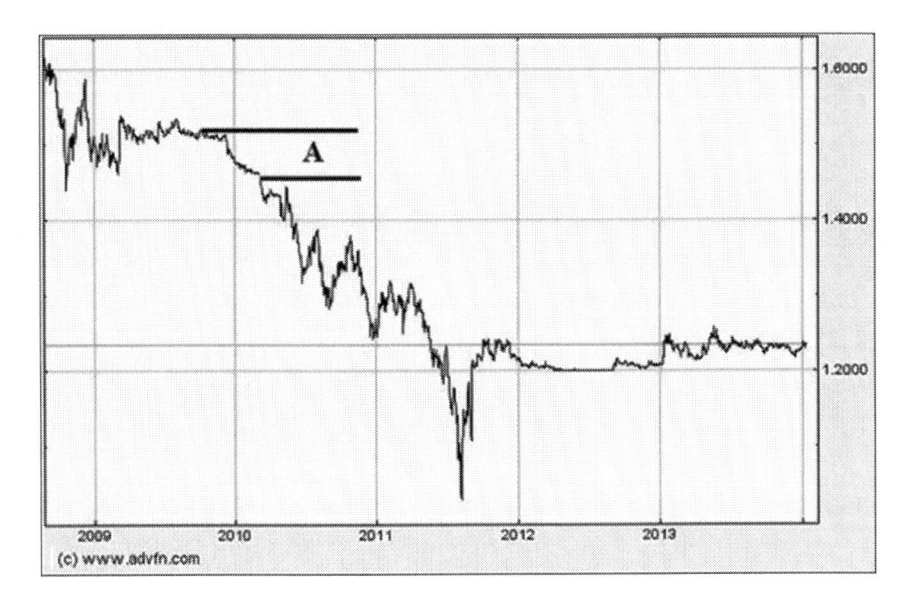

[chart]

[Chart Key:
A = Overall, with just a flat long EURCHF position the trader is only down 250-300 pips but he can get rid of this entirely by re-weighting]

In the above example, **he could also have sold EURCHF,** which would have given him a flat position, as:

1. +EUR -USD

2. +USD -CHF

3. Therefore, net long EURCHF

4. Therefore, sell EURCHF = flat.

However, there were **many other options available whilst he was long EURUSD and long USDCHF:**

1. Increase the relative weighting of the long USDCHF position (as described above) or he could think more laterally still and buy the USD against something else as well.

2. This would have increased his net long USD position but also it would have allowed him to insulate himself against any CHF-specific good news that might cause it to rally and thus lose him money on his long USDCHF position – for example, if the central bank of Switzerland (SNB) raised interest rates unexpectedly.

3. Therefore, he would have looked around for other currencies where the outlook was grim and good news was not expected on the horizon. At the time, GBP looked especially ropey, so he could have sold GBP and bought USD.

4. This again could be reweighted in terms of amount.

5. And so the process goes on.

Cross-Asset Hedging

Sticking with the failing long EURUSD position example for the time being, the trader need not have just hedged his bets with currencies.

Let us recap on the basic situation: he had gone long EUR, expecting some turnaround in the fortunes of the currency, based perhaps on the notion that future figures might show that the weaker Eurozone members (Greece, Spain, Portugal, Italy, Ireland) might be turning themselves around.

So, what else could he do to capitalise on the continued poor performance of the Eurozone that was crucifying his long EURUSD position?

1. Sell the major stock indices associated with the individual countries performing especially badly in the EUR region (as shown above).

Greece Athens Stock Exchange (Historical)

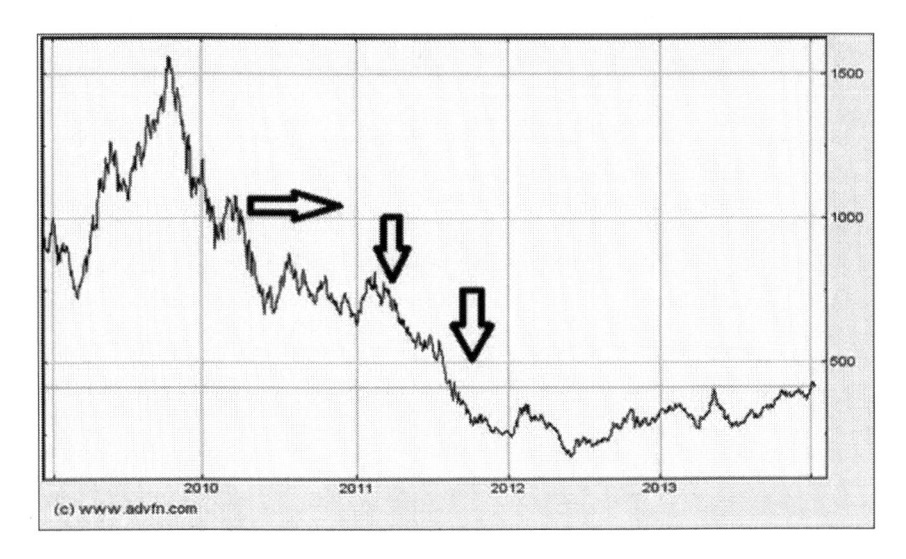

Had he sold the ASE as above, say another USD1 million worth, his entry price at the time would have been around 2,250 and falling fast. He could also have sold the other major indices of troubled Eurozone countries.

2. Looking at it another way, he could have bought US stock indices instead/as well as.

Dow Jones Industrial Average (Historical)

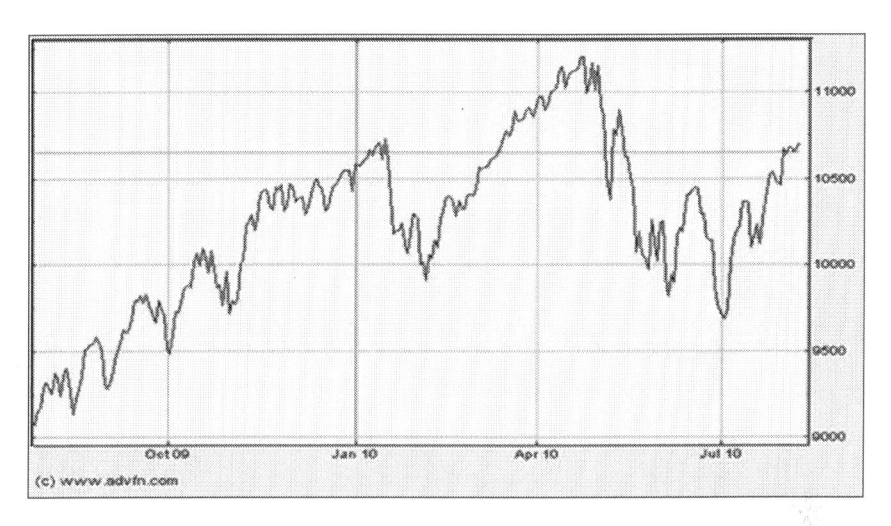

3. If he was, in the meantime, suddenly concerned about his net short CHF position then he could hedge out the CHF risk, by buying the major Swiss stock index.

4. He could have done a currency option to hedge risks either side (we will discuss options later on).

Cross-Sovereign/Credit Rating Hedging

Given that the credit risk for the troubled Eurozone members was increasing over the period when the EUR was falling out of bed, the trader could have bought credit default swaps (CDS) on the countries worst affected. CDS are basically like insurance policies on entities going bankrupt (for example, companies or, in this case, countries). The more technical definition is: CDS pay the buyer face value in exchange for the underlying securities or the cash equivalent should a government or company fail to adhere to its debt agreements; the higher the likelihood, the higher the price of the CDS.

Again, this would have hedged the EUR exposure as, broadly speaking, the more money that was lost on being long EUR, the more money was made on being long Greek CDS (that is, in essence, buying the likelihood of Greece defaulting on its debt).

Options

Options are best used as a form of hedging, although many traders deal in them as they would any other standalone asset class. It should be pointed out at this juncture that trading options is an exceptionally risky business and one which retail traders would best avoid in their first five or so years of trading, at minimum. The reason for this subsection is that options positions sometimes have a significant effect on the overall trading patterns of a market, so a trader needs to know what they are when they read market reports stating that x and y options are weighing on/supporting key levels.

Key Types

An option is the right, but not the obligation, to buy or sell an asset at a particular price (the 'exercise price') on or before a specific future date (the 'exercise date').

The two most common types of option are called an **American style option** (which can be exercised at any point up to the option expiration date) and a **European style option** (which can only be exercised on an exact exercise date).

For the more 'exotic' **Asian options** the payoff is determined by the average underlying price over some pre-set period of time, conceptually different from both the American and European option types in which in both cases the payoff of the option contract depends on the price of the underlying instrument at exercise.

Barrier options, meanwhile, that often have a significant effect on market trading patterns, are a type of option whose payoff depends on whether or not the underlying asset has reached or exceeded a predetermined price. A barrier option can be a knock-out, meaning it can expire worthless if the underlying exceeds a certain price, limiting profits for the holder but limiting losses for the writer. It can also be a knock-in, meaning it has no value until the underlying reaches a certain price.

Key Terms

An option to buy an asset is called a 'call' option and an option to sell one is called a 'put' option. A trader can buy or sell either type of option (that is, he can buy the right to sell or buy, and he can sell the right to sell or buy). If he sells an option then he receives a premium from the buyer (a bit like an insurance premium), however, he is obligated as the seller to pay out to the buyer in the event that the option is exercised (and these payouts can be limitless, depending on how the option has moved). If he buys an option then he receives these premiums.

Options are extremely useful as hedging tools (this was their original purpose, as a type of insurance against unforeseen movements in asset prices) but, as with all financial assets, they can also be used for purely aggressive speculative purposes.

In a currency option, then – let us stick with the EURUSD example that we have been predominantly using in the last few pages – if a trader bought a EURUSD call then he would be buying the right (but not the obligation) to buy EUR and sell USD, and if he bought a EURUSD put then he would be buying the right (but not the obligation) to sell EUR and buy USD. And vice-versa if he was selling a call or put; he has a liability then to meet the obligation implied in the option if the buyer decides to exercise it.

Although we are not going to go into huge details about the pricing of options, one thing that it is useful to be aware of is that the premium paid to buy an option is a reflection both of the exercise price of the option (and whether it is currently in profit, ITM, or out of profit, OTM, see above) and also the volatility of the market for the currency pair.

Looking at options in terms of them being insurance policies is quite helpful in a number of regards. Let us say that someone has bought a house and wants to insure its contents against theft for GBP10,000. The insurance company has to decide on a range of factors in determining the level of premiums. Has the house got window and door locks, is it backing onto a secluded area, is it an area known for burglaries etc? So, let us say that the answers are: yes to locks, no to secluded area, no to burglaries. The insurance company decides that overall the person seeking insurance will only have to pay them their GBP10,000 back over 20 years. This implies zero risk volatility or thereabouts.

One year into the policy and there are a spate of burglaries in the area, so the premiums go up, as there has been an increase in the risk and so on and so forth. The area in which the house is located now has a private security firm patrolling your grounds 24/7, so premiums go down again due to lower risk.

In the EURUSD example, **the trader had gone long EUR short USD at 1.5063 and the position had started to go against him almost from the beginning. The near-perfect hedge here would have been to buy a EURUSD put (the right but not the obligation to sell EUR and buy USD) at a strike price of 1.5063** although the price would have to be adjusted slightly to take into account the premium that the trader would have paid to the seller of the option, but basically that is the idea.

He could, conversely, have banked money in advance if he had sold a EURUSD call option (giving someone the right but not the obligation to buy EUR from the player, therefore the player is selling them and buying USD) also at 1.5063.

Key Legislation

A key part of why more investors in general are now looking at options (and futures) investment than they were before the new slew of market regulations (Basel III, Mifid, Dodd-Frank etc), of course, is that they appear to fall outside the confusion of precisely what will and will not be actively managed within the scope of the new FX regulatory environment.

For example, one key idea was that the traditionally bilaterally-traded over-the-counter (OTC) FX derivatives markets would be migrated into a mandatory electronically-executed environment, all under the auspices of central counterparties (CCPs) that act as middlemen between the trading parties and the central clearinghouses. Moreover, participants would be obliged to post initial and variation margin to the CCPs on a daily or intra-day basis, so the need for easily accessible capital to enable such trading would also increase dramatically.

However, timing remains a problem for the futures markets, given that the dates of the contracts are much more specific than those of spot and forward outright contracts, which are completely flexible, and liquidity is also a problem for the futures markets, which is very small compared to the global FX markets.

The massive risk in writing options was highlighted in the Nick Leeson case. Leeson was in charge of both Barings Bank's front-office dealing operations on the Singapore International Monetary Exchange (SIMEX) and its back-office function so that when a trade went wrong at the front end he personally could simply rubber-stamp it at the back end. He continued to do so until he lost Barings around GBP830 million, bringing the bank down in the process; this being a reminder of over-confidence in one's abilities.

Also, in order to cover his mounting trading losses he decided to write vast numbers of options essentially betting on the Nikkei stock market rising. He had pocketed millions of dollars in 'insurance options' from others and all was looking good as Japan boomed, until the Kobe earthquake hit Japan in January 1995, whereupon the Nikkei fell like a stone and his customers wanted their insurance payments back; thus illustrating that markets are not always predictable.

Basic Structures (Long-Only Options)

Buying a call option

This is used most simply by those who believe that an asset is going up in value (it is buying the option to buy a certain asset). If the asset price is higher than the strike price plus the premium paid then the trader makes a profit. The only risk here, as with all options bought, is that the trader loses the premium paid.

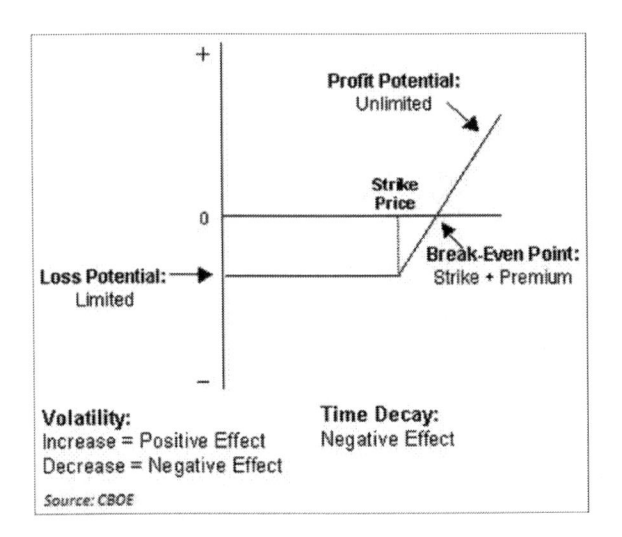

```
                    +
                           Profit Potential:
                              Unlimited

                              Strike
                              Price
                 0
                              Break-Even Point:
 Loss Potential:              Strike + Premium
    Limited

                    −

 Volatility:                Time Decay:
 Increase = Positive Effect  Negative Effect
 Decrease = Negative Effect
 Source: CBOE
```

Buying a put option

This is used by those who believe that an asset is going down in value (it is buying the option to sell a certain asset). If the asset price is lower than the strike price plus the premium paid then the trader makes a profit. The only risk here, as with all options bought, is that the trader loses the premium paid.

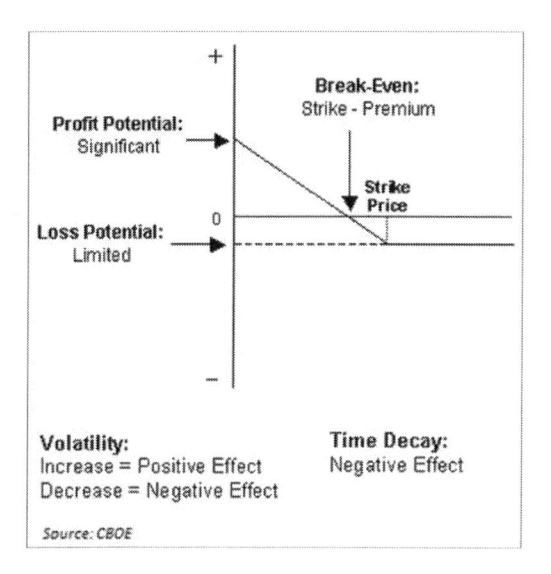

Long Straddle

This is used by investors who think an asset is going a long way in one direction but are unsure as to which direction that might be. It involves buying both a put and a call option at the same strike price and the same expiration date. This offers unlimited potential upside but limited downside.

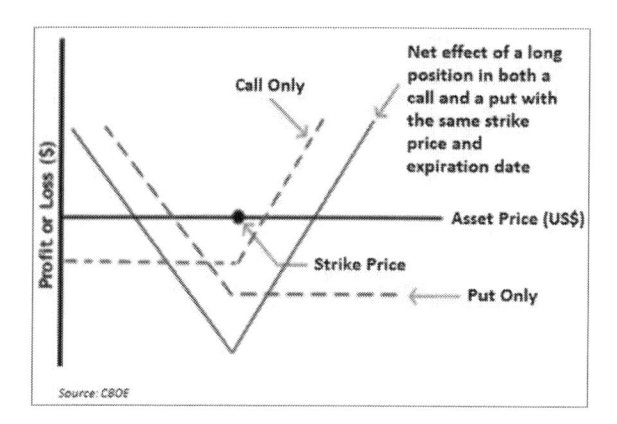

Long Strangle

This is for investors similar to those in the Long Straddle strategy but with the differences that both are usually some way out of the money and the call option and put option elements have different strike prices (but the same expiration date).

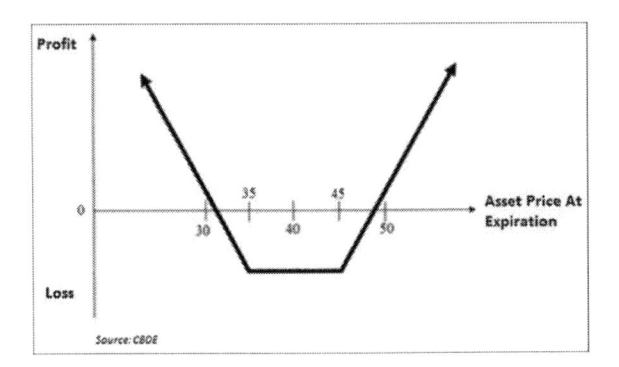

As mentioned, sometimes big options positions (generally, those sold by financial institutions) have a major effect on markets. This occurs as those who have sold them understandably attempt to avoid an asset reaching the exercise price of the option, at which point they would face massive payouts to those who have bought them. In practical terms, the level of these exercise prices are often located just below key support levels or just above key resistance levels respectively, and protective buying or selling in order to avoid option exercises often reinforce the strength of these support and resistance levels.

Risk-On/Risk-Off And Other Correlations

Even in a more 'normal' market environment – that is, one with clear overall trends – simply 'jobbing' in and out of an asset in isolation in search of a few pips here and there is almost certain to result in trading disaster. Indeed, **this style of dealing is a key reason why 90% of retail traders lose all of their trading funds within 90 days of beginning to deal.** Not being one of these and, rather, being one of those that makes life-changing serious money requires self-discipline, knowledge of trading fundamentals, a sound grasp of technical analysis and risk management and extensive knowledge of risk management techniques; all of which are covered in depth earlier. The ability to discern what patterns are in play across the global financial markets at any given point is also crucial and this is what this section is about.

What Is RORO?

In general terms, 'RORO' is a function of the risk of systemic failure across the global financial system. When the risk of this failure rises there is a shift towards less risk-exposed assets ('Risk-Off') and when it falls there is a move towards more risk-exposed assets ('Risk-On'); both conditions together being acronymically termed 'RORO'. More specifically, RORO means that the price action of all major financial markets assets is correlated positively or negatively to a greater or lesser degree.

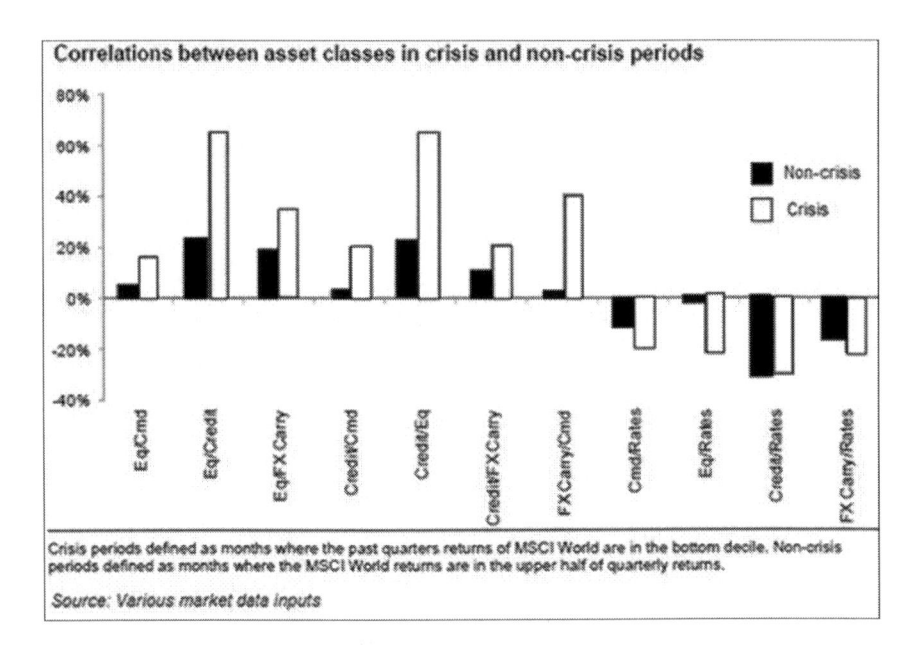

Correlations between asset classes in crisis and non-crisis periods

Crisis periods defined as months where the past quarters returns of MSCI World are in the bottom decile. Non-crisis periods defined as months where the MSCI World returns are in the upper half of quarterly returns.

Source: Various market data inputs

The RORO trading paradigm first fully manifested itself after the collapse of Lehman Brothers in 2008. In the aftermath of this and the blow-up of a full global financial crisis thereafter, there were two diametrically opposed potential outcomes. One was that the dramatic actions undertaken by policymakers and governments around the world – which ranged from huge cuts in interest rates, currency devaluations and quantitative easing, or all three – would successfully result in a global economic recovery. The other was that these measures would not work, at least not quickly, in which case there would be at least a continuation of the global depression, if not a worsening of it.

At that point it was recognised that either of these would have a major impact on the price of different assets. Therefore, when confidence was running high that the measures would work in effecting at least an upturn in the world's economic fortunes, global investors moved towards more risk-exposed (risk-on) assets and when the opposite was the case they moved towards less risk-exposed assets (risk-off). **This meant that there were very pronounced synchronised price moves – up or down – across**

varying asset classes, depending on whether they were regarded as more risky (risk-on) or less risky (risk-off).

Over the past two years, much of 2015 saw the predominant market view that the US economy was ready to take off, marking a definitive end to the lingering effects of the Great Financial Crisis. This meant a shift towards risk-on assets. However, when the US Federal Reserve did actually raise rates – and signalled that they would continue to do so at a quicker pace and to a higher degree than many had previously thought – fear set in that these interest rate increases might choke off the tentative recovery. This meant a shift towards risk-off assets.

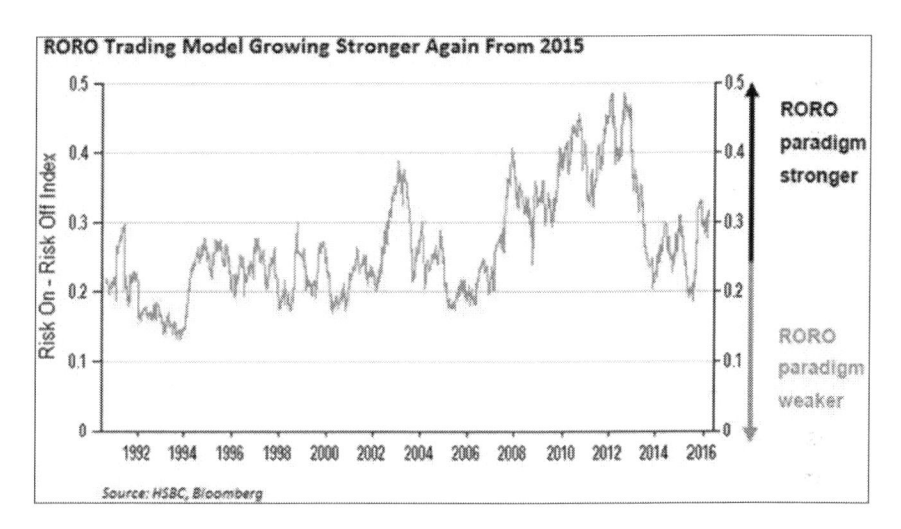

These fears – and the corollary move into risk-off assets – were exacerbated by additional heightened concerns over weakening oil prices, decreasing economic growth in China and the near-zero real growth occurring in the Eurozone, plus further worries over what Britain's exit from the EU would mean for the geopolitical bloc and an apparent stalling of Japan's growth ambitions.

It is extremely important for the trader to realise that these correlations not only remain a very significant common price component of all assets in all regions across the world but also

that they change with great frequency – both on a minor level, intraday even, and on a major level, over weeks and months.

As at the end of 2016, the RORO trading model was a dominant theme again, as shown below.

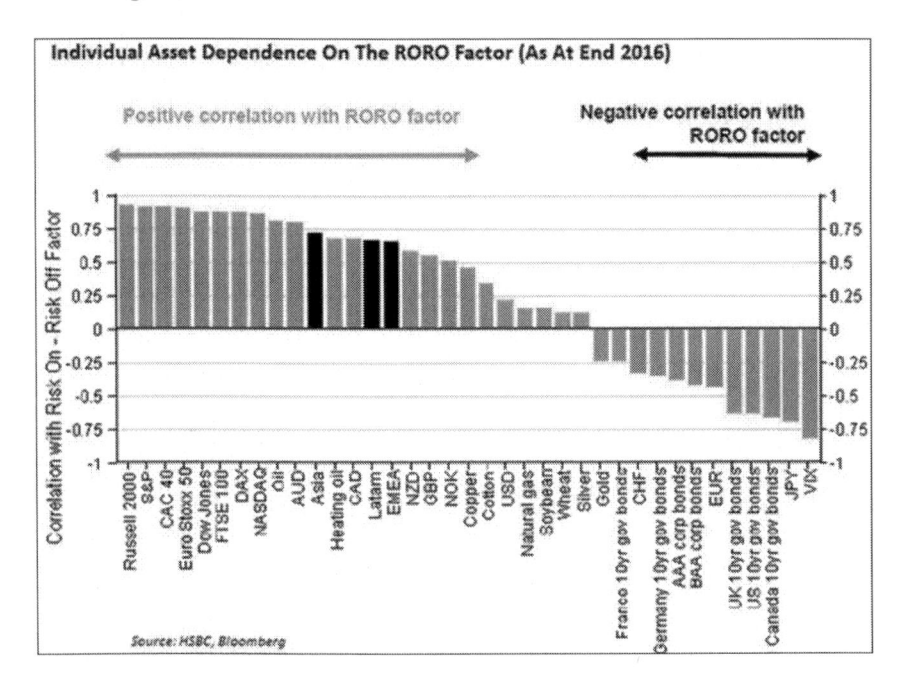

Individual Asset Dependence On The RORO Factor (As At End 2016)

Source: HSBC, Bloomberg

The fact that the prices of apparently disparate individual assets move in tandem (either positively correlated or inversely correlated) means that **classical methods of maximising returns whilst minimising risk will remain sidelined for the foreseeable future, calling for shrewder and nimbler investment approaches going forward.**

This is even truer in periods when these correlations change on a proverbial dime, as they have been doing for some time now, although there are much longer-term cycles of which a trader must be aware in order to understand the base point from which they are operating and these were identified earlier *(The Business Cycle, The Kondratieff Wave and The Minsky Cycle).*

Changing Bond And Equity Correlations

As mentioned earlier, there is a **general rule of thumb that early on in a market cycle when interest rates rise (or are expected to rise shortly) then bonds are bought and equities are sold. As the cycle progresses, increased buying of bonds reduces the yield (the simple mathematical formula mentioned earlier) resulting in money then flowing back into equities.** Both of these phases have corollary effects on the FX and commodities asset classes (see later). Over the past few months in particular, though, there have been enormous swings in these movements, principally as a result of dramatically shifting market views on where interest rates will be in any of the major world economic groups (US, the Eurozone, Japan and China), tempered by growth outlooks in these areas, and by the relative position of each on the quantitative easing curve, with the US having ended QE whilst it still continues in one form or another in the Eurozone and Japan, and for China massive investment stimulus packages are the usual way in which growth is underpinned.

In broad terms, correlations heatmaps are a good starting point to see how the relationships between bonds and equities have changed over the relatively recent past, as shown in the following charts.

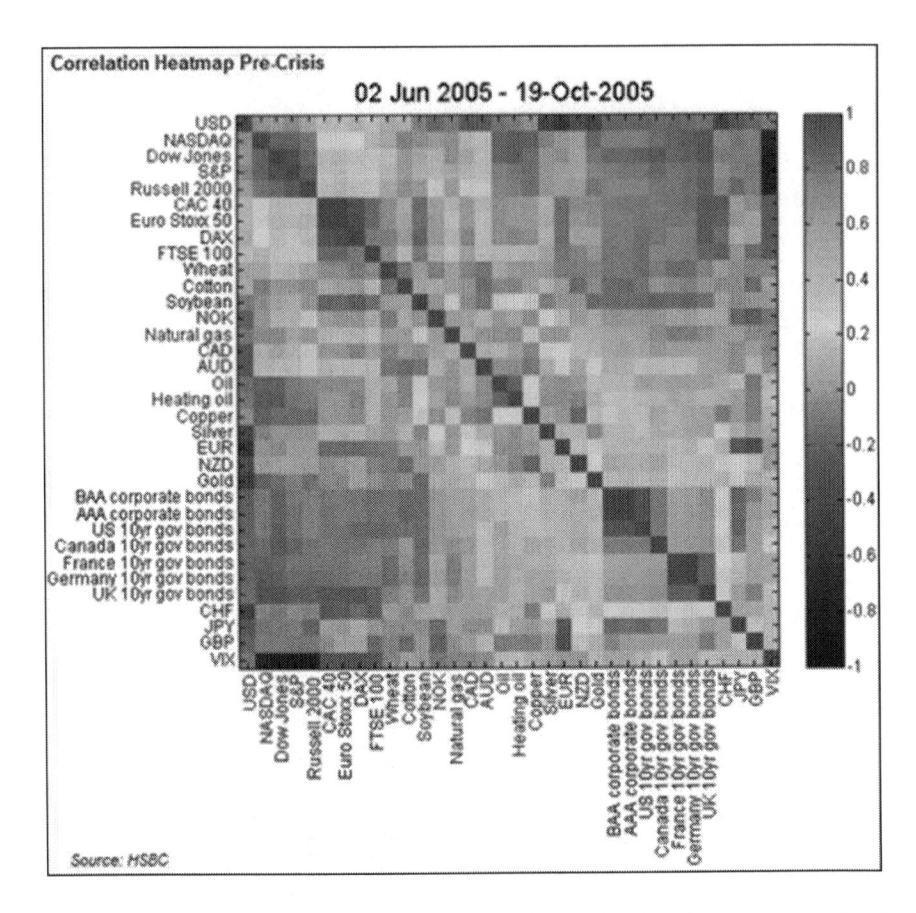

Correlation Heatmap Pre-Crisis
02 Jun 2005 - 19-Oct-2005

Source: HSBC

In the chart above, it is obvious that the RORO phenomenon had not fully manifested itself, with the only noticeable correlations being between assets of the same class, such as various bonds and various stock markets and even in respect of the latter, the correlations are really only between the different stock markets of the same country.

After the Lehman's failure, though, the situation, as shown in the chart below, had radically changed, with correlations – positive and negative – establishing themselves across the board.

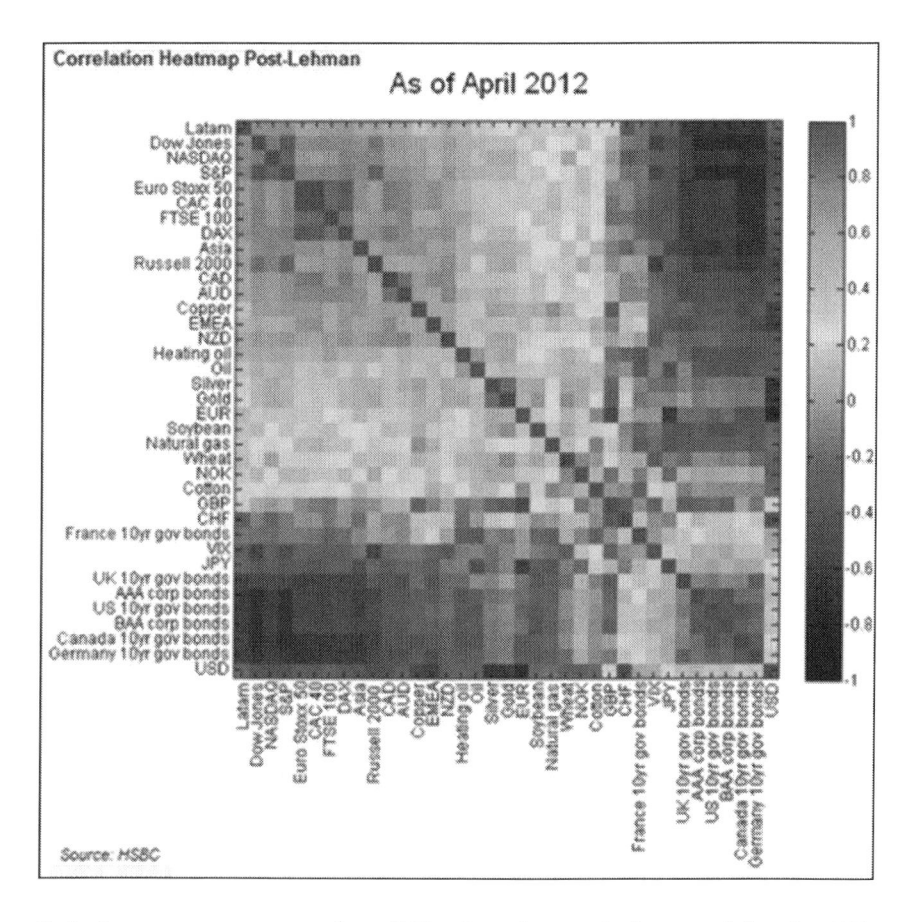

Correlation Heatmap Post-Lehman
As of April 2012

Source: HSBC

It is important to note that QE when it was being used by the US, the Eurozone, Japan and indeed the UK, is not the same as RORO and does not have the same effect. In fact, the typical RORO correlation structure came into being way before QE was seriously considered by the market and rather than QE being a cause of RORO, it exists as a separate driver of markets. For example, QE was positive for both equities and bonds whereas RORO moved these asset classes in opposite directions, and these differences are highlighted in the charts below.

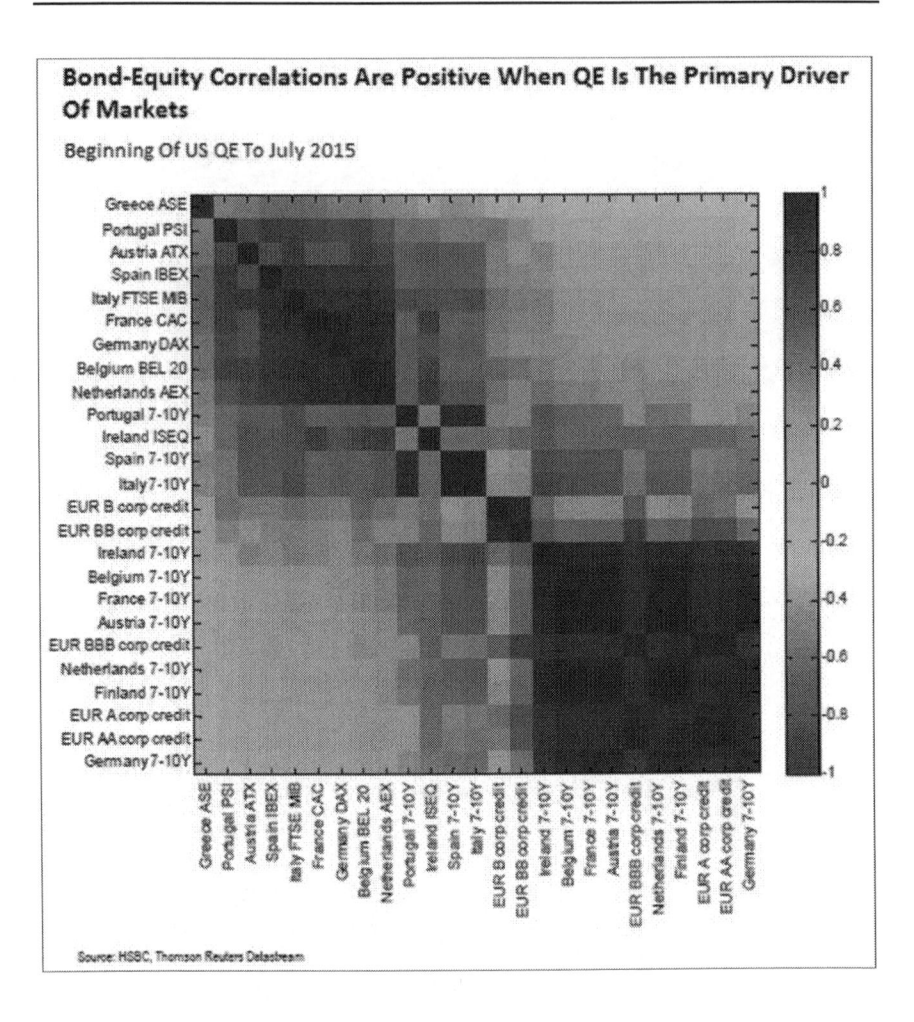

Bond-Equity Correlations Are Positive When QE Is The Primary Driver Of Markets

Beginning Of US QE To July 2015

Source: HSBC, Thomson Reuters Datastream

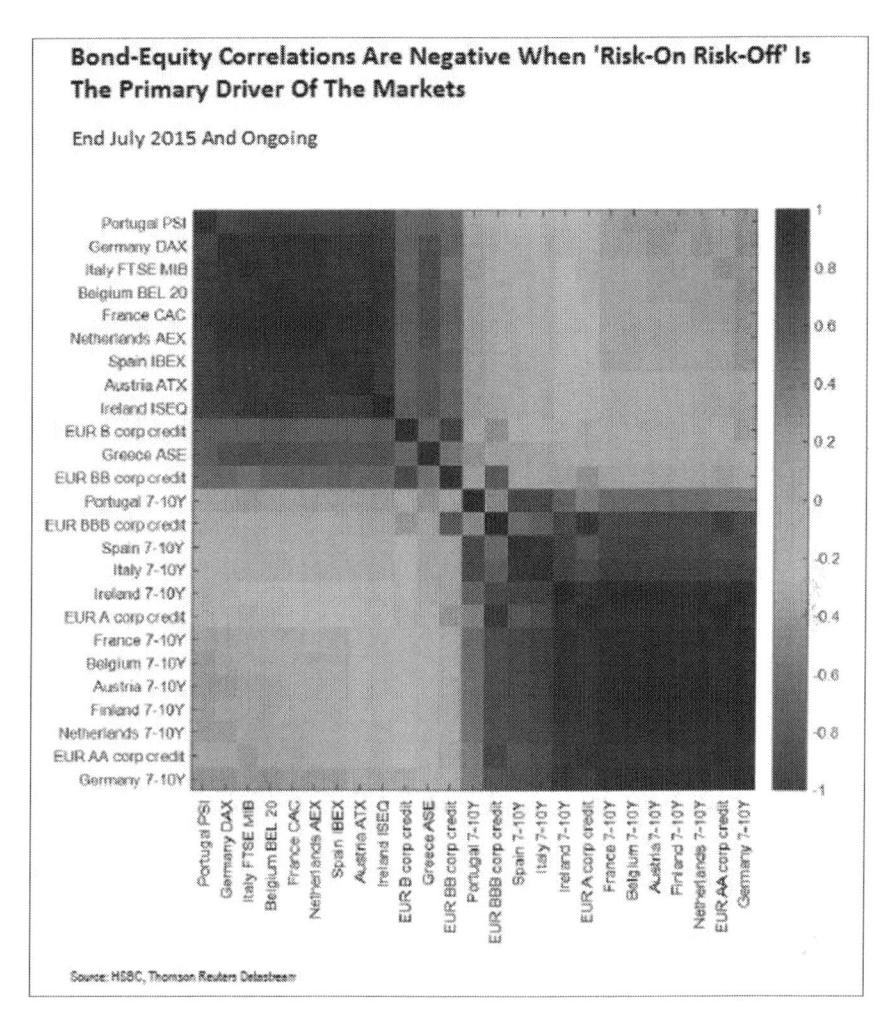

Bond-Equity Correlations Are Negative When 'Risk-On Risk-Off' Is The Primary Driver Of The Markets

End July 2015 And Ongoing

Source: HSBC, Thomson Reuters Datastream

Risk-on risk-off is arguably easier to deal with in the overall bond-equity context because generally in this environment they do what they 'should' do, which is move in opposite directions. **When QE dominates, though, a wider range of assets rise and fall together.** In practice, both environments are difficult in this particular market paradigm because it can be difficult to discern at any given time which of the two key trading factors – QE or RORO – is prevalent and which will be prevalent within the next few hours even, depending on upcoming data releases or statements from central bankers or politicians.

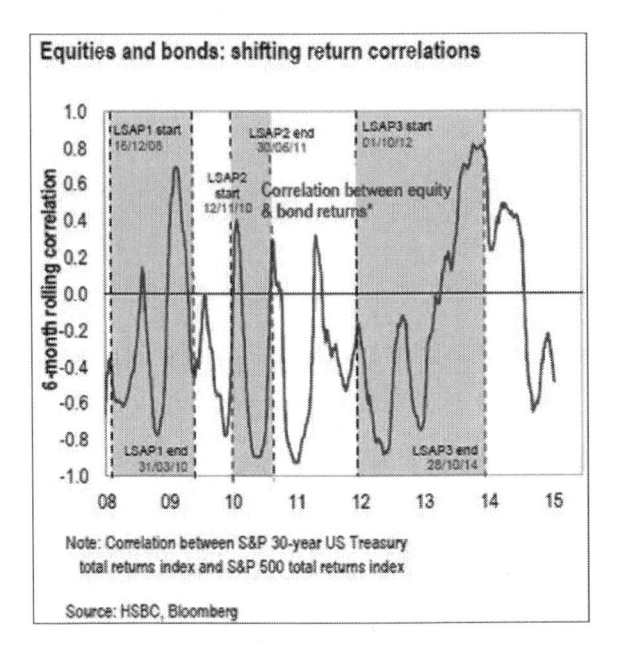

Equities and bonds: shifting return correlations

Note: Correlation between S&P 30-year US Treasury total returns index and S&P 500 total returns index

Source: HSBC, Bloomberg

These changing relationships within financial markets are suggestive not only of recent regime shifts but of future ones that are imminent as well. In the early days of QE, benchmark bond curves (like US Treasuries and German bunds) would steepen and there was no discernible trend in inflation expectations. Now we have seen both a flatter curve and lower expectations and this is essentially the market telling the central banks that recession risk has increased and the inflation target is less likely to be hit. Indeed, the past few months have already seen numerous radical policy shifts from central banks (from negative rates employed by the Swiss National Bank to changes in the renminbi currency regime by the People's Bank of China), and it is very likely that equally dramatic moves are on the cards for reasons outlined later.

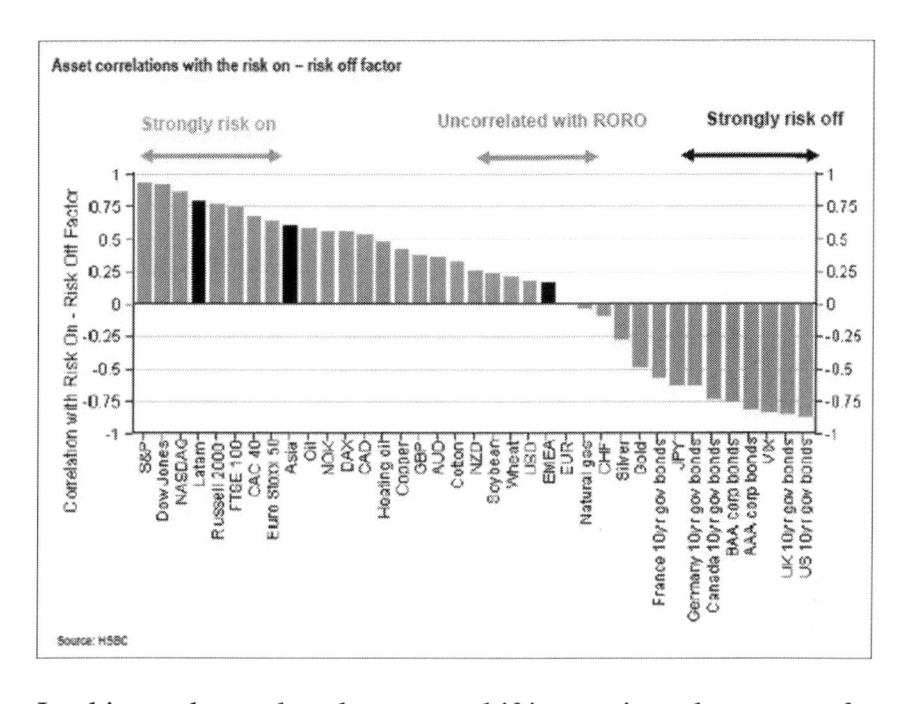

Asset correlations with the risk on – risk off factor

Strongly risk on — Uncorrelated with RORO — Strongly risk off

Source: HSBC

Looking only at what the recent shifting regimes has meant for the US markets, with knock-on effects elsewhere, of course, the reduction in USD holdings and Treasury sales, has seen at least a USD2 trillion swing in foreign exchange flows. This could be regarded as a recycling operation between public and private sectors. Whatever the state of play of QE now is in the Eurozone – whether it is close to peak or not – a return to a more 'usual' market will not occur any time soon. It has taken the world's central banks around eight years to inflate and distort the globe's liquidity to where it is now and there is no reason to expect that it will not take another eight years for it to be unwound and normalised.

Having said all of this, it is possible to establish some key trading points dependent on which trading factor – QE or RORO – is dominant at any point (and working out which is dominant is discussed throughout this book). **Looking at shorter-term (15-day) correlations over the past two years, it is clear that bond yields (as opposed to prices) have been positively correlated with equities for most of the time.** This implies that it is primarily growth expectations as opposed to liquidity ones that has been driving the relationship, although there was a notable exception during 2013 with the 'Taper Tantrum' that was focussed on how much and when the US Fed would begin to wind down its QE. Aside from this period, generally inversions of this relationship tend to be brief, as equities initially pull back on the pure uncertainty fuelled by momentary bond market disorder but then (when dealers revert back to basics and are struck by the reality that strengthening reflationary demand remains intact) the correlation tends to revert to its normal negative value and equities are able to re-rate via a discounting of future growth expectations.

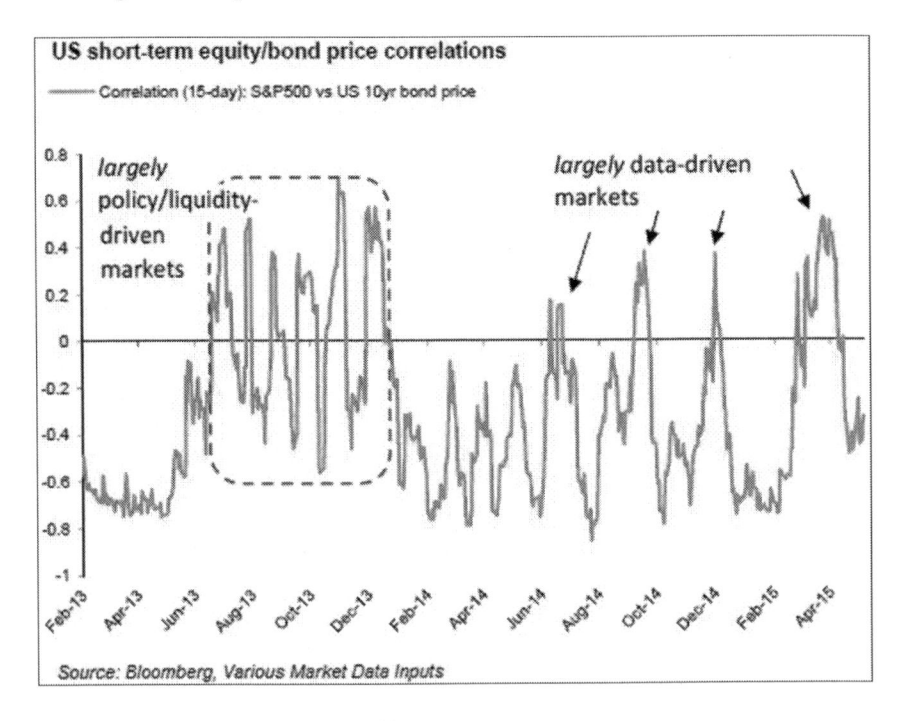

The pullbacks the equities markets saw over the past two years, aside from those based on pure uncertainty fuelled by momentary bond market disorder, occurred primarily as a function both of the likelihood of Greece being forced out of the Eurozone and on the likelihood at any given point in time of the onset of a US interest rate tightening cycle (usually spurred by some statement either from Chair of the Federal Reserve, Janet Yellen, or by another high-level member of the monetary policy structure).

A notable example of this – that was not also subject to the influence of other major market factors, so it can be regarded as a 'clean' example – was when the Fed initially prompted market speculation that a rate tightening cycle was going to begin imminently in June 2004. This was preceded by two MSCI World pullbacks (and then similarly-sized rebounds) of 5-6% in the few months before the first hike and another 7% pullback shortly after. In the following three years through to October 2007, however, the MSCI World went on to rally some 65% from those troughs, even as the Fed progressively raised interest rates by 425 basis points through to the middle of 2006.

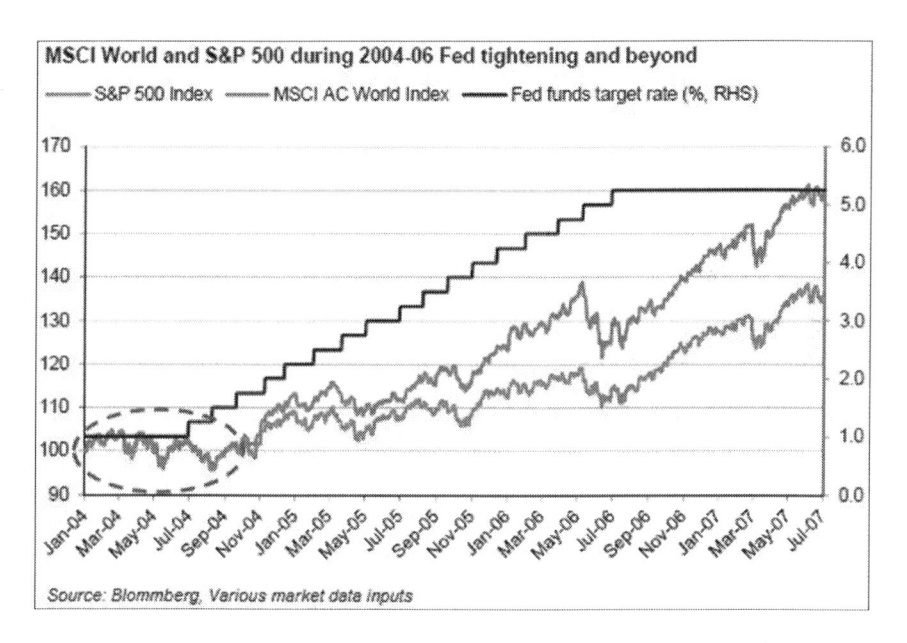

MSCI World and S&P 500 during 2004-06 Fed tightening and beyond

Source: Blommberg, Various market data inputs

Interestingly, though, the absolute level of bond yields also matters for the equity-bond relationship, and certain yield levels are the tipping points at which bond yield rises negatively impact equities prices or bond yield falls positively impact them. As shown below, with US Treasuries it has historically only been when yields exceed roughly 5.0-5.5% that higher yields (i.e. lower bond prices) seem to have a negative impact on equities.

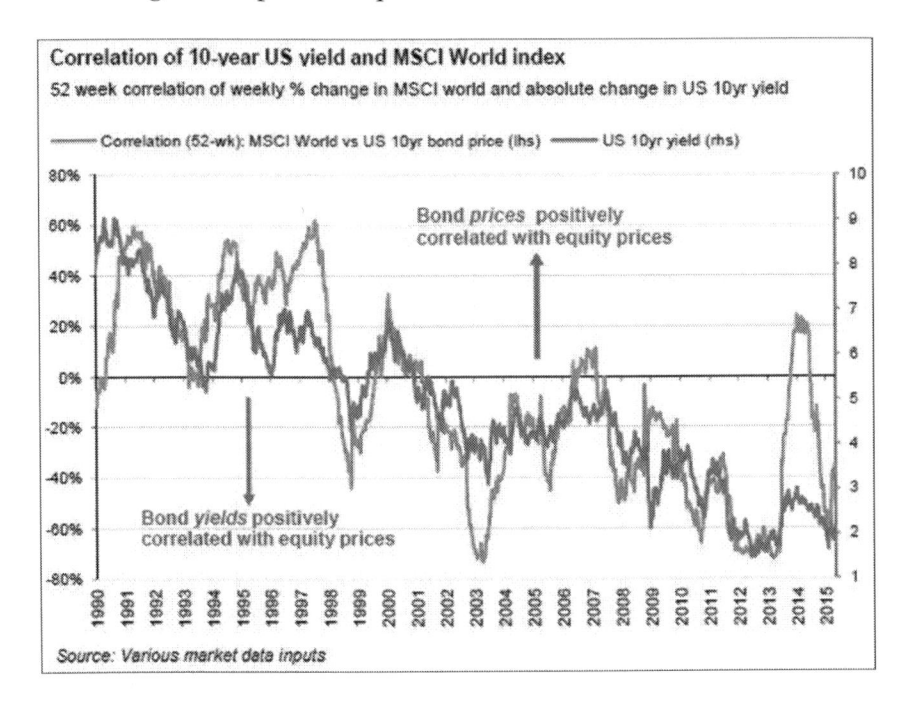

Correlation of 10-year US yield and MSCI World index
52 week correlation of weekly % change in MSCI world and absolute change in US 10yr yield

Chart showing Correlation (52-wk): MSCI World vs US 10yr bond price (lhs) and US 10yr yield (rhs), 1990-2015. Annotations: "Bond prices positively correlated with equity prices" and "Bond yields positively correlated with equity prices".

Source: Various market data inputs

Below that yield range bond prices (rather than yields) have historically been negatively correlated with equity markets, and these reflect strengthening growth prospects and/or reduced deflation risks that should be consistent with equity upside.

Looking at the current position on the US rates tightening expectations curve, two scenarios may manifest themselves in trading terms, but each will accord with one or other of the key patterns already described. First, US interest rates continue to rise and trigger an increase in risk premiums across bonds and rates markets globally, which, in turn, pushes up yield curves and forces a de-rating of equities. Second, in the absence of continued higher interest rates, or perhaps because further US rate tightening is put on hold (as a result of slower growth, a stronger dollar and low inflation), the outcome would be for investors to be pushed further up the risk curve into equities, and valuations could rise further. This second pattern would continue until such point as equity markets eventually became severely overvalued, thereby offering a very poor prospective return.

Equities Trading In A Rising US Interest Rates Scenario

Historically, periods marked by rising US interest rates have generally supported Growth stocks more than Value stocks, not just in the US but globally, and particularly relative to Income-delineated value styles (i.e., Dividend Yield). Indeed, since mid-2014, Growth has been consistently the top-performing equity style, while Value and its subset Dividend Yield have been the weakest, as shown in the chart below.

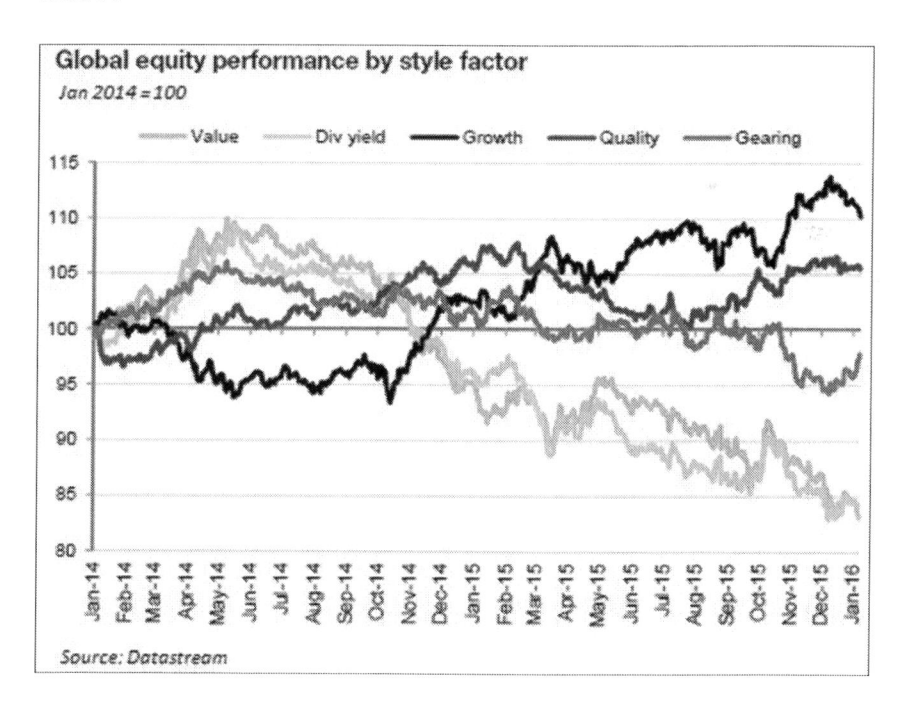

Global equity performance by style factor
Jan 2014 = 100

Source: Datastream

Factoring in the broader economic patterns discussed above (K-Wave, Minsky, Business Cycle), there is reason to believe that the 2017 US interest rate outlook should continue to support a portfolio bias for Growth (i.e., cyclical sectors) over Dividend Yield. Moreover, looking at previous data patterns, it appears that Yield stocks actually do best when investors are moving into bonds (seeking incremental safety rather than incremental risk) rather than the common view that they do best when investors are initially moving out of bonds and into equities.

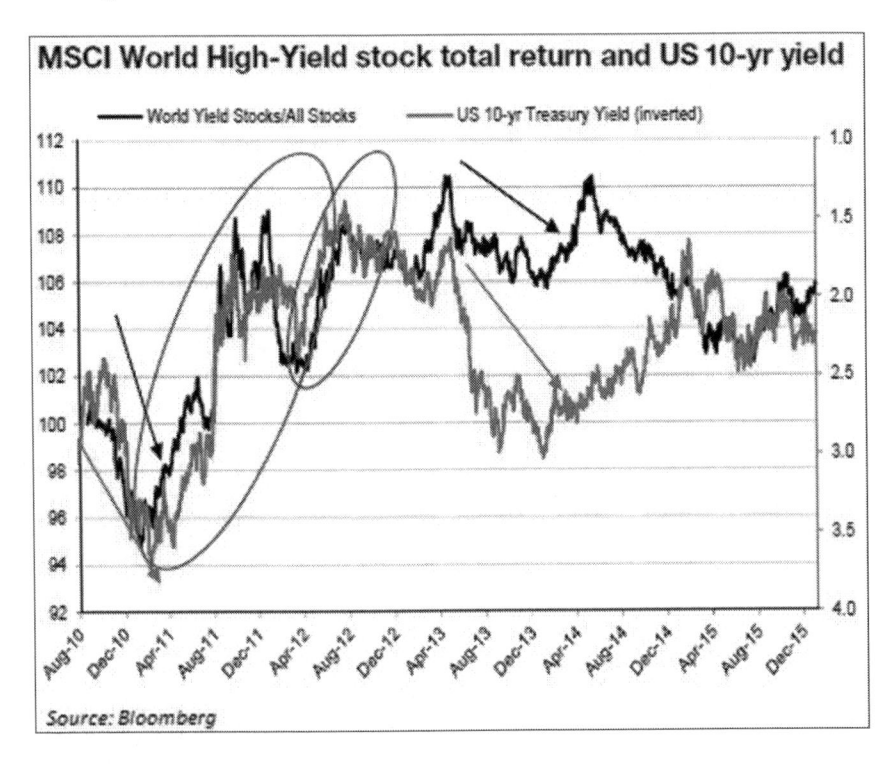

MSCI World High-Yield stock total return and US 10-yr yield

Source: Bloomberg

Moreover, the fact that Growth as a style currently offers a 10% or so valuation discount versus long-term averages suggests that the style remains under-owned by portfolio managers and, given the aforementioned factors, is likely to benefit from rotational buying in the quarters ahead, as rates rise, whereas the highly crowded nature of

Dividend Yield plays is highlighted by this type of stocks' elevated valuation premium of more than 25%.

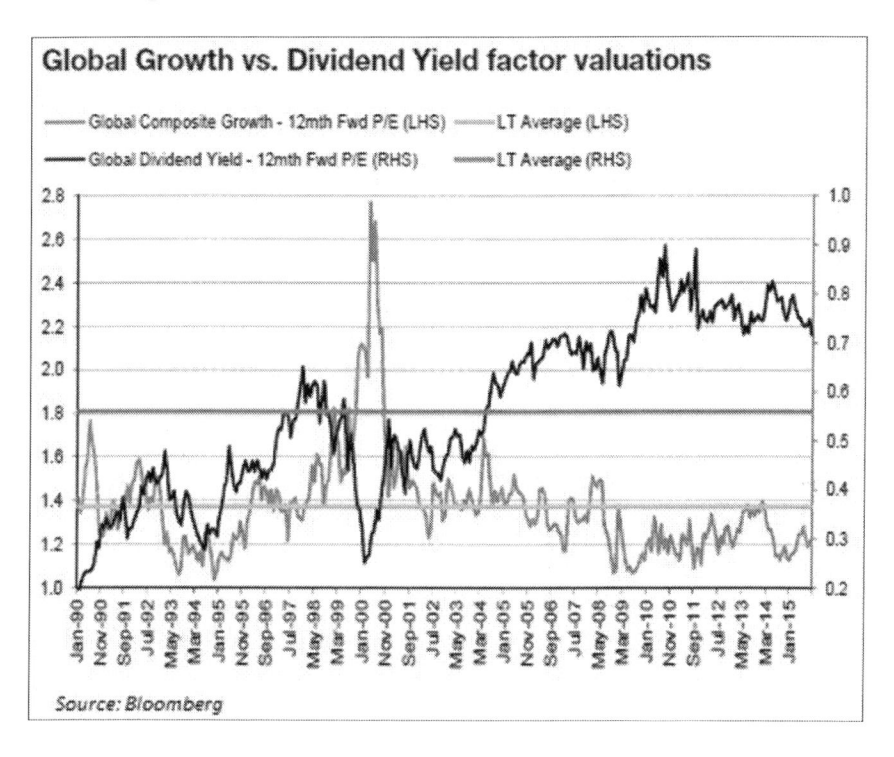

Global Growth vs. Dividend Yield factor valuations

- Global Composite Growth - 12mth Fwd P/E (LHS)
- LT Average (LHS)
- Global Dividend Yield - 12mth Fwd P/E (RHS)
- LT Average (RHS)

Source: Bloomberg

It is also critical to note that **the current depression in the global hydrocarbons pricing complex (this will be discussed in much greater detail later) is not beneficial to Dividend Yield stocks but is benefitting Growth stocks.** In this context, inflation expectations have historically also usually displayed a strong directional correlation with the relative performance of Growth vs. Income (i.e. Dividend Yield) in the global equities arena. This is a product mainly of the positive relationship between inflation expectations and demand strength (which benefits cyclical stocks) and between inflation expectations and interest rate expectations (which, when rising, undercut the relative performance 'bond proxy' Yield stocks).

However, **despite lower break-even inflation expectations together with declining oil prices since mid-2014, Growth stocks have continued outperforming Income ones (i.e., Dividend Yield), which appears to underline that the market is looking more at the demand-positive element in the oil price decline rather than its deflationary element.** In this respect, on the one hand, it is true that the oil price decline means that for oil exporters there is a crunch on revenues (which has ramifications discussed later) but, on the other hand, for oil importing nations the reduction in the oil price means first that its costs are reduced (in transport costs and/or manufacturing costs) and that the domestic population has more money in their pockets to spend on products and services. **In this latter regard, for example, it is estimated that every USD10 per barrel change in the price of crude oil results in a 25-cent change in the price of a gallon of gasoline and, according to the American Automobile Association in Washington, every cent that the national average price of gasoline falls, more than one billion dollars per year in additional consumer spending is estimated to be freed up.**

Global Growth/Income relative performance vs. inflation

Source: Bloomberg

Given all of this, for equities, the greatest beneficiaries of such a style bias for Growth over Yield in the current rising US rates environment would historically appear to be Technology and Industrials, whilst Energy and Utilities are likely to fare particularly poorly. Additionally, whilst it is obvious that many financial stocks will do badly (especially those with connections to high-risk areas, such as the Eurozone and China), property stocks in general virtually always underperform when the US Treasury curve steepens.

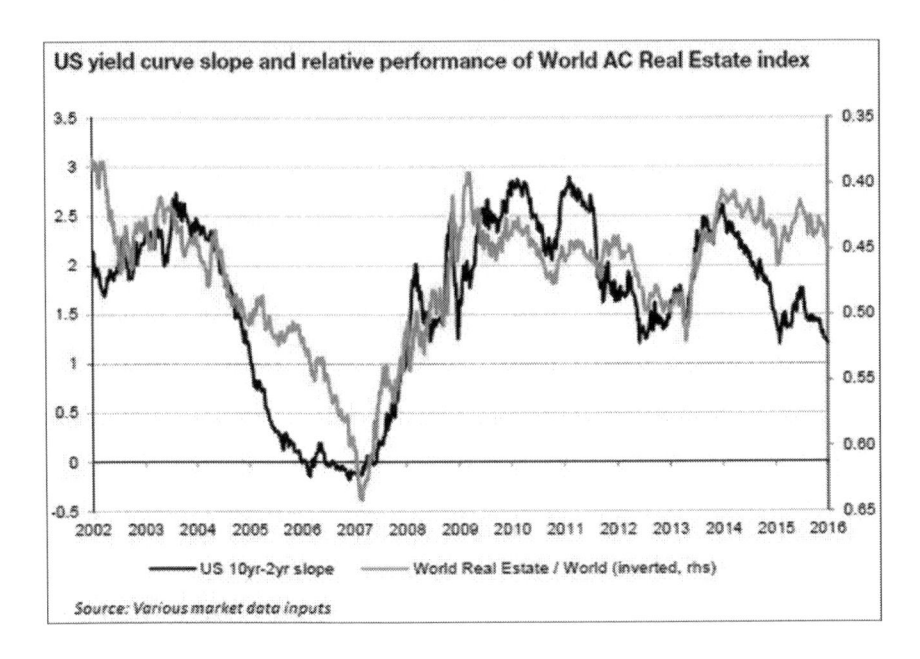

US yield curve slope and relative performance of World AC Real Estate index

Source: Various market data inputs

On a more general front, as highlighted recently by major global ratings agency Moody's, it is apposite to note that December 2015 and January 2016 were the only two months since at least 1982 where the 10-year Treasury yield was up from the same month a year earlier. This was despite a deeper than 15% year-over-year plunge by the base metals price index's moving three-month average (usually, such pronounced decelerations trigger remedial declines by benchmark Treasury yields). Also, prior to December's Fed rate hike, Fed Funds had never been raised in the context of both: (i) a deeper than 15% annual plunge by the base metals price index's three-month average; and, (ii) a wider than 650 bp spread for high-yield bonds (recently, the high-yield bond spread was an exceptionally wide 873 bp).

Historical records show that the high-yield bond spread's month-long average has climbed above 800 bp on only four previous occasions: August 2008, July 2002, November 2000 and October 1990. In three of those four incidents, the US was about to enter or already in a recession, with the only exception being July 2002 (which was the beginning of an economic recovery that only survived for five years).

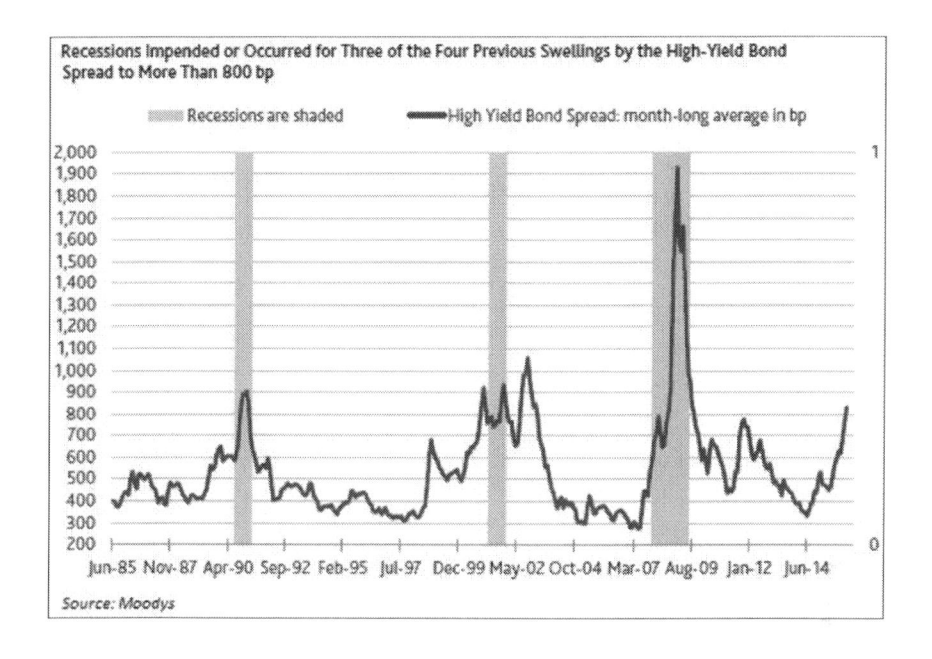

Recessions Impended or Occurred for Three of the Four Previous Swellings by the High-Yield Bond Spread to More Than 800 bp

Recessions are shaded — High Yield Bond Spread: month-long average in bp

Source: Moodys

Bond Trading In The Current Economic Environment

For the moment, despite the December 2016 and March 2017 interest rate hikes in the US, the country's benchmark bond yields have moved in an opposite direction to that taken by the Federal Funds rate. The drop by the 10-year Treasury yield following the two Fed rate hikes was in response to reduced expectations for GDP growth that partly stemmed from the diminished likelihood of meaningful fiscal stimulus.

The US equity-implied consensus now looks for nominal GDP growth of 4.3% in 2017, which is only slightly higher than early November 2016's pre-election forecast of 4.2%. This is despite the apparently economy-boosting rhetoric of President Trump. In the meantime, the 10-year Treasury yield eased from mid-December's 2.6% to less than 2.4% and, in the absence of any meaningful increase in the outlook for the US' nominal GDP, a sustained move below 2.25% looks entirely possible.

Having said that, if and when the US equity bubble bursts, the resulting reduction in systemic liquidity will lead to costlier capital for businesses and then an increase in corporate defaults. **This, in turn, will result – if and when it happens – in a drop in both the Fed Funds rate and Treasury bond yields.** In this context, the bursting of the equity bubbles of 1987 and 1999-2000, the high-yield and commercial real estate bubbles of 1989-1990 and the housing bubble of 2004-2006 were followed by substantially lower benchmark interest rates. **In the meantime, the deep drop by equity prices will lead to a ballooning of high-yield bond spreads, which currently under-compensate for the long-term default risk.**

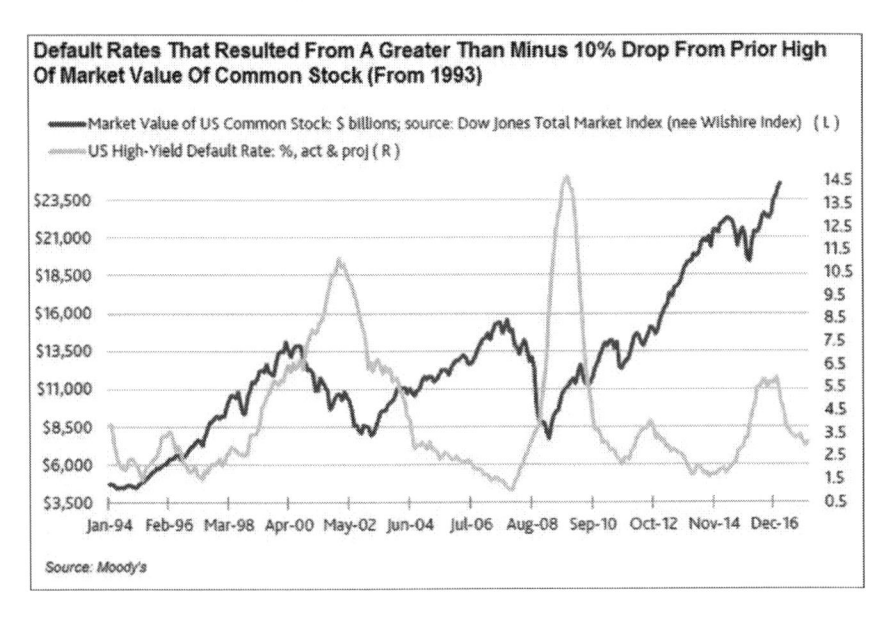

Default Rates That Resulted From A Greater Than Minus 10% Drop From Prior High Of Market Value Of Common Stock (From 1993)

Market Value of US Common Stock: $ billions; source: Dow Jones Total Market Index (nee Wilshire Index) (L)
US High-Yield Default Rate: %, act & proj (R)

Source: Moody's

Oil In The Correlations Mix

Oil And The US Dollar

The most obvious correlation to note is between the oil price and the US dollar, as oil is priced in the US currency. **Twenty years ago,** it seemed that there were fairly clear principles for investors to follow with regard to the link between the oil and USD prices: **the higher the crude oil price, the higher the USD (the rationale being that as oil prices rose then the demand for dollars to buy it would increase and thus the USD would strengthen).**

Over the past ten years or so, this relationship has completely reversed, as **rising oil prices have coincided with a broadly weaker dollar, and this has been explained by the idea that rising oil prices lead to deterioration in the US trade deficit (oil and oil products historically represented around 50% of the entire US trade deficit) and thus a negative outlook for the USD and corollary selling of it. The reverse, of course, is equally true, in that a downward trending oil price has coincided with a rising USD.**

Although some of this is due to a cessation in the vast number of dollars being released into the US economy (in the three QE programs) and a consequent rebalancing of supply and demand rules in favour of the historical norm, it is also due to the fact that a lower oil price is a huge spur to growth in the US, as it both increases consumer spending and also lowers manufacturing costs (thus, in turn, making exports more competitive in the global market).

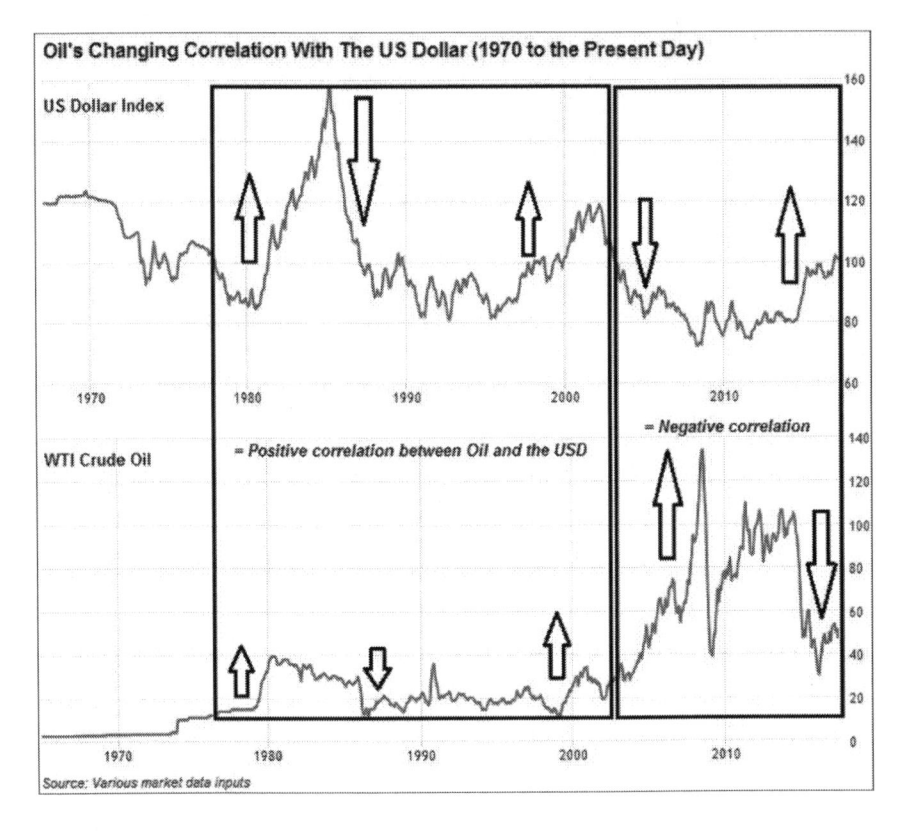

Oil's Changing Correlation With The US Dollar (1970 to the Present Day)

Source: Various market data inputs

Simply knowing this correlation between the oil price and the value of the US dollar would have netted a trader spectacular gains over the past three years in particular (since the beginning of 2014 when Saudi began its shale-destruction strategy and then reversed it), and had the trader been doing what he should have been doing on a daily basis (i.e. reading up on all markets from all major sources, watching the key business channels and looking at the trading charts from a technical analysis perspective), then his point of entry for the short oil trade and/or the long USD trade would have been very early on in this major trend change.

Oil And Other Currencies

The inverse relationship between the oil price and the value of the USD, then, is clear but the **relationship between oil and other currencies is slightly more nuanced: part of it is a function of the macroeconomic profile of countries whose asset values are defined in significant part by their major role that oil (or other commodities) play in their balance of payments, and part of it is a consequence of the trajectory of the USD.**

In respect of the latter to begin with, the end of the three rounds of QE by the US Federal Reserve has meant that the usual rules of supply and demand have led to a natural strengthening of the USD across the board (as seen in the USD Index chart above), with less dollars in the system and fairly constant demand putting a premium on the US currency. The end of QE and the corollary robustness (to a degree) of the US economy (at least, it has not yet tanked in the absence of extra money being pumped into the system) has also led to market expectations of further rises in interest rates from the Fed at a faster pace than previously thought. Given that money goes to where it is best rewarded for the concomitant risks involved, the USD has benefited from inflows looking for a relative safe-haven offering some yield (and will continue to do so).

Three years ago in my book *Everything You Need To Know About Making Serious Money Trading The Financial Markets* I predicted the broad-based sustained rise in the USD and also that it marked the beginning of an enduring long-term uptrend, and this view is still intact. Here was the chart from back then:

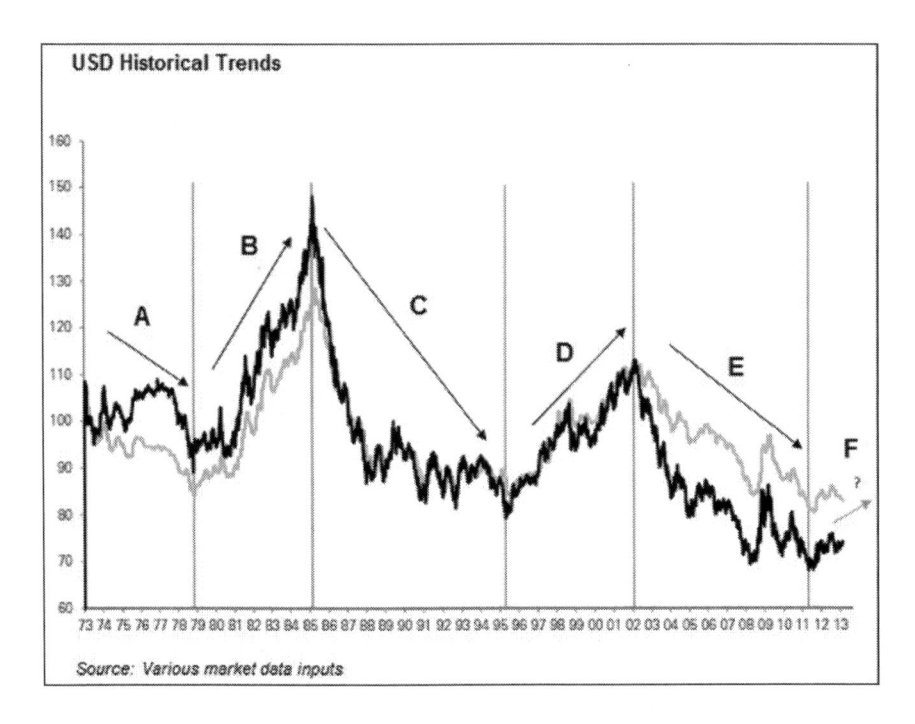

[Chart Key:
Lines:
Upper dark black from left to right = Nominal US dollar versus majors
Lower light black from left to right = Real broad US dollar
Vertical lines = Key trend turning points
Arrows From Left To Right:
A = 6 years, down 18%
B = 6 years, up 67%
C = ten years, down 46%
D = 7 years, up 43%
E = 9 years, down 40%
F = Next big trend ... UP?]

And here is the chart since then:

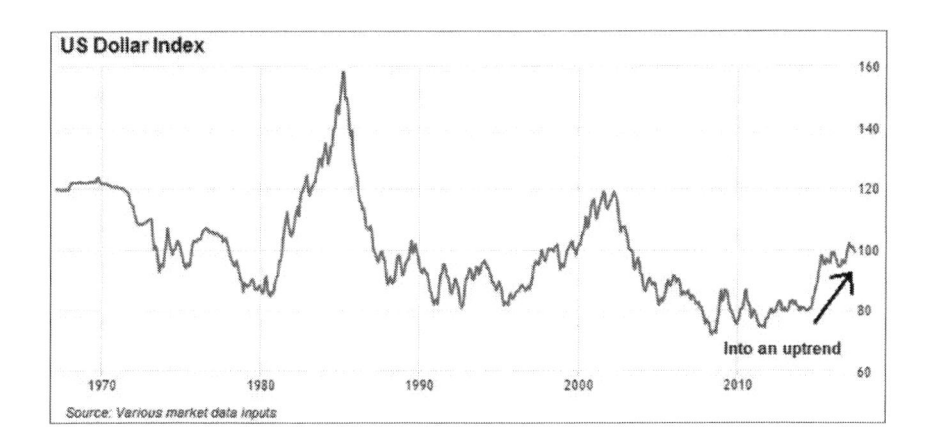

Moving Along The Risk Curve, By Market- And Asset-Type

Whilst, by definition, many currencies in the world have depreciated as the USD has risen, expectations of interest rates rises in the US and the end of QE in the country has also meant a shift in general away from 'riskier' investments, both by asset class and by country. In general terms, **the risk curve moves from least risky asset class to most risky asset class as follows: cash (in a solid currency), bonds (in a solid country), equities (in a solid country), FX (riskier than the previous three categories but extremely liquid) and commodities (riskier than the first three categories and relatively extremely illiquid).** In general terms as well, **the risk curve moves from least risky country type to most risky country type in the following fashion: developed market, emerging market, frontier market.** Consequently, in addition to the decline in oil and the concomitant strengthening of the US dollar, there has been both a move away from emerging markets (and frontier markets) towards developed ones and away from commodities in general to assets with less risky profiles.

To deal with this last point first (stripping out the country-type component) the developed markets of Canada and Australia have notably suffered against the USD, given the significant part that commodities play in the economies of both countries (oil, gold, liquefied petroleum gas and coal being in the top five of Canada's global exports; mineral ores, oil and precious metals being in the top five of Australia's).

To recapitulate, here is the WTI oil chart:

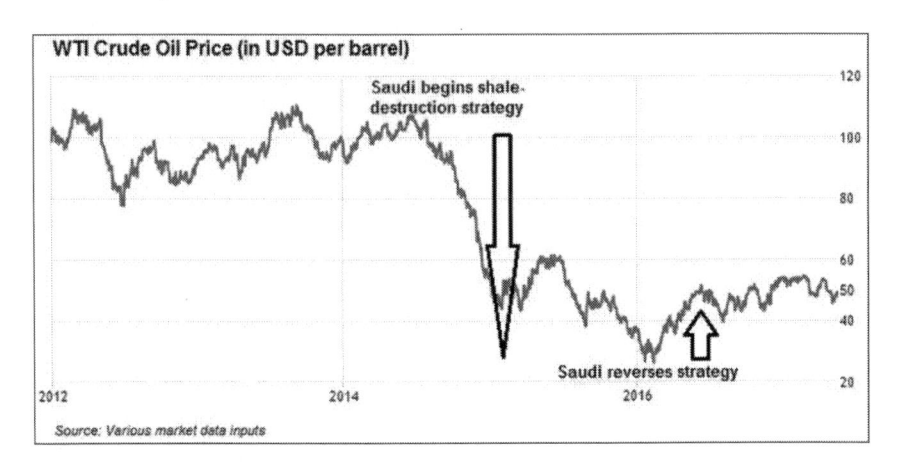

[Chart: WTI Crude Oil Price (in USD per barrel), 2012–2016, showing "Saudi begins shale-destruction strategy" and "Saudi reverses strategy" annotations. Source: Various market data inputs]

Below shows the break to the upside that occurred with the announcement of the OPEC (plus a few key non-members) announced in December 2016 to cut production in order to bolster the oil price.

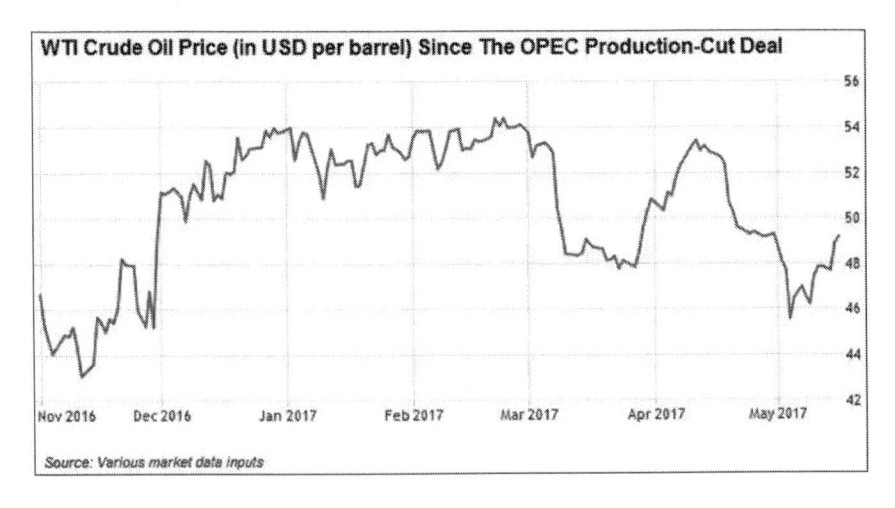

[Chart: WTI Crude Oil Price (in USD per barrel) Since The OPEC Production-Cut Deal, Nov 2016 – May 2017. Source: Various market data inputs]

Below are the USD against the CAD and the USD against the AUD charts (please note here that the CAD has been used as the base currency to show more clearly how it has weakened against the USD but, of course, in market tradition the USD is the base currency against the CAD), but the AUD chart shows the AUD as the base currency, as in market tradition. **Both, in fact, have tracked the trajectory of oil and consequently have an almost perfect positive correlation with it and an almost perfect negative correlation with the USD.**

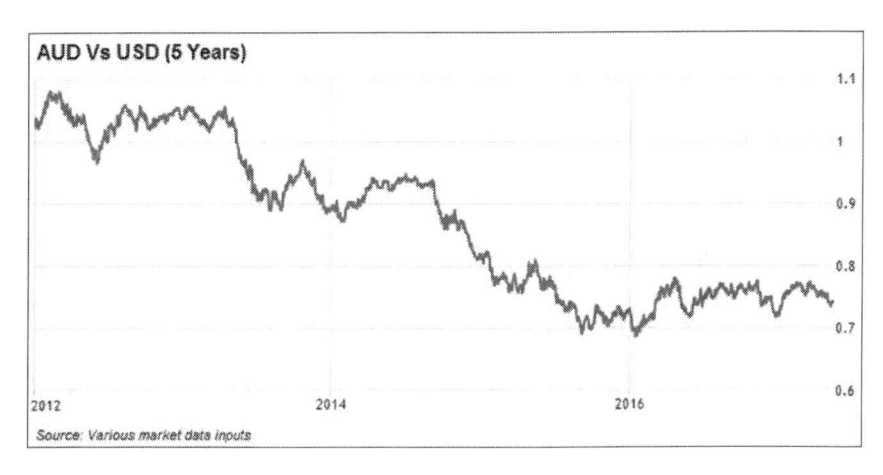

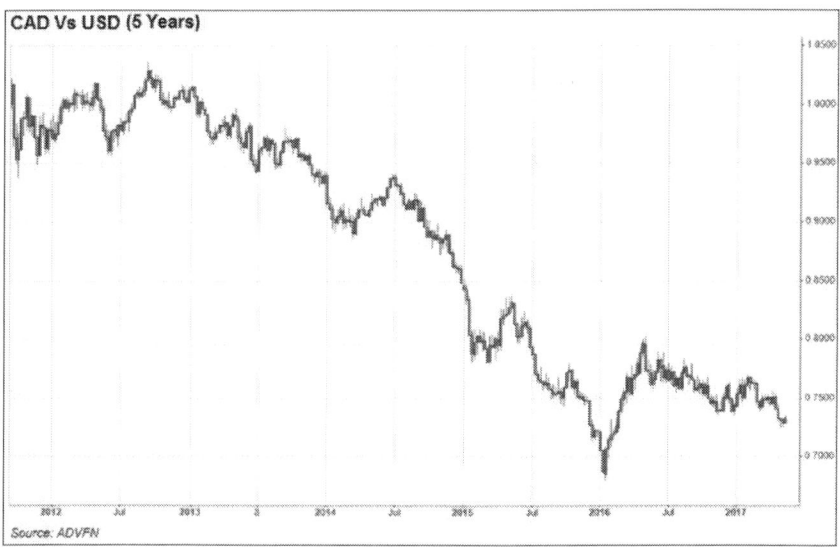

Looking then at the former point, **this rotation away from buying into EM growth and back towards developed market growth (in particular that of the US) without a heavy representation of commodities in their economic mix has also been clearly evidenced in EM currency trends,** even those of the once much-vaunted BRIC (Brazil, Russia, India and China) nations and of the almost as previously much-hyped MIST (Mexico, Indonesia, South Korea and Turkey) group of countries.

Risk Rotation Currently Reinforces US Economic Growth

This weakening of the currencies of other energy producers and of other emerging markets – particularly those that are major commodities producers (much of South America, for example, notably Chile and Peru) – reinforced the US economic growth investment paradigm, as it reduces the costs to the US's manufacturing base, because the price of raw materials falls, making exports more competitive and boosting demand at home, as mentioned above.

From the viewpoint of boosting consumer demand, quite aside from cheaper goods being available in shops (electronics that utilise commodities from emerging markets, for instance), demand for the biggest product that most people will buy in their lives – housing – is also inclined to be boosted, as steel and copper costs fall relative to the USD. For example, in an average US house enough copper is used to fill an Olympic-sized swimming pool.

Trading Strategies Off The Current Saudi Fix

Short Oil

The consensus view of smart money investors is that OPEC needs to continue to extend production cuts – in tandem with selected major non-OPEC producers, notably Russia – simply

to keep oil around the USD50 pb level rather than to realise its ambition of getting oil to the US$60 pb level or above and sustain it there. Given this, the risk is clearly to the downside again, so a short oil position looks like the optimal play, especially with the prospect of a strong USD for the time being. In the context of determining downside (or upside) potential in an asset, it is vital to look at long-dated charts, as below, to see where serious factors have resulted in long-standing support ('S') and resistance ('R') levels, as below for WTI crude oil.

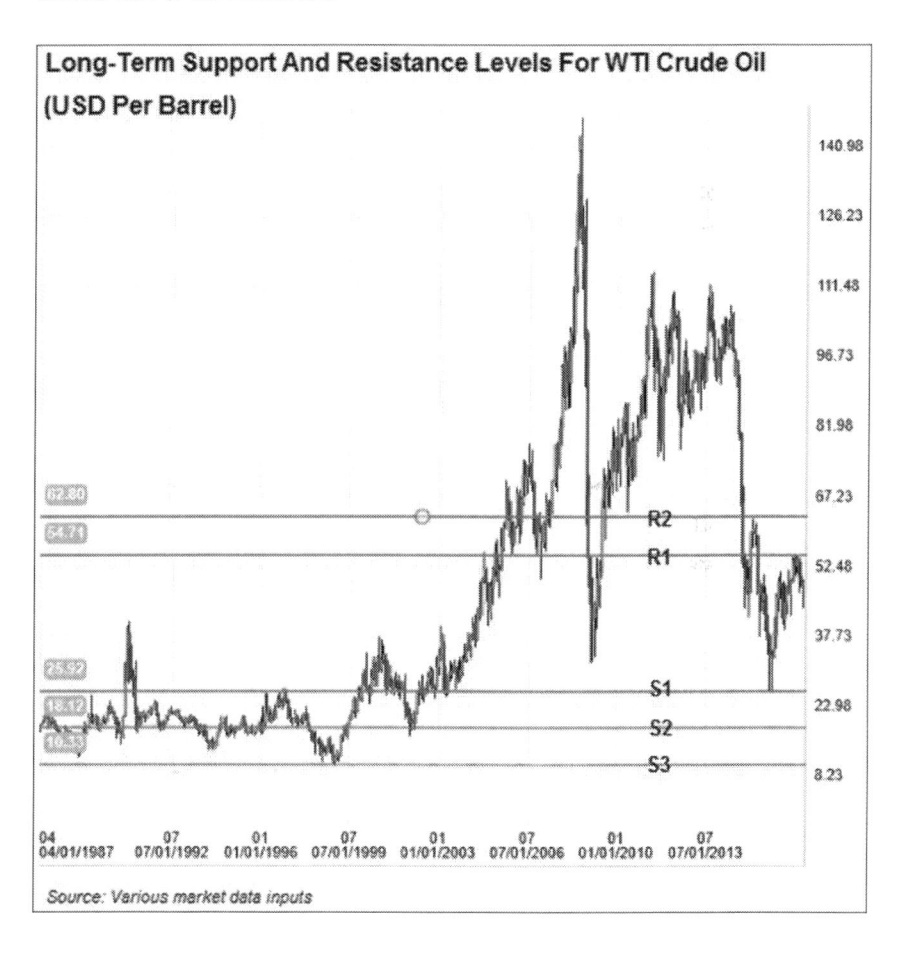

Long-Term Support And Resistance Levels For WTI Crude Oil (USD Per Barrel)

Source: Various market data inputs

Short Middle East Hydrocarbons Producers' Stock Markets

Clearly, given the aforementioned market conditions for oil, **shorting the stock markets of countries dependent on oil (and/or gas) for a significant proportion of their revenues – either directly or through an exchange traded fund (ETF) – would be a winning trade in an ongoing oil price downturn.** When thinking about the potential scope for oil-driven local economic damage, the size of the local energy sector – without regard for the destination of that production – is an important metric, and oil accounts for around 50% for some of the Gulf States: **Kuwait, Saudi Arabia and Iraq** (see chart below).

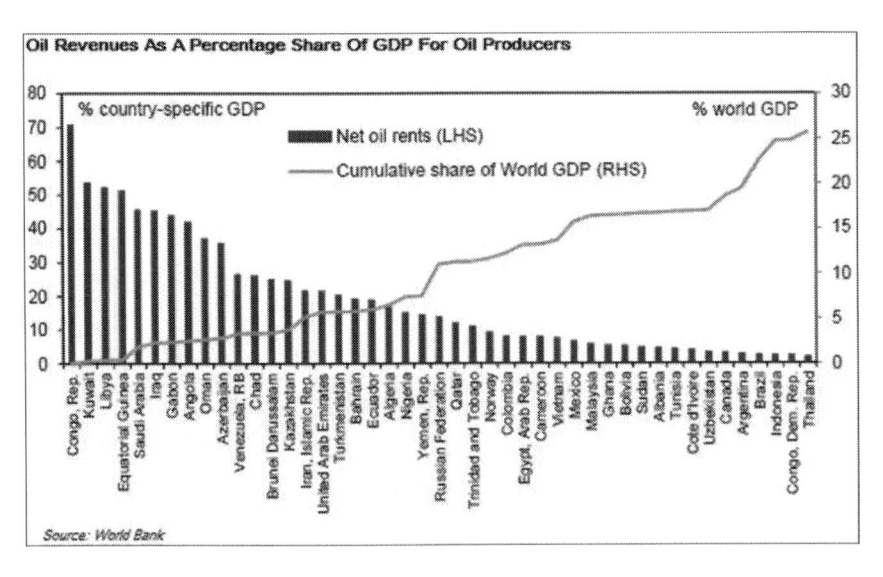

A simple back of the envelope calculation that directly translates a decline in oil prices into a proportional decline in GDP suggests that **every USD10 per barrel drop in the oil price shaves 3.4% and 4.2% of gross domestic product (GDP) off fiscal and current account balances, respectively, in the Gulf Cooperation Council (GCC) economy as a whole.** Given the view that the oil price will remain subdued, selling any pullbacks on the stock markets of the key

Middle Eastern hydrocarbons producers is likely to remain a profitable strategy.

In this context, it is – as always with everything being traded – highly advisable to keep an eye on the latest announcements relating to them, as major ones will often afford the opportunity to 'buy the rumour, sell the fact' on these bourses. A good example of this was **the announcement by Saudi Arabia that it was to open up its benchmark Tadawul All Share Index (TASI) to direct foreign non-Gulf investment participation.**

With a capitalisation of around USD530 billion at the time – more than the combined capitalisations of the other six major domestic exchanges in the Gulf Cooperation Council (GCC) and only slightly less than Brazil's (USD600 billion) but more than Russia's (USD490 billion) – the mere fact that it was to open to foreigners prompted a brief flurry of buying before it fell back markedly again, allowing investors to add to short positions at better levels.

Adding to the initial buying flurry was the view – quite reasonably – that opening up the TASI to such foreign participation would be a precursor to Saudi Arabia being included into Morgan Stanley Capital International's (MSCI) Emerging Markets Index (EMI) within just two years after the adjustment. This would bring with it big block buying from fund managers who are required to mirror the index's composition under the investment mandates of their funds and provide a concomitant lifting of valuations across the board in one fell swoop.

As for how much money might flow in as a result of this was evaluated on the basis that MSCI launched a provisional Saudi index based on the draft rules published the previous year. If this was used as the basis for incorporation into its EMI then Saudi Arabia would have a 1.5-2.0% weighting immediately, on a par with previous investment darling Turkey and larger than perennial global funds' favourites Poland and Chile. With USD1.7 trillion benchmarked against MSCI's EMI according to latest figures, on a straight weightings-alone valuation then such a move would be expected to attract between USD25.5-34.0 billion in new funds in the very short term.

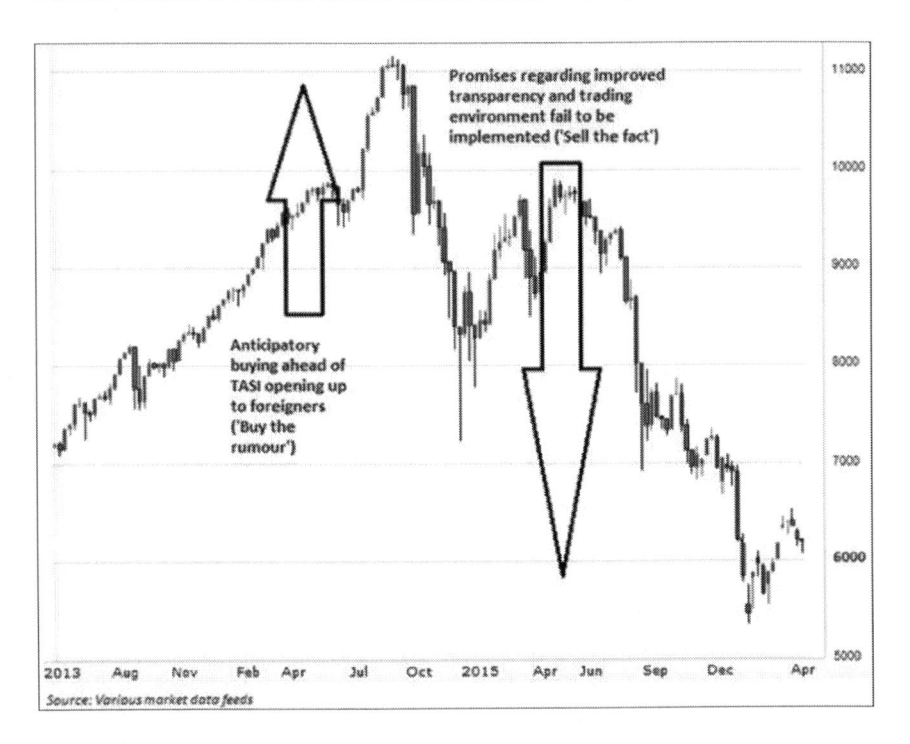

Saudi Arabia's Tadawul All Share Index Performance

In reality, though, other considerations are factored into the overall investment equation of a major global fund manager, particularly operational efficiency, geopolitical risks and a country's macroeconomic picture. In each of these respects major questions remain over the Saudi bourse, and these have been reflected in its trading trajectory since the TASI was opened up. It is also instructive that similar concerns have come into play with the region's other major stock markets, even those – like the UAE and Qatar – that have already been included in the MSCI indices.

Operationally, it is not surprising that given the Kingdom's tightly-regulated political system, the adjustment to such new capital inflows looks like it will be done in a very conservative and incremental way. The Capital Markets Authority stated prior to the TASI liberalisation that, in general terms, each foreign institution would need to have at least USD5 billion of assets under management and investment experience of five years. It added that there would be a 10% cap on combined foreign ownership of the market's value. Additionally, each such Qualified Foreign Investor (QFI) would only be able to hold a maximum of 5% of issued shares in any one listed company; all foreign investors (including resident and non-resident) would have a combined ceiling of 49% ownership of issued shares in any one listed company; and QFIs together would only be able to own a maximum of 20% of issued shares of any one listed company.

Clearly, therefore, the bullish runs that we have seen in anticipation of market-liberalising moves in the Middle East are more often than not the product of a belief from inexperienced retail investors (a large proportion of the shares traded in these stock markets are from this investment type) who believe that in and of itself a move such as liberalisation and/or inclusion in key benchmarks, like those of the MSCI, will lead to long-term stock market gains. Indeed, according to Saudi Arabia's Capital Market Authority, as at the end of 2014 there were 4.3 million of these 'hot money' investors in the TASI, accounting for around 35% of total Tadawul share holdings by value, but a near 90% of all volume (compared to 60% of volume in China, 35% in India and less than 2% in the US, according to local bourse figures). **For experienced players, bullish runs at the moment are best regarded as selling opportunities, at least until accompanied by hard and fast rules that point towards greater transparency, ease of trading and improved corporate governance at the key constituent companies of the indices.**

Short Saudi Aramco After 2018 IPO

For some time now the idea of floating Saudi Arabia's flagship hydrocarbons company – Saudi Aramco – via an initial public offering (IPO) was mooted and recent weeks have seen more details emerge on this. Specifically, at its most basic level, **up to 5% of the company will be offered in 2018, probably in the first half of that year.** The reason for the IPO, as delineated by the person now effectively in charge of Saudi's economy, Deputy Crown Prince Mohammed bin Salman, is to reduce the Kingdom's long-running dependence on hydrocarbons for the vast majority of its revenues, under what is call the 'Vision 2030' plan.

Although the past few weeks have seen a number of apparently positive steps taken to increase the appeal to international investors of the much-vaunted initial public offering (IPO) of up to 5% of Saudi Arabia's flagship firm next year, major questions still remain over the offering, pointing to the final valuation coming in a lot lower than had initially been expected. In this context, when the IPO was first announced in January last year, it was broadly accepted that it would place **the overall value of Aramco around at least USD2 billion but recent estimates have put that figure instead – for the entire company – at around 500% less than that, at USD400 million,** and even that number may be optimistic.

As market expectations have fallen, there have been a series of announcements designed to bolster this increasingly bearish outlook on the offering. First was the removal of doubts over when and how much of the company would be offered. Second came the comment in Riyadh from Aramco chief executive officer, Amin Nasser that the offering would include the company's 'concession' that consists of the oil and gas reserves of the Kingdom (almost a fifth of the oil world's entire reserves). And third was the Royal Order that Aramco's income tax rate would be cut to 50% from the previous 85%, although the 20% royalty on gross revenues that it pays to the Saudi government will remain the same.

The clarification on the concession was a vital piece of information for international investment managers, adding some marginal value to Aramco. However, its overall impact has been reduced by ongoing questions over the extent of Saudi Arabia's actual reserves, given that Saudi Arabia has claimed exactly the same amount of oil reserves, 265-266 billion barrels, for the past forty years, despite the facts that it has pumped an average of nearly three billion barrels of oil every year from 1973 to the end of 2016 – which totals 129 billion barrels – and has not during that entire time made any new significant oil finds. **This sort of claim, which looks to most people to be mathematically impossible, makes it very difficult for international investors to believe anything that Saudi says about any subject.**

Indeed, shortly afterwards, any positive effect that the initial announcement may have had upon international investor sentiment was reduced further when Salman clearly stated that although the IPO will include Aramco's 'concession', the actual oil wells "will still be owned by the government . . . this is the same as before, and there are no changes to that."

In the same vein, the actual impact of the tax cut looks to be near-zero on Aramco's bottom line, with the firm set to pay out almost exactly the same amount to the Saudi government indirectly in new share dividends as it did directly in the tax. Indeed, this point was tangentially confirmed by a comment at the time from Saudi Arabia's Finance Minister, Mohammed al-Jadaan, in Riyadh that: "Any tax revenue reductions applicable to hydrocarbon producers operating in the kingdom will be replaced by stable dividend payments by government-owned companies, and other sources of revenue including profits resulting from investments." It is possible to believe that shifting the payout structure to one based on dividends rather than straight tax – in and of itself – would be a positive for international investors but in practice it makes no difference to the bottom line of the firm.

In fact, on this basis – private investors valuing Aramco based on the free cashflow it generates rather than on the basis of a multiple of reserves– global consulting firm Wood Mackenzie stated recently that it valued Aramco's core production business at USD400 billion, using a standard 10% annual discount rate. In addition, the key issue here is that no one has revealed what the new dividend policy will be, and international investors will be aware that the Saudi government will still be completely in charge of Aramco's operations, which will continue to be a product of the state's overall geopolitical policies, as the state will still own at least 95% of the entire company.

In this context of operational transparency, it is apposite to note that in recent months Aramco's already convoluted and opaque structure has been further twisted by the government's overriding concern to bring its business in line with the socially-oriented 'Vision 2030 Plan'. Since then, aside from its core businesses of oil, gas and petchems production, Aramco has been forced into getting involved in big industrial projects that are too big for the private sector that have little or nothing to do with that core business. These include developing a USD5 billion ship repair and building complex on the east coast, working with General Electric on a USD400 million forging and casting venture and executing government-directed projects that have social goals, such as building industrial cities, stadia and cultural centres, and creating the King Abdullah University of Science and Technology. Clearly, this begs the question of who would want to buy into a situation like this and, worse, if Saudi Arabia again orders Aramco to cut production to support the oil price, or uses income from the firm to prop up Saudi military efforts in Yemen. **This 'state-interference factor' means that other listed state-directed companies, such as Russia's Gazprom and Rosneft, and Brazil's Petrobras, for example, trade at multiples far below those of their non-state peers.**

Moreover, bringing Aramco more into line with international standards – the declared aim of shifting more towards a dividend-based from a tax-based payout profile – raises further valuation issues, all of them negative. Using the same rationale as Wood Mackenzie, other industry analysts have further highlighted in recent weeks that these assumptions are based on all of Aramco's barrels being sold at best world market prices. However, this is not the case: of its 12 million barrels per day of crude oil and natural gas liquid production, almost 4 million is consumed at home where, despite 2015's subsidy reforms, gasoline still sells at around US$32 per barrel. For natural gas as well, even though Saudi Arabia has doubled its pricing of this – to US$1.50 per million British thermal units (Btu) – it still remains well below the US's US$2.84/Btu level and even further below current prices in Europe and Japan.

Happily for canny investors, amongst the recent changes made to the structure of the TASI – including, positively, a move to adopt the developed market standard two-day settlement for trades ('T+2') – **was the idea to allow short selling, which seems rather in the same ilk as a turkey voting for Christmas.**

Short Canada

For those investors who, for one reason or another, do not want to trade Middle East assets, **the oil price can also be proxy traded to a degree through both the currencies and stock markets of more usually traded sovereigns, as highlighted below.** In this context, Canada is extremely interesting in that, like the US, its manufacturing base and consumption has benefited from a lower oil price environment but, unlike the US, its benchmark stock index – the Toronto Stock Exchange (TSX) – has a much greater proportion of its overall composition made up of companies directly or indirectly negatively exposed to lower oil prices than their US counterparts. So the TSX has theoretically been more prone to a downside move than the DJIA.

This disconnect between two key elements of a country's economic profile as exhibited in its principal stock market – and as has happened elsewhere in connection with the oil price,

which is for some countries both a key cost in manufacturing but also a key part of income – offers clear hedging and arbitrage possibilities.

To see this more clearly, it is necessary to superimpose the cumulative returns profile of the TSX and of Brent crude as occurred in the aftermath of the onset of Saudi's shale industry-destruction strategy at the beginning of 2014.

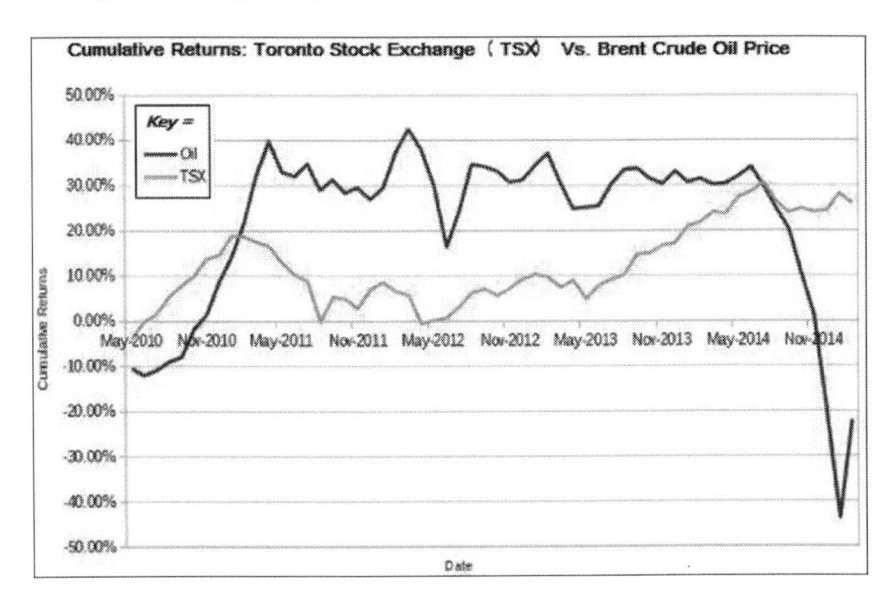

Cumulative Returns: Toronto Stock Exchange (TSX) Vs. Brent Crude Oil Price

As can be seen above, for much of the past five years or so the TSX and Brent crude returns have been very closely correlated in trend terms. At the beginning of the Saudis' negative comments over the oil price direction in 2014, the TSX's and Brent crude's cumulative returns directions markedly diverged, with the TSX buoyed up (relative to the Brent price) by the factors mentioned above and by other non-energy sectors performing well.

Given that the TSX index and oil prices had not diverged to such a degree in a very long time, but that the TSX has a very heavy weighting of energy stocks, historical correlations suggested that this relatively recent divergence would narrow

over time, and this is precisely what has happened, as shown below.

Brent Crude Oil Vs. Toronto Stock Exchange

For the longer-term trade, then, any discrepancy in trend should continue to be rectified in one of two ways: either oil prices rise with a concomitant increase in returns to match the TSX's or oil prices remain low and the TSX falls accordingly to reflect this.

This is an illustrative example of the way in which such divergences between energy-heavy stock markets (see above) and the oil price can be utilised to generate alpha returns with very little inherent risk having to be dealt with through further risk management strategies. **This can also be found in other similarly constructed markets, although rarely to such a degree, including most notably perhaps Australia, Mexico, Norway, Venezuela and Russia. Unsurprisingly, given the equities flows involved, the Canadian dollar has been broadly pressured during the severe oil price depression** (see chart below).

CADUSD (CAD Base)

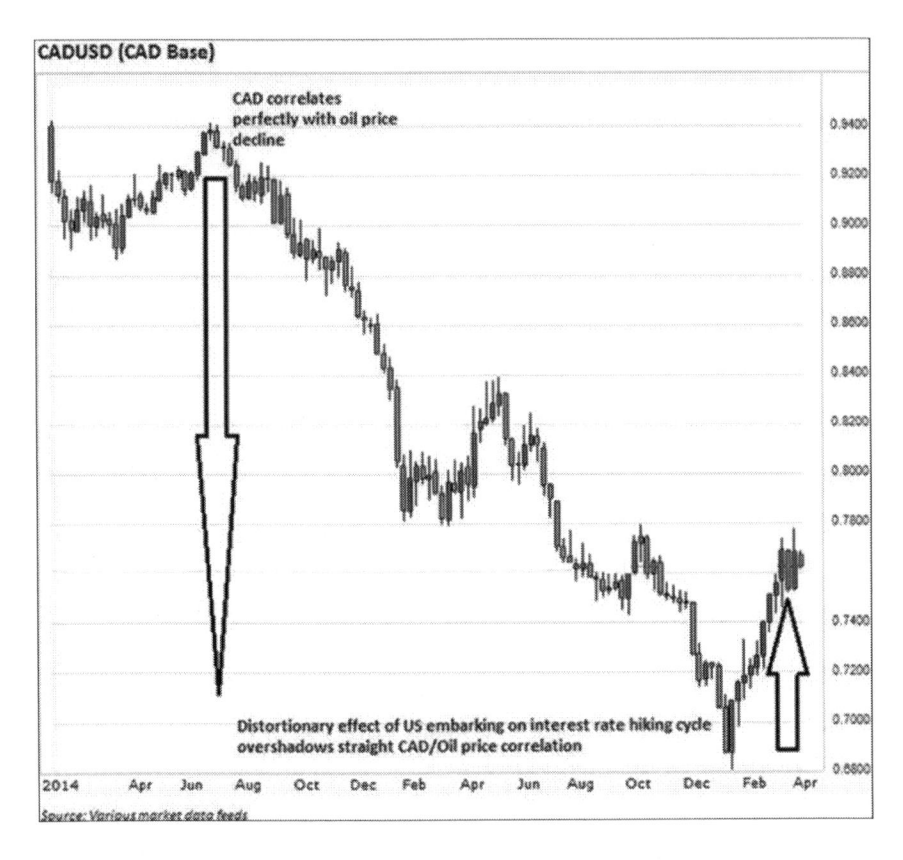

CAD correlates perfectly with oil price decline

Distortionary effect of US embarking on interest rate hiking cycle overshadows straight CAD/Oil price correlation

Source: Various market data feeds

The same can be said for the currencies of those countries just mentioned, whilst the effect on the currencies of most major Middle Eastern oil producers has been militated against by the fact that they have pegs to the US dollar. **Nonetheless, spectacular gains could be made by trading against the possibility of these pegs enduring, albeit in a slightly more tangential fashion than usual.**

In this context, the **first quarter of 2016 was marked by consistent pressure on forward Saudi riyal prices all the way out to one year duration on the curve,** indicating speculation over whether the riyal's 3.75 effective currency peg to the US dollar, which has existed since 1986 and has been regarded as a cornerstone of the country's economic stability, will survive intact. Interestingly, with the Saudi Arabian Monetary Authority (SAMA) having been active in attempting to shore up the value of the riyal across all dates, short and long, since the beginning of that year, **hedge funds in particular have been looking to effectively short the riyal – and by implication bet against the survival of the peg at 3.75 – by buying interest rate swaps (IRS).** At the end of March 2016, for example, Saudi IRS hit multi-year highs, with the idea being that as SAMA eventually runs too low on USD reserves to prop up the riyal (selling the USD to buy the Saudi currency) then it would have to embark on interest rate hikes to bolster the currency instead. In this vein, two-year Saudi IRS climbed by around 100 basis points (bps) from the end of September 2015 to the end of March 2016, to over 2% by the end of the first quarter 2016 – their highest since January 2009 – a massive number, given that the Saudi central bank has raised official interest rates by only 25 bps over the same period. Although the first part of 2017 has seen some reduction of pressure on the riyal, the prevailing market view is that the riyal is vulnerable.

This trading view has been exacerbated by negative ratings moves on Saudi Arabia, including the downgrade last year by S&P of its long-term foreign currency debt rating. The problem with the downgrade was not just that it occurred very quickly in ratings agency terms after the earlier downgrade in the previous October, nor even the new rating itself (A-), but rather that it was an unusual double-digit cut (from A+), as opposed to the single digit moves that ratings agencies usually use. The fact that Moody's had a materially higher credit rating for Saudi than did S&P – three notches more, in fact, at Aa3 (and Fitch Ratings' was four notches higher, at AA) is completely irrelevant from the international investor perspective, as they take the lowest rating into account and not the highest.

The ratings curve, as mentioned earlier, is essentially a risk curve for global investors and the speed at which a country's rating changes is seen as a function of how volatile the risk situation in it currently is, so a double-digit cut implies that the risk inherent in Saudi – and therefore in investments into it – is extremely high. Moreover, **at A** minus, Saudi is now at the lowest rung of upper medium grade investment status, with one further move down putting it into lower medium grade territory, with the next category being non-investment grade, which would be catastrophic from the perspective of 'real money funds', many of which would not be allowed under their investment mandate to invest in a product with such a rating.

Long USD

Another currency trading correlation to note is between the oil price and the US dollar and the full analysis of this is mentioned above. Suffice it to recap here: as it now stands, this historical relationship has been somewhat distorted by the US embarking on an interest rate hiking cycle (this virtually always results in its earlier phases in a weaker USD, as explained in depth a little later). Nonetheless, stripping out this factor, which will be taken out of the equation as the interest rate hiking cycle develops, **the flipside to the straight short oil trade, as the correlations showed, is a long USD trade. The cleanest way to trade this is going long the USD Index** – established in 1973 (based at 100) as a measure of strength of the US currency against the currencies of six major other currencies: the euro, the Japanese yen, the Canadian dollar, the British pound, the Swedish krona and the Swiss franc. **Obviously, added profits can also be made by buying USD against currencies of countries that are highly dependent on oil for their trade revenues, such as those mentioned earlier (for example, Canada and Mexico offer the easiest trading opportunities in this regard).**

Short Emerging Markets FX

Whilst, by definition, many currencies in the world depreciated as the USD began its major rise ahead of the first US interest rate hike in 2015 ('buy the rumour'), expectations of interest rates rises in the US (and the end of QE in the country) also meant a shift in general away from 'riskier' investments, both by asset class and by country. This was then reversed markedly once the US had actually hiked interest rates, as the US lost ground ('sell the fact') and riskier investments benefitted to a degree. **Since then, as highlighted earlier in this book, there has been an ebb and flow of investment into and out of 'safer' and 'riskier' assets, depending on which investment factor has been prevalent at any one time in the markets, and the speed and degree of swing of these moves has been unprecedented in market history.** Even during the Great Financial Crisis there were extended periods where investment broadly favoured safer or riskier assets. In general terms, the risk curve moves from least risky asset class to most risky asset class as follows: cash (in a solid currency), bonds (in a solid country), equities (in a solid country), FX (riskier than the previous three categories but extremely liquid) and commodities (riskier than the first three categories and relatively extremely illiquid). It also moves from least risky country type to most risky country type in the following fashion: developed market, emerging market, frontier market.

As it now stands, though, **the relationship between commodities and EMFX is more nuanced, with a feedback loop that plays back into where in the global economic cycle differing market payers believe we are.** Notably in this regard, while the supply story in commodities (most visibly evident in the oil market) has received significant attention over the last year and a half or so, it does not fully explain the entire investment picture. Specifically, the extended fall in commodities prices that the markets have seen might usually have been expected to have fed through into a re-acceleration in global economic activity by this point; that is, the 'recovery phase' mentioned earlier in this book in the section looking at *Economic Patterns*.

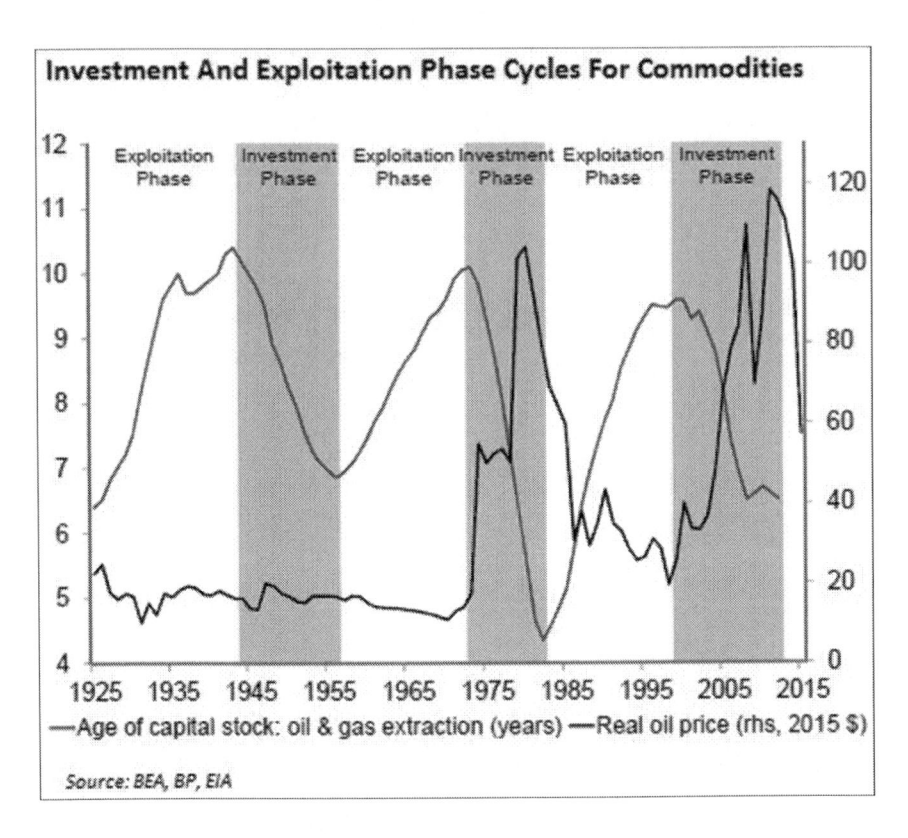

Investment And Exploitation Phase Cycles For Commodities

[Chart showing Age of capital stock: oil & gas extraction (years) and Real oil price (rhs, 2015 $) from 1925 to 2015, with alternating Exploitation Phase and Investment Phase periods labeled.]

Source: BEA, BP, EIA

In fact, though, this broad-based global economic recovery has proven to be much more elusive than initially expected, and demand weakness has been compounding the negative returns associated with the ongoing supply shift, militating into a situation that might better be characterised as being in a much earlier stage of economic re-development than thought; in many key economies, in fact, the 'contraction phase'.

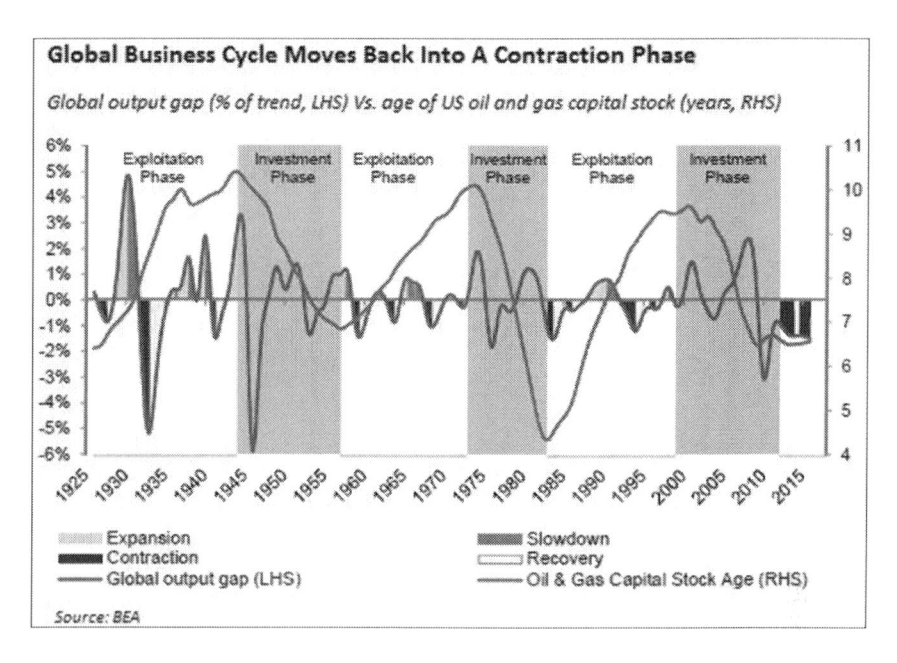

Global Business Cycle Moves Back Into A Contraction Phase

Global output gap (% of trend, LHS) Vs. age of US oil and gas capital stock (years, RHS)

[Chart showing global output gap and oil & gas capital stock age from 1925 to 2015, with alternating Exploitation and Investment Phases marked]

Legend: Expansion, Contraction, Global output gap (LHS), Slowdown, Recovery, Oil & Gas Capital Stock Age (RHS)

Source: BEA

A key factor in this stalling of recovery has stemmed from emerging markets, with growth weakness having been driven by the nature of the private credit involved (see later focus on China) and sovereign debt and terms of trade shocks depressing activity. This could be regarded as the third phase of the Global Financial Crisis, with the first being the crisis in developed markets and the second being the sovereign crisis in Europe. In China – the major source of metals and oil demand growth for the last decade – economic expansion is not just slowing but is also re-balancing towards being consumption-led (through the development of a larger middle class) and away from fixed investment-led (through government-supported infrastructure projects).

Three Phases Of The Global Financial Crisis

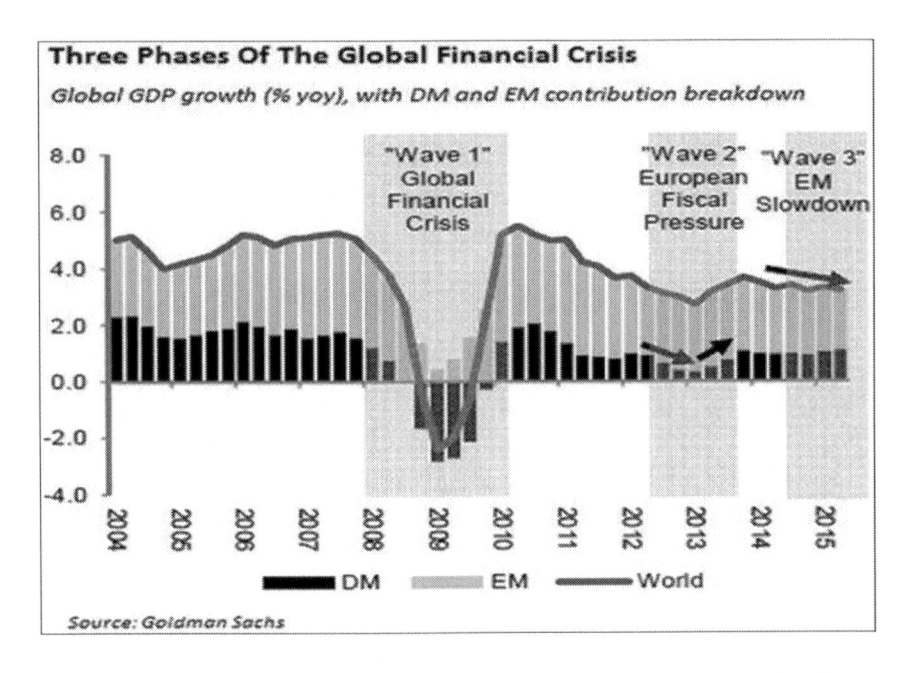

Global GDP growth (% yoy), with DM and EM contribution breakdown

[Chart showing global GDP growth from 2004 to 2015 with three highlighted phases: "Wave 1" Global Financial Crisis, "Wave 2" European Fiscal Pressure, and "Wave 3" EM Slowdown. Legend: DM, EM, World.]

Source: Goldman Sachs

This weak global growth – and worsening terms of trade – has been feeding back into commodity price falls through significant EMFX depreciation, including amongst commodity producers. Specifically, as the local currency costs of production have fallen, commodity cost curves have been pushed lower and flatter (in USD terms) and this, in turn, has been exacerbating oversupply and making new equilibrium price levels a moving target, to the downside.

Weak EM Demand Feedback Loop Into Global Commodity Supply Through The FX Channel

- Shale Revolution
- US (positive) income effect channels
- Lower US Energy Prices
- More US Economic Growth
- More Commodity Supply
- EMFX (weakness) channel
- US monetary policy channel
- More US Economic Growth
- Less Emerging Markets Demand
- Less Accommodative US Monetary Policy

Source: Goldman Sachs

Metals In The Correlations Mix

Gold

Historically, gold has been the usual beneficiary of heightened risk across the globe, on the basis that, unlike currencies, more cannot simply be produced at the drop of a central bank's printing presses (as in QE). So, for example, the correlations for gold were fairly simple: if the USD looked weak then gold would be strong, and this generally still holds true.

Given that an earlier recommendation in the sub-section above is to go long the USD, this would, therefore, appear to be a counter-intuitive trade but, in fact, a long gold position is a good hedge against the sort of uncertainty that surrounds the oil price, especially from a geopolitical perspective. Indeed, gold has been regarded as the archetypal **'safe-haven' commodities asset in times of political uncertainty** (troubles in the Middle East, for example, sparking buying not just in that area but around the globe) **and economic uncertainty** (ongoing anaemic growth in some key global economies) in the same way that the Swiss franc is seen as such in currency terms.

Additionally, it has been seen as a hedge against inflation concerns that have risen sharply on the basis of the QE policies adopted by the Fed, the BOJ, the ECB – the long-term refinancing operations (LTRO) was QE by another name – and until recently the BOE as well.

Recently, as well, gold is seen as a good buy in the unusual interest rates scenario that we are seeing playing out around the world (negative rates, that is, as mentioned at length earlier). One factor in this context is that, although the uncertainty and distress associated with negative rates would tend to increase interest in gold anyway, the more pronounced shift of monetary policy in this direction by central banks is encouraging even greater flows into bullion.

In particular, **there is no sense yet that negative rates could not be cut even further, so the opportunity cost of holding gold (which has no yield attached to it) is reduced.** To this depression of the global yield curve has been added a flattening as well, with risk-off plays. **A flattening yield curve often presages an economic slowdown, which may continue to trigger policy responses that generally support gold. Indeed, the last time the differential was that low was in January 2008, in the early stages of the Global Financial Crisis, which, in turn, produced one of the biggest bull runs in gold for many years.**

Gold Price In USD (end 2015 to present)

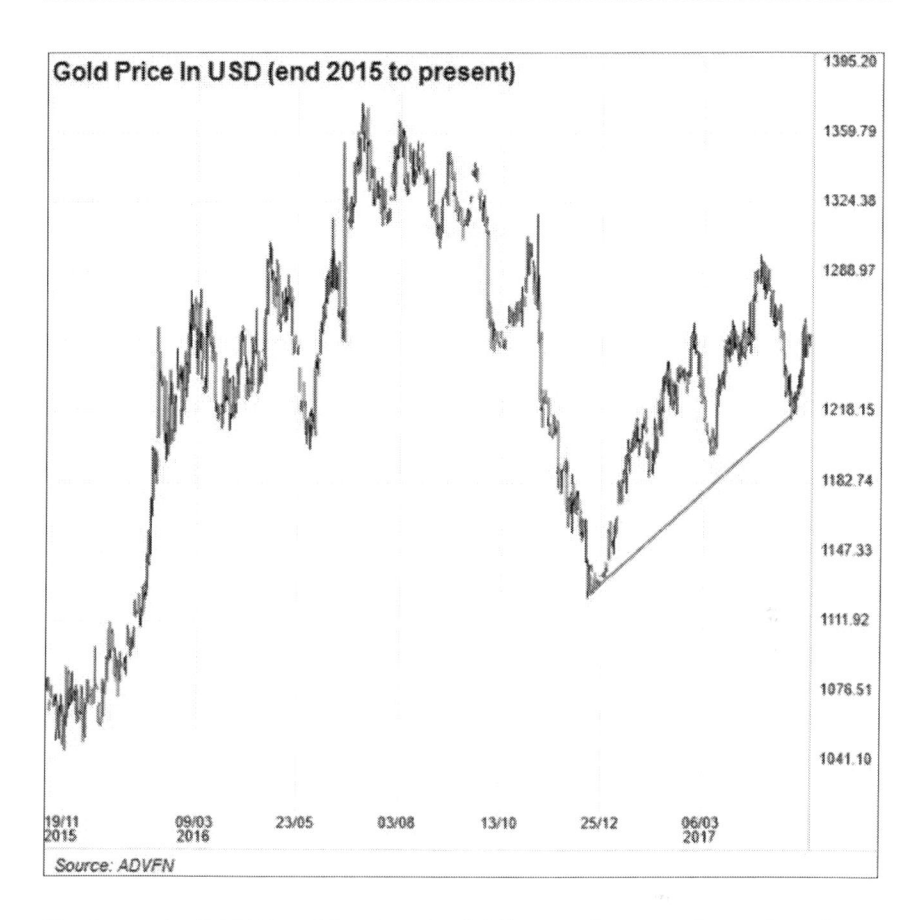

Source: ADVFN

By the end of 2015, gold prices had fallen to five-year lows, largely on the back of renewed USD strength, with the generally inverse correlation to the USD re-asserting itself. However, there were three other **factors that came into play in support since then: various periods of EUR strength against the USD; rising buying from central banks (against a broadly static supply profile); and various periods of rising market volatility overall (as measured by the VIX).**

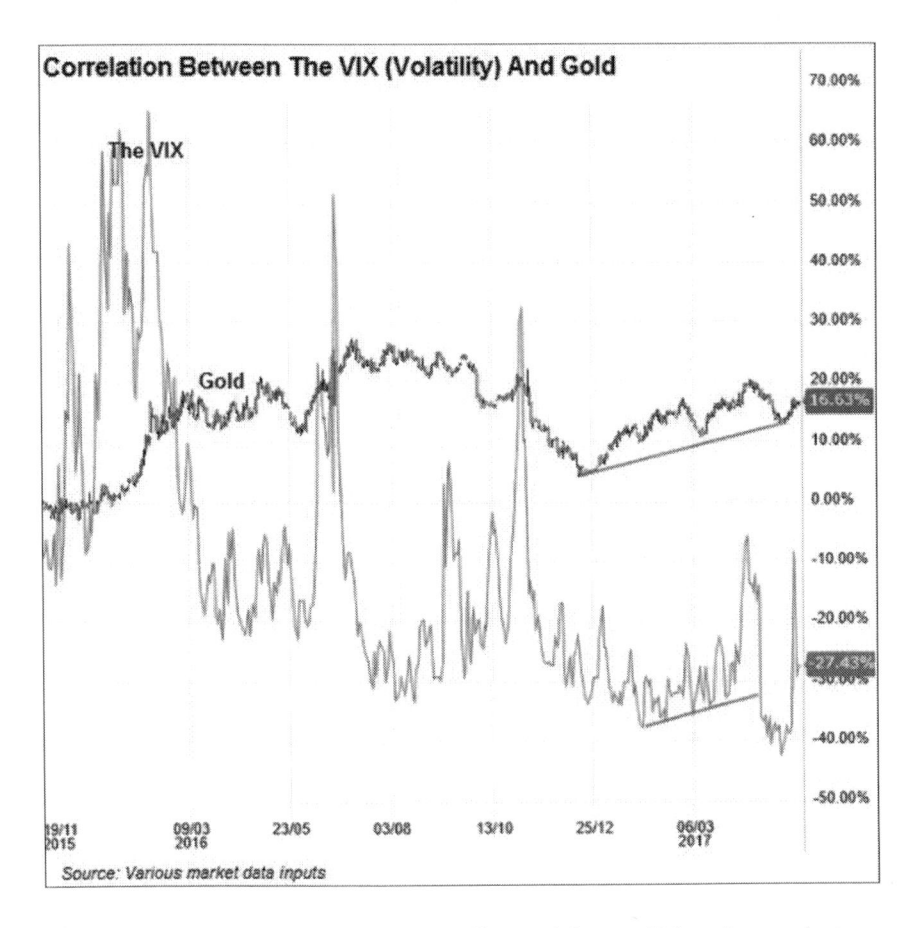

Correlation Between The VIX (Volatility) And Gold

Source: Various market data inputs

While investor flows in large part dictated by traditional correlations dominate gold prices in the near to medium term, **the locus of physical demand continues to shift from West to East.** Nearly two-thirds of all the physical bullion purchased is consumed by India and China, who trade the number one and two spots for greatest consumer and importer between them. While economic growth in China and other EMs may be slowing, it is still strong by historical standards and rising incomes in these countries are likely to support a rolling higher floor price for gold.

Also interesting **from a historical perspective – and a point that reinforces the changing relationship at times between the USD and the gold price – is that a US rate rise may, in itself,** also be supportive of gold at times. **During the last four Fed tightening cycles, gold prices tended to weaken going into a rate rise and rally for the next 120 days afterwards.**

Silver

The same correlations that apply to gold apply to silver, although they are less marked for two reasons: first, silver has more of a broader industrial application than gold, as well as its store of value investment theme; and, second, silver is regarded lower down the chain of 'flight to safety' assets than gold.

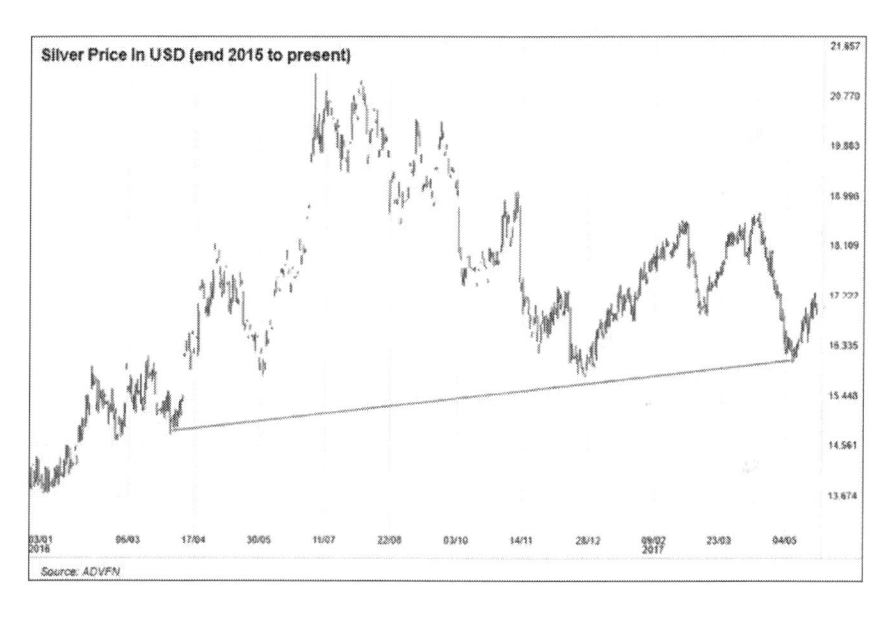

In terms of the supply and demand side, then, the recent bounce in silver price has been partly driven by an easing in mine production after a decade of significant output increases, whilst industrial demand, which comprises half of total silver consumption, has seen something of a bounce as well, after a weak 2015, due to increasing uptake in Asia. Additionally, the low prices of 2015 sparked demand for coin and small bar demand, plus jewellery-related uptake, and holdings in silver ETFs have been steady.

In 'normal' market conditions, when risks are not seen as being high, the **ratio between the silver and gold price – which can serve as an indicator to determine when to buy or sell the metals** – remains relatively steady at around the USD40/oz level, although the longer-term historical average is around USD15/oz. At times of perceived heightened risk, though, gold outperforms silver (as a safe-haven), pushing the gold to silver ratio higher as seen below.

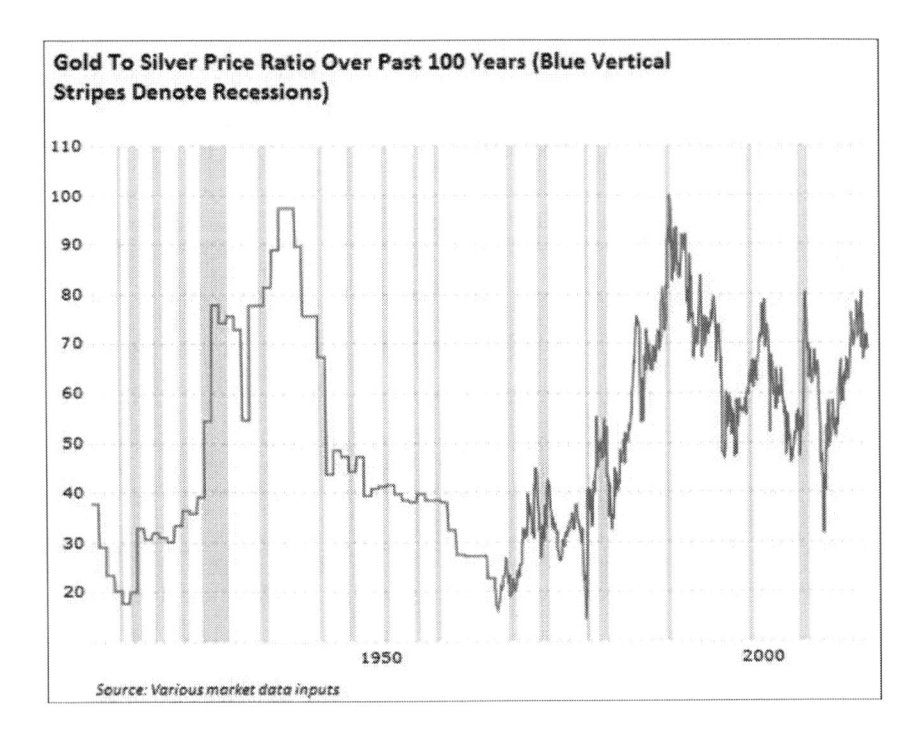

Gold To Silver Price Ratio Over Past 100 Years (Blue Vertical Stripes Denote Recessions)

Source: Various market data inputs

PGMs

Of the platinum group metals (PGMS), platinum itself is the most interesting from the trading perspective. **Historically platinum has usually commanded a premium correlation to gold of around USD200-400/oz or so, giving regular opportunities for divergence trading.**

Gold to Platinum Ratio

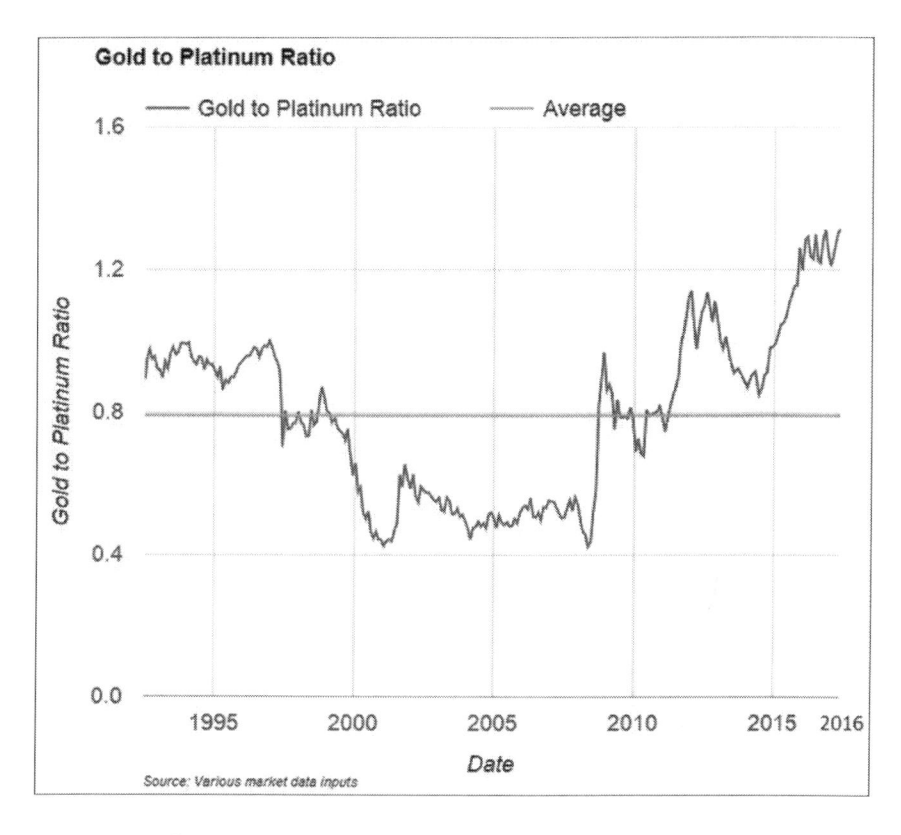

Source: Various market data inputs

In terms of general trends in this ratio over the past few years, the gold-to-platinum ratio decreased in the second half of the 1970s, reaching nearly as low as 0.5 in February 1979, implying that platinum was overvalued to gold. The ratio rose in the beginning of the 1980s, reaching a peak of nearly 1.5 in September 1982, indicating that platinum was undervalued compared to gold. Then the ratio generally fell for the rest of the 1980s, whilst during the 1990s the gold-to-platinum ratio was slightly below 1:1 for most of the time. **The behaviour of gold and platinum prices, then, clearly shows again that gold is the predominant safe-haven asset in times of financial distress.**

Even more specifically, **gold tends to outperform platinum when the confidence in the government, economy and currencies is deteriorating, while it underperforms platinum** during periods of monetary stability, economic growth and high confidence in the financial system.

During 2015, platinum fared poorly due to falling commodities prices in general (as a consequence of reduced demand from China), concerns over future diesel vehicle demand (the emissions scandal) and weak jewellery demand from Asia. This slowdown in demand also coincided with a rebound in mine production.

These lower prices over the period led to restructuring programs across the mining industry, which, over time, should constrain mine supply growth, tighten supply/demand balances and eventually support prices.

Other Metals

Whilst gold is a key 'safe-haven' asset, outperforming in times of heightened global uncertainty, the metal that is a key to indicate a stable global growth environment is copper. As was touched on earlier, copper is a key industrial metal that is used globally in a wide range of industrial applications, outperforming when the global economy is in good health and optimism over continued world GDP expansion is high.

Like the gold-to-oil ratio, **the gold-to-copper ratio is an indicator of the health of the global economy against the fear of failure.** As the chart below illustrates, the ratio has been in decline since hitting a seven-year high in early January 2016.

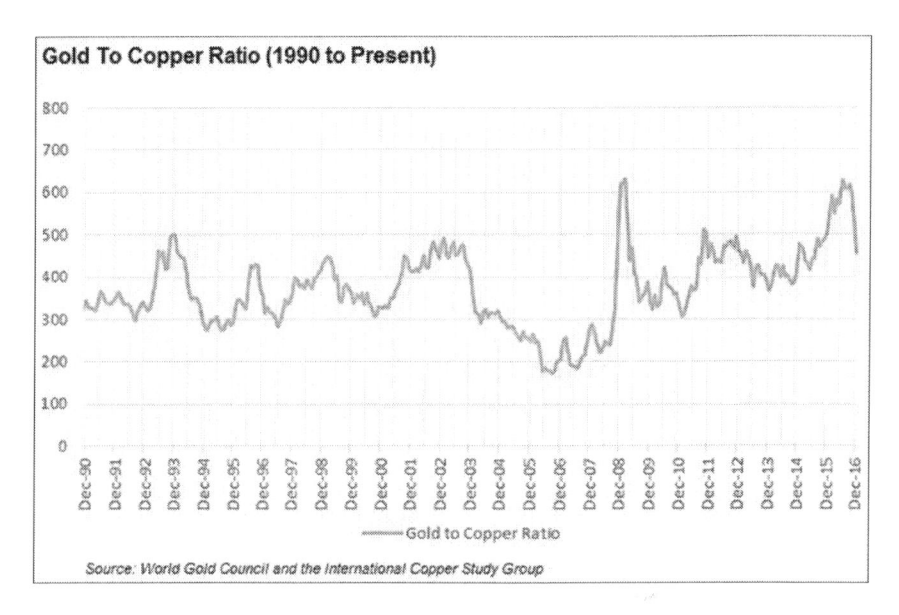

Gold To Copper Ratio (1990 to Present)

Source: World Gold Council and the International Copper Study Group

This close correlation between the gold to copper ratio and the level of fear in the market can be seen from the chart below, which shows the former plotted against the measure of fear, represented by the volatility index, the VIX.

Although in recent weeks this ratio has fallen, the trend is still rising, which indicates that there is rising fear that increased risks may well again re-assert themselves in practical market terms in the near future.

Gold To Copper Ratio Vs The Vix (1990 to Present)

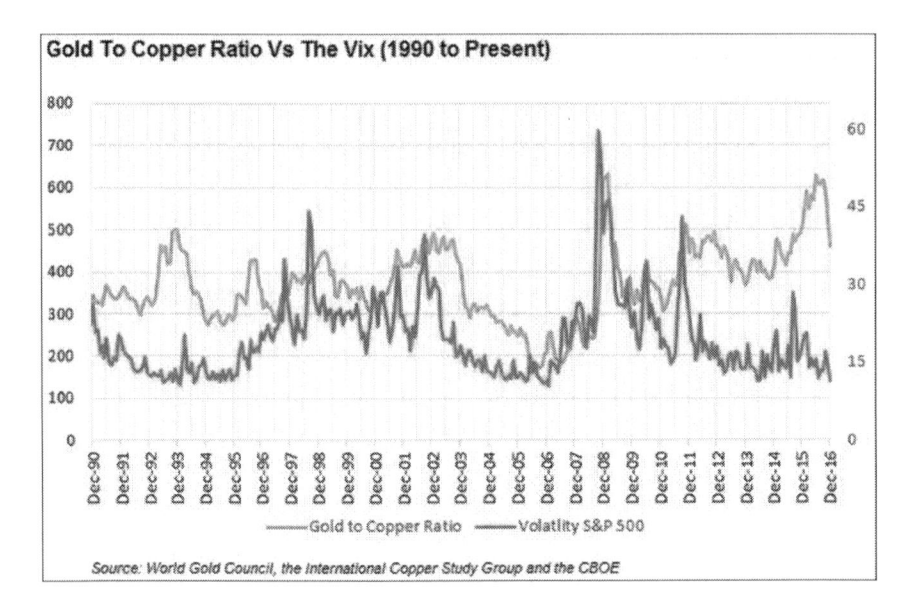

Source: World Gold Council, the International Copper Study Group and the CBOE

In fact, **the metals complex often yields some surprising – but potentially extremely valuable – correlations that the vast majority in the market do not notice and consequently are a proverbial 'licence to print money'.** A case in point was the **longstanding correlation between the price of iron ore and the value of the Australian dollar, which, in turn, was a superb way of playing the economic slowdown in China.**

From the moment that China started to show signs that its growth rate was declining below the key 8% level in 2011/12, the AUD began to show serious signs of rolling weakness. The reason was that at that time at least 30% of all of Australia's exports had been going to China since 2008 when China injected CNY4trn (USD635bn) into its economy as a stimulus.

China Annual GDP Growth Rate, % (2007 to Present)

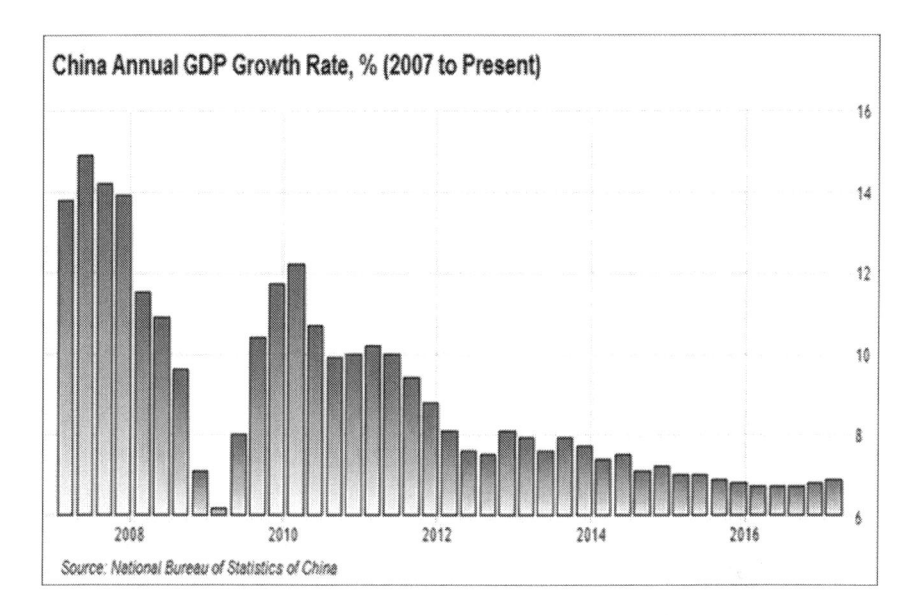

Source: National Bureau of Statistics of China

The **key pointer to the relationship between China and Australia showed up unequivocally in the price of iron ore, as the metal is a vital component used in steel, which was a direct indicator of infrastructure growth in China. Moreover, iron ore at that time, in itself, constituted around 20% of Australia's total exports.**

Given the recent decision by China to renew massive infrastructure investments – the 'One Belt, One Road' initiative promising more than USD1 trillion in infrastructure and spanning more than 60 countries – it may well be that this correlation dramatically re-asserts itself.

Uncovering this type of relationship through lateral thinking is an excellent way of generating alpha returns going forward, of course.

Key Risks On The Horizon

There are a number of major factors that individually could continue to twist financial markets into trading patterns that swing exceptionally quickly into wildly contradictory modes and lead to substantial trading losses, if they are not thoroughly understood in terms of accurate historical precedent, correlations and geopolitical dynamics. These risks are rising again, as can be seen in the charts below developed by economists from the US's Federal Reserve Board.

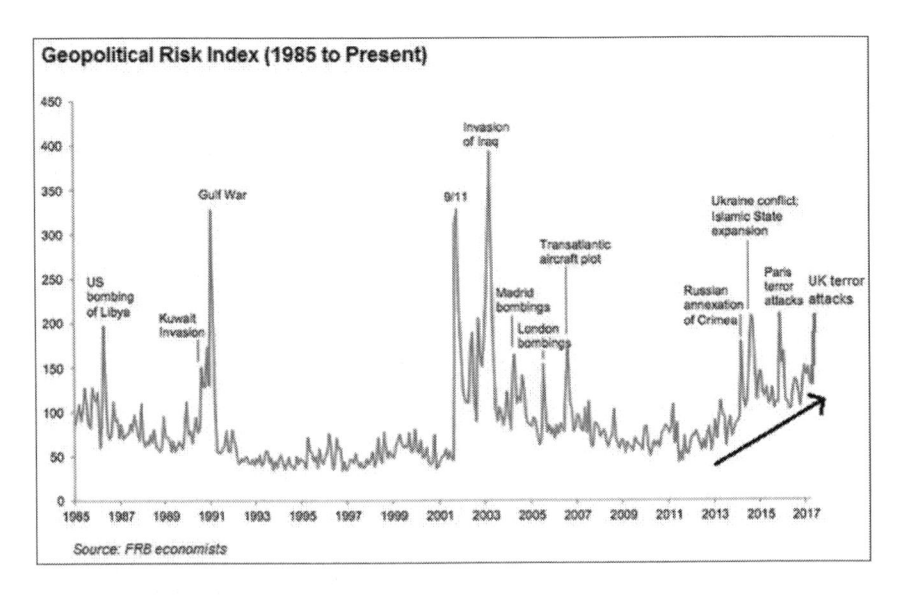

Geopolitical Risk Index (1985 to Present)

Source: FRB economists

These 'ghosts in the machine' are questions of growth and QE-inspired crashes in the US (with new President, Donald Trump, now in place), the Eurozone (with Brexit now factoring into the equation), China and Japan, with corollary concerns over the global hydrocarbons market, in addition to fears over global security pressure points.

At any one moment, one or more of these take precedence in dealing terms over the others but the order can change in a split second, so thoroughly understanding these 'ghost' factors is vital to ensuring correct portfolio positioning in order to skew the risk/reward balance in a trader's favour and this is what this section is about. This is all the more important as the average level of risk has risen to levels approaching more than a 100-year high.

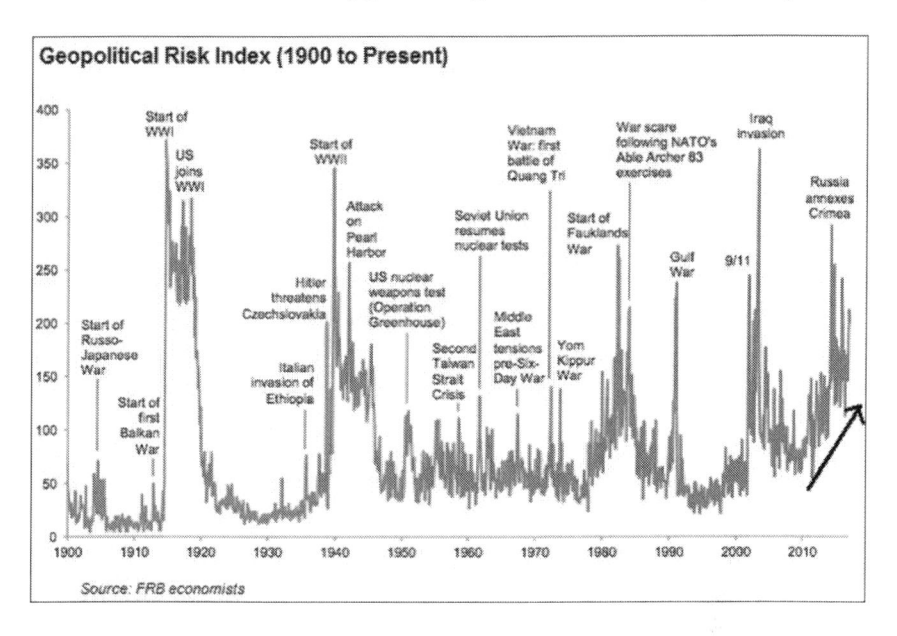

Geopolitical Risk Index (1900 to Present)

Source: FRB economists

The US

Every consistently successful trader in the world since trading began has left his personal political views behind the second he logs into his trading terminal and this applies today as much as it ever did. Irrespective of a trader's personal view of political developments – and the past year or so has seen some extraordinary developments in this respect, of course – a trader who wants to continue to generate consistent profits over time should disregard personal preferences and the preferences of the crowd over any political developments and focus simply on what the development means in practice: especially in economic and geopolitical terms.

A case in point is US President Donald Trump. Contrary to the hysterical predictions – as with Brexit – that the election of Trump would be a major risk-off event, markets of both the equities and bond varieties have gone from strength to strength. This, by the way, shows how dangerous it is to trade based either on knee-jerk personal reaction to an event or on the prevailing collective 'wisdom' in a society. **It also underscores the age-old trading maxim of going with the flow in the run-up to an event and then doing the exact opposite when the event has actually happened; that is, 'buy the rumour, sell the fact' in a market rising ahead of an event or 'sell the rumour, buy the fact' in a market that is falling ahead of an event.**

Since Trump settled in, markets have started to factor in expectations of major positive growth at the expense of only a slight rise in inflation. In reality, the consensus view of the smart money is that Trump's administration will implement an impact-reduced version of the more dramatic measures that were flagged in Trump's election campaign.

Specifically, on the fiscal side, there is likely to be a much more modest easing of less than 1% of GDP that should set in during the latter part of 2017, given that there will be caution even amongst Republicans about adding sizeably to the budget deficit (as they only have a four-seat majority in the Senate). The tariff effect on trade is also likely to be minimal, as is the GDP effect of any actual reductions in immigration.

US GDP Annual Growth Rate (%)

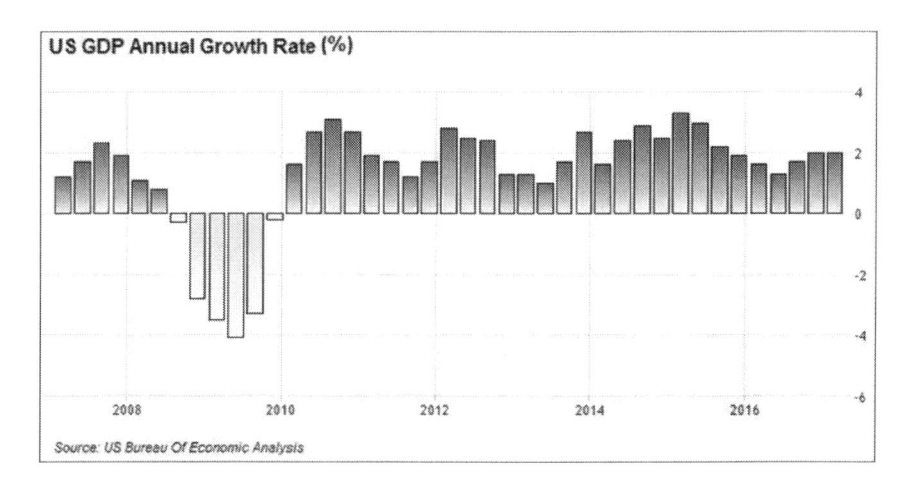

Source: US Bureau Of Economic Analysis

Overall, the planned fiscal stimulus programme should lead to a boost to the economy, a relatively small rise in inflation but also more interest rate rises at a higher pace than many had previously expected. **This, in turn, will put further upward pressure on global long-term interest rates. At the same time, faced with ongoing low growth and low core inflation, the European Central Bank is likely to extend even further its QE (asset purchase programme) and the Bank of Japan will do the same. This greater divergence in interest rates will push the USD up even more.**

The Risk Of A Major Equities Correction

These factors, though, will exacerbate the risk of a crash in the US equities markets down the line, with the knock-on effect that this will have on other developed countries' equities markets.

The reason why a crash is on the cards already, initially in the US before it spreads out, is that the current rally is being driven by the vast wall of money that was pumped into the developed market economies – so far – during their QE programmes. In this context, it is estimated that at least USD18 trillion from various developed market central banks has ended up in equities and bond markets since the QE programmes began.

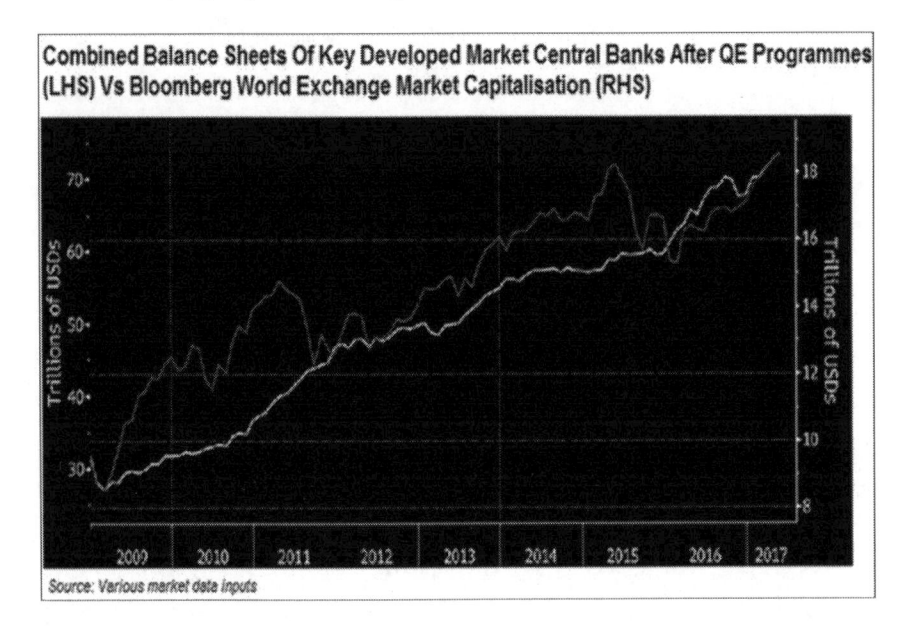

Combined Balance Sheets Of Key Developed Market Central Banks After QE Programmes (LHS) Vs Bloomberg World Exchange Market Capitalisation (RHS)

Source: Various market data inputs

Even prior to the bounce in US equities, and the corollary bounce in the equities markets of similarly highly-rated developed markets that came in the wake of the election of President Donald Trump as President, **these markets were looking overvalued but now they look dangerously so.** The ratio of the market value of US common stock to year-long pre-tax operating profits rose to 11.5:1 in Q4-2016, which was the highest such ratio since Q2-2002's 12.5:1, according to figures from Moody's. Indeed, the current market value of US common equity is now at a multiple of pre-tax profits from current production that was unheard of prior to 1998.

Also of concern is that US stocks are very highly priced relative to actual corporate earnings. According to market data, as of Q2-2015, the market value of US common stock rose to a cycle high of 218% of corporate gross-value-added (GVA), where the latter is a proxy for total corporate revenues. During 2002-2007's business cycle upturn the ratio failed to reach 200% and the market value of common stock crested at 185% of corporate GVA in Q2-2007. After falling to Q1-2016's 192%, the market value of common stock has since risen to 214% of corporate GVA in Q4-2016.

The current high level of over-valuation of US equities means that they are **vulnerable to a deep slide in the event that profits contract or interest rates undergo a disruptive climb, with a knock-on negative effect for other closely correlated assets, especially the equities markets of other similarly developed markets.**

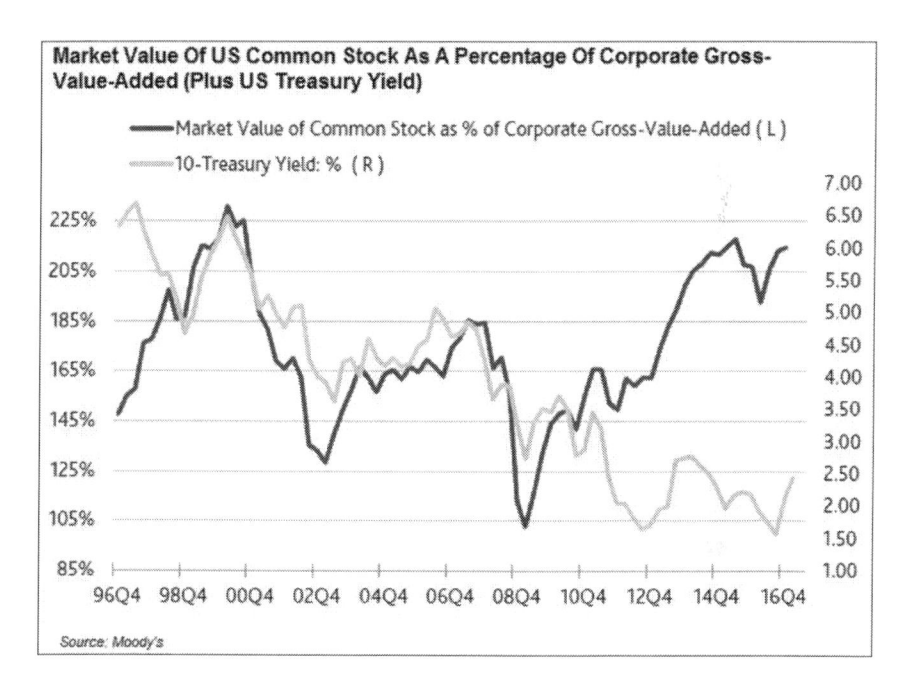

Market Value Of US Common Stock As A Percentage Of Corporate Gross-Value-Added (Plus US Treasury Yield)

Source: Moody's

China

The twin announcements at China's annual National People's Congress (NPC) in March 2017 from Premier Li Keqiang, in Beijing, that the world's second-largest economy has cut its growth rate target to the lowest level in 27 years and that "developments both inside and outside China require that we are ready to face more complicated and graver situations" have **heightened longstanding concerns that China will trigger the next global financial crisis.**

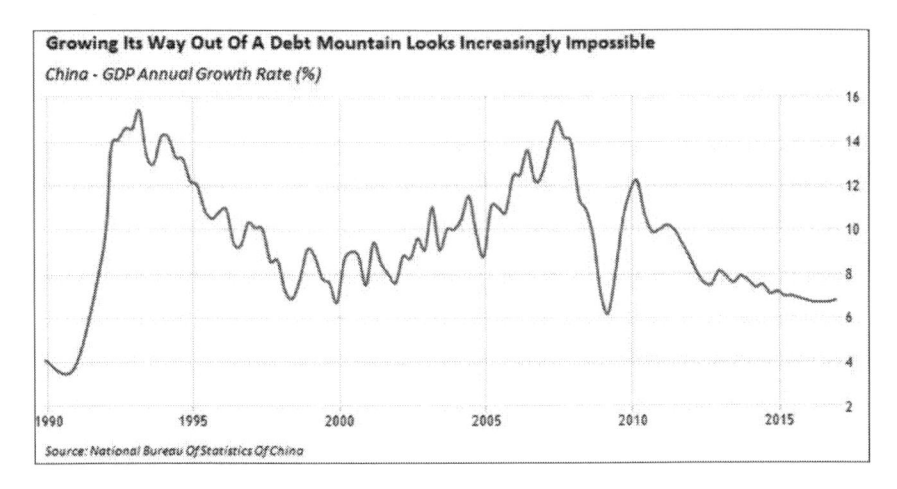

Growing Its Way Out Of A Debt Mountain Looks Increasingly Impossible
China - GDP Annual Growth Rate (%)

Source: National Bureau Of Statistics Of China

Even before this acknowledgement by Li, the markets were aware that **China has for a while been demonstrating the three key symptoms that have preceded all of the major financial crises of the past three decades – the 1997 Asia Crisis, the 1998 Russia Crisis and even the Great Financial Crisis that began in 2007 – which are: a high degree of debt leverage, a rapid rise in asset prices and a decline in underlying growth potential.** There is an analogue in China to every critical element that precipitated these other crises but, given the greater magnitude of each of them in China, when the crisis there unravels it will make the Great Financial Crisis and depression look like a picnic.

Huge And Growing Debt Leverage

In terms of the debt leverage to begin with, **China's debt-to-GDP ratio rose to 237% as at the end of 2016 from 225% the previous year.** Moreover, according to the People's Bank of China's own data, 'total social financing' (which measures overall credit supply to the economy) doled out a record CNY17.8 trillion (USD2.3

trillion) **in new credit in 2016,** with an increasing share of this being used to pay debt servicing costs.

Worrying though these figures are, they pale into relative insignificance when compared to the **debt being hidden in lenders' off-balance-sheet portfolios of loans that have been re-packaged into 'wealth-management products'** (WMPs) that typically offer a high rate of return but are effectively unregulated. These used to be mainly sold to the public but in recent years have been sold increasingly to banks and other financial institutions.

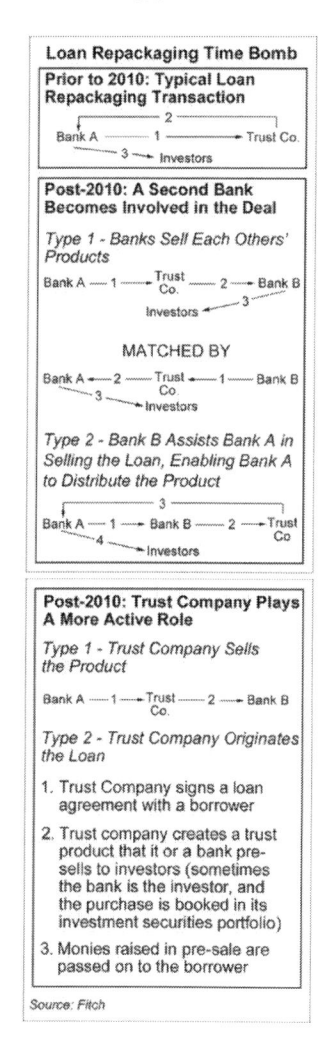

Loan Repackaging Time Bomb

Prior to 2010: Typical Loan Repackaging Transaction

Bank A —1— Trust Co., with arrow 2 between them, 3 → Investors

Post-2010: A Second Bank Becomes Involved in the Deal

Type 1 - Banks Sell Each Others' Products

Bank A —1— Trust Co. —2— Bank B, 3 → Investors

MATCHED BY

Bank A ←2— Trust Co. ←1— Bank B, 3 → Investors

Type 2 - Bank B Assists Bank A in Selling the Loan, Enabling Bank A to Distribute the Product

Bank A —1→ Bank B —2→ Trust Co, 3 connecting, 4 → Investors

Post-2010: Trust Company Plays A More Active Role

Type 1 - Trust Company Sells the Product

Bank A —1→ Trust Co. —2→ Bank B

Type 2 - Trust Company Originates the Loan

1. Trust Company signs a loan agreement with a borrower
2. Trust company creates a trust product that it or a bank pre-sells to investors (sometimes the bank is the investor, and the purchase is booked in its investment securities portfolio)
3. Monies raised in pre-sale are passed on to the borrower

Source: Fitch

In practical terms, **there are layers of liabilities built upon the same underlying assets, much as was seen with subprime asset-backed securities and collateralised debt obligations in the US in the lead up to the onset of the Great Financial Crisis that began in 2007/2008. However, the range of assets is much greater and less safe than mortgages and there is significantly less visibility on the assets in each WMP than there was in the subprime sector.**

Despite numerous rounds of regulatory crackdowns on WMP activity, issuance continues to soar. The stock of Chinese banks' off-balance-sheet WMPs have grown 158% since 2014 – compared to 34% growth of on-balance-sheet assets during this time – and stood at CNY26 trillion at end-2016.

These WMPs constitute a hidden second balance sheet, similar to the Special Investment Vehicles and conduits that the Western banks had in 2007/2008, which nobody paid attention to until there started to be bankruptcies. When everything fell apart, these off-balance-sheet liabilities had to be incorporated on balance sheets, magnifying the banks' losses.

Their capacity to magnify the scale of the domino-effect of bad debt that also crippled the global financial system during 2007/2008 crisis is all the more concerning given that, even as it stands, as much as 25% of all of China's outstanding credit may be in non-performing or problem loans by the end of this year. This compares to an official bad-loan number for banks of 1.75%.

The scale of the WMPs is exacerbating the already stretched finances of financial institutions that occurred as a consequence of the rapid rise in asset prices, most notably in the property and stock markets. These took off after the CNY4 trillion stimulus package unveiled in November 2008, aimed at mitigating the worst effects of the global recession that was gathering pace at that time.

Stockmarket Bubbles

In theory, this money was to have made its way into government-mandated infrastructure projects via state-owned enterprises (SEOs) but in reality a lot of it instead was 're-directed' by individuals into personal investments in the stock and property markets, which is why both of those rose very rapidly from 2008 onward.

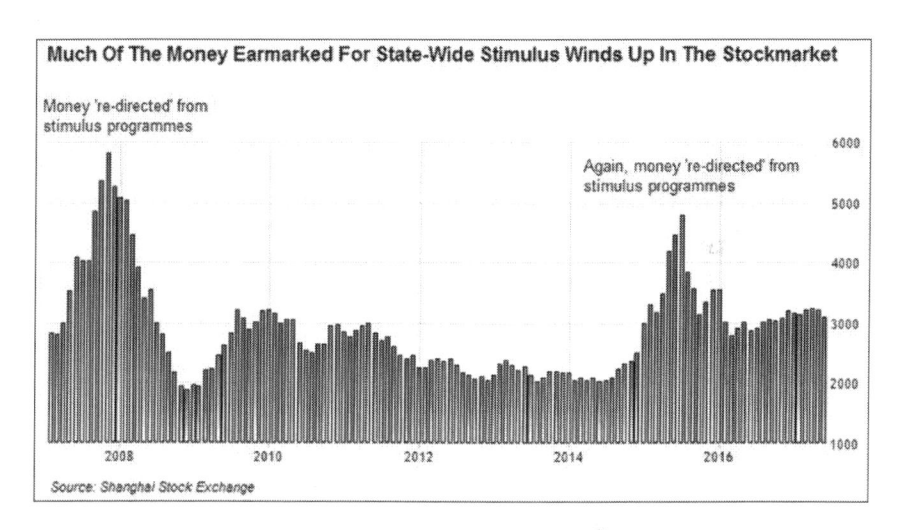

Much Of The Money Earmarked For State-Wide Stimulus Winds Up In The Stockmarket

Money 're-directed' from stimulus programmes

Again, money 're-directed' from stimulus programmes

Source: Shanghai Stock Exchange

Although the benchmark stock markets in Shanghai and Shenzhen have seen mixed fortunes over the past year, as a result of the large proportion of 'hot money' retail investors in the country, property market values in China's major cities continue to rise inexorably.

Housing Bubbles

According to global data provider, Numbeo, **property prices are now 44 times the level of income in Shenzhen, 33 times in Beijing and 32 times in Shanghai, which compares to eight times in Tokyo during its 1980s credit bubble and to 6.4 times in the US at the time of its own housing bubble prior to the sub-prime catastrophe.** Even rental prices in China's key cities are much higher than the 22.8 times level in the US prior to the onset of the 2007/2008 financial crisis, at 43 times in Shenzhen, 34 times in Beijing and 33 times in Shanghai.

This disparity between prices and incomes means that banks and other financial institutions will be unable to repair their balance sheets by liquidating property assets at current prices, as there is going to be a chronic lack of potential buyers.

Three years ago, the Chinese Academy of Social Sciences in Beijing estimated (based on electricity meter readings) that **there were around 64.5 million empty apartments and houses in the urban areas of China, which was just over five times the level in the US at the height of the US sub-prime mortgage bubble.** Despite various government initiatives (including buying properties itself and turning them into public housing), this figure has not meaningfully altered and has simply moved debt from one set of balance sheets to another.

Mathematical Impossibility Of Current Debt Management/ Growth Strategy

Historically, China has taken the view that it could simply grow its way out of potentially devastating debt overhang but, as signalled in March by its own official downgrading of growth projections, this strategy looks even more flawed than ever.

The amount of credit in China is about 2.7 times the size of its GDP and it is increasing twice as fast as economic growth, so in purely mathematical terms the idea of growing its way out of trouble just does not compute. We are also seeing diminishing returns in this context as it is now taking even more credit to generate each unit of economic growth, which again is unsustainable.

A bailout would require trillions of dollars' worth of yuan being spent, which would create a massive capital shortage for much of the system overnight and, for China, with a much weaker social safety net and a much poorer population than the West had at the onset of its crisis, social and political instability would be a real concern in that situation.

Indeed, around 140 million people have migrated from China's rural areas to its cities over the past 20 years and another 300 million are predicted to follow suit in the next 20 years, according to Unicef. Consequently, the Chinese government has to provide these economic migrants with jobs, housing and food in order to avoid the sort of social unrest that we have seen in recent years in other countries, which means sustaining a sufficiently healthy economic growth rate, but most of that is being done through state-directed spending, which, in turn, adds to the debt mountain.

Catalyst For Catastrophe Could Be US Rates Rises

The catalyst that is currently most likely to cause a major debt crisis in China is **the likelihood of the US raising interest rates more than had originally been expected** as a consequence of an improving domestic economic outlook.

In order to avoid money moving out of China in search of higher returns elsewhere, the **central bank would need to keep the interest differential between China and the US as it is, which would mean raising interest rates in line with the States, but this could well trigger defaults on this debt.** Because of the interconnectedness of China's shadow banking system a default here would knock on to another default on a WMP which then cascades through the system and produces a wave of further defaults and so on, and then there is a full-blown crisis.

The initial effects of this would probably be felt in the rest of the world via plunges in China's benchmark stock markets that would prompt parallel falls in markets around the globe, as happened last year, which gave the world's stock markets the worst start to the year since the great financial crisis.

More fundamental, though, would be that **a crashing China would no longer be a key driver of global economic growth for** the foreseeable future, banks would be forced to liquidate assets around the world to mitigate losses, exacerbating initial stock market falls, and the government would have to sell some or all of its trillions of dollars' worth of US Treasury bonds to boot, with likely disastrous consequences for US markets and the world as a whole.

Indeed, **last year the IMF warned that such an economic crisis in China could result in a world-wide recession** because of its increasing financial links with the rest of the global economy and added that these are only set to accelerate as China continues to open up its local bond and other markets to foreign investment, as it is doing.

Brexit And The Eurozone

There are two distinct elements to the United Kingdom's withdrawal from the European Union – Brexit – that are discussed below. First, the impact of Brexit on the UK, which is included not because of its standalone influence on global finance (which is minimal) but because the reaction to it in some quarters is a perfect illustration of how emotions can warp the reality of a situation and are to be avoided at all costs when trading assets. Second, the potential for it to lead to other countries leaving the Union and the effect that a break-up of the Eurozone would have on global finance (which would be major).

Brexit

In and of itself, Brexit – whether soft or hard – has its positive and negative aspects, just as remaining in the EU would have involved the same. In very general terms, **remaining in the EU would have tied the UK to an entity that has no coherent economic or monetary policy and is subject to an enduringly low growth profile.**

Moreover, staying in the EU but with its own currency, **the GBP, continuing to act as a safe-haven from Eurozone turmoil**, would have resulted in a continued increase in the value of sterling relative to the euro (fair value for GBPUSD is around 1.2200, by the way, based on a range of historical real effective exchange rate, purchasing parity and economic factors), which would have led to further declines in exports and the balance of payments, a worsening debt burden, ongoing underperformance from the corporate sector, rising unemployment and a sustained drop in benchmark stock indices.

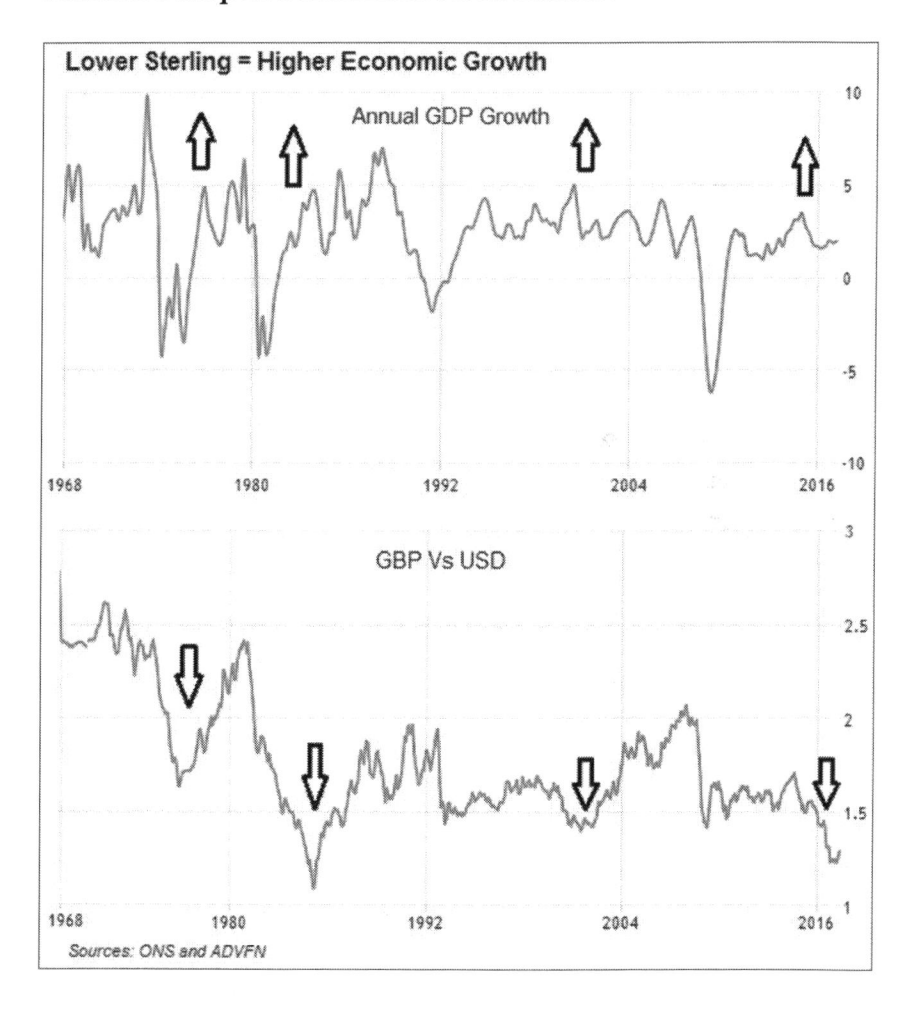

On the other hand, **leaving the EU will result in a relative rise in cost-push inflation as sterling buys UK producers less in the way of raw materials, a corollary adjunct squeezing of real incomes, and the possibility of a temporary drop off in exports if the UK is unable to negotiate an exit deal that leaves tariffs at a level comparable to those currently enjoyed with the EU states and instead go along the lines of WTO rules.** This latter element, though, would be more than compensated for over time if the UK concluded free trade deals with other major trading countries in the world, starting by leveraging relationships with Commonwealth countries such as India, Australia, Canada and New Zealand, and with longstanding ally the US.

Overall, it is likely that in the short term the implementation of Brexit will be subject to uncertainty that may prompt falling investment, further currency weakness, rising inflation and squeezed real incomes. All of these, though, are likely to be temporary effects, with European negotiators likely to take a more pragmatic approach after the initial knee-jerk reaction has concluded, allowing for a transition period should it be required. A tariff war on goods remains extremely unlikely, given the mutually advantageous nature of the relationship and the oft-cited concern over the non-tariff barriers (for example, customs checks if the UK is outside of the customs union and checks on UK compliance with EU regulations) are also unlikely to manifest themselves as the UK is likely to be able to negotiate a deal which reduces the administrative burden on British exporters.

Even if the deal does present some additional costs and inconvenience for UK firms, these will be offset by greater investment flows into the UK by dint precisely of its not being a part of the structurally unsound EU and, more particularly, of the inherently unsustainable euro. Given this, business investment will continue to rise, sterling steady, stock markets maintain a very healthy tone, real wage growth strongly re-emerge and consumption stay robust.

The Eurozone

Ever since European Central Bank President Mario Draghi stated that he and the ECB would do 'whatever it takes' to preserve the euro – a red rag to the global markets' trading bull if ever there was one – **the Eurozone has delivered barely any growth, the worst labour market performance among industrial countries, double digit unemployment rates, more than 20% youth unemployment, unsustainable debt levels and inflation rates far below the central bank's own target.**

Indeed, despite him adding last year that for seven years they have 'countered the threat of a new great depression', **by some measures, the situation is worse than during the Great Depression:** unemployment in France and the periphery is around 13%, higher than the 10% French average from 1930 to 1938, despite the support offered by Germany's economy and sustained QE (via the Public Sector Purchase Programme and its related Covered Bond Purchase Programme and Asset-Backed Security Purchase Programme), which has well surpassed EUR1tn of support). For the EU, there are massive risks at every turn, as delineated below.

To begin with, **any necessity to undertake reforms amongst Eurozone countries to prevent the vast squandering of money that had occurred since the Eurozone came into effect in 1999 was eliminated in 2012 when in July of that year the ECB guaranteed to bail out countries in need via Outright Monetary Transactions (OMT).** Although it has not been used, the mere fact that it is there, and the corollary loose QE for countries that were basically bankrupt – Spain, Italy, Ireland, Portugal and Greece – has meant an almost complete absence of any meaningful reform. Prior to 2012, high interest rates and refinancing threats forced governments to become serious about reforms and so, over that period, more than half of the growth initiatives recommended by the OECD were implemented across the Eurozone. Since then, though, this figure has dropped to around one fifth.

This has resulted in a situation in which the peripheral countries mentioned above do not generate enough growth to reduce high levels of indebtedness and unemployment, and there is no prospect of their ever doing so, meaning that a massive default is inevitable sooner rather than later, threatening the very existence of the Eurozone itself. There are two prime candidates currently for this existential crisis: Greece and Italy.

The reckoning for other EU member states when one of these fragile states goes under will be gigantic. In theory, a core country is liable for its own debts but in practice it is inconceivable that a member state would not be bailed out as the contagion would spread throughout the entire Eurozone; witness the lengths that the ECB went to prevent Greece from doing so, despite its appalling financial position in recent years.

In practical terms, then, **the tax payers and savers of other member states would currently be liable** for the following, and these are very conservative estimates based on both the ECB's balance sheet and the Target2 balances between eurozone countries (the 'Trans-European Automated Real-time Gross Settlement System' is a reflection of capital flight from the countries in Southern Europe to banks in Northern Europe). On the former, assuming an extension until March 2018 and share of sovereign bonds between EUR55bn and EUR60bn in the monthly total of EUR80bn, the Eurosystem's holdings of government bonds would roughly double compared with the level reached end August 2016, to about **EUR2tn.** In the case of Target2, last year saw unprecedented levels, with Germany running a surplus of around EUR750bn, while the largest deficits were recorded by Spain (about EUR330bn) and Italy (around EUR360bn). **In short, Eurozone Target2 imbalances have touched or exceeded the crisis levels hit in 2012 when Greece was on the verge of leaving the Eurozone.**

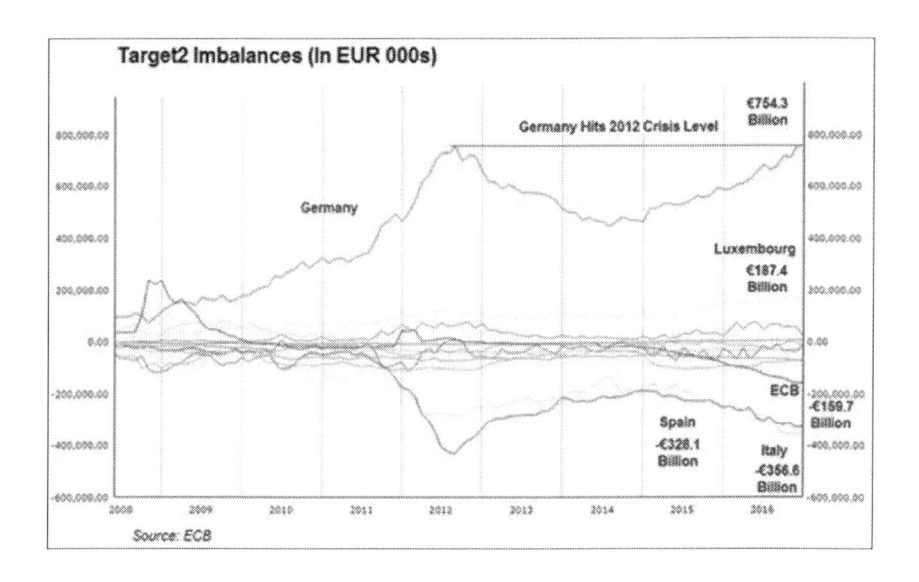

Black Swan Events

There is a common error among investors to describe any extreme market-moving event as being a 'Black Swan Event' but this is not true as, for example, a systemic collapse in China as outlined above, although certain to have a very high impact on markets is, nonetheless, predictable. **Black Swan Events can be defined as those that come as a complete surprise. In addition, they will have an extreme effect on the world and also, after one has manifested itself, it is rationalised in hindsight.**

Initially coined by the first and second century Roman poet, Juvenal, the term 'Black Swan' to illustrate **the innate fragility of any commonly held assumption** was then applied to the financial markets by Nassim Nicholas Taleb, a former highly-regarded trader and risk analyst himself, meaning that he actually knows something about the market worth knowing.

By definition, Black Swan Events in their purest sense cannot be foreseen so would not include, for example, some of the major risks outlined earlier – China crisis, Eurozone crisis, US crisis –

or indeed potential military conflicts, such as between the US and China prompted by the Senkaku Islands or North Korea, or between the US/Western Europe and Russia prompted by either continued Russian expansion into the West or NATO expansion into the East, or an accident in Syria, and so forth.

However, the best traders – and there is absolutely no reason why some readers should not fit into this group down the line – should be on the lookout for the very earliest signs of a Black Swan Event in the making. In practical terms, this involves three things:

1. Enormous curiosity over world events.
2. Exceptional ability for lateral thinking.
3. Extreme single-mindedness (although in this latter regard, absolute adherence to the key risk/reward principles and principles mentioned earlier is vital).

Again on a practical note, if the trader comes across something like this that he thinks may portend a disaster at some point, then the first move should be to buy volatility (through going long the VIX, for example) either spot (if the disaster looks imminent) or by buying longer-dated call options (the right but not the obligation to buy volatility at a predetermined price at some point in the future).

A case in point, for example, was well before a small number of people started noticing the pricing discrepancy specifically between CDSs and CDOs and the general creditworthiness of banks and other financial institutions before the Great Financial Crisis, there was a tiny mention in a bar in Liverpool Street in the City of London in July 2007 that major French bank Societe Generale was having trouble honouring a CDO payment, partly because of a fund squeeze and partly, it was rumoured, because the banks' risk managers did not really understand the bank's true exposure on the CDO product. **These two elements were vital in seeing that a major market cataclysm might be in the offing. It was impossible to say with** certainty at the time precisely what would happen or when but rather one could conclude that something very serious was going to occur. This is the nature of Black Swan Event trading.

Reviews

Review Of The Complete Guide To Successful Financial Markets Trading

This is the best book I have read on trading the markets, as it deals with all trading scenarios, allowing for making money whether markets are going up or down and even making money when they're stuck in sideways action. For beginners it's good because it gives the basics in terms of background on each of the main markets and how to actually make trades and make trades that will make money and for those of us who've been around for a bit it offers great trading insights that I haven't seen before in any book.

Sam Barden, SBI Markets

Reviews Of The Great Oil Price Fixes And How To Trade Them

(Watkins') ethos is knowledge equals power equals money, so in other words, the more information you have, the better decisions you can make when it comes to trading... Watkins goes to great lengths to lay the groundwork of what he calls 'the oil market'... Watkins explains how traders can capitalise on the oil market to make large amounts of money using various trading mechanisms and techniques. These are equal parts intimidating and enlightening for the uninformed but would no doubt prove empowering for those who understand trading and the terms used here more explicitly. This book is an incredible journey into the heart of trading on the oil markets, one that for those who heed it wisely, could potentially lead to millions earned in oil market trades. Highly recommended.

'The Edge' finance and business magazine

I had originally purchased The Great Oil Fixes since there was such a paucity of material related to oil trading and speculation... (all your books are) uniformly excellent. I have learnt a tremendous amount from them, despite already having been in the business for several years... The technical analysis aspects provide simple but robust tools to keep one on the right side of the major market moves.

Gerard de Condappa, Head – Asia Pacific at REFCO Trading Services

About The Author

After graduating from Oxford University with BA (Hons) and MA (Hons) degrees, Simon Watkins worked for a number of years as a senior Forex trader and salesman, ultimately achieving the positions of **Director of Forex at Bank of Montreal and Head of Forex Institutional Sales for Credit Lyonnais.** He has since become a **financial journalist, being Head of Weekly Publications And Managing Editor and Chief Writer of Business Monitor International, Head of Global Fuel Oil Products for Platts, Global Managing Editor of Research for Renaissance Capital (Moscow)** and **Head of Developed Market Bond Analysis for Bond Radar.**

He has written extensively on Forex, equities, bonds and commodities for many publications, including: *The Financial Times, Euromoney, FT Capital Insights, FX-MM, CFO Insight, The Edge Middle East Finance, International Commerce Magazine, The Securities And Investment Review, Accountancy Magazine, The Emerging Markets Monitor, Asia Economic Alert, Latin America Economic Alert, Eastern Europe Economic Alert, Oil And Gas Middle East, European CEO, Global Finance*

Magazine, World Finance Magazine, The Emerging Markets Report, FTSE Global Markets, VM Group Energy Monthly, VM Group Metals Monthly, Islamic Investor Magazine, Finance Europe, Finance Emerging Europe and *CIMA Financial Management.*

In addition, he has worked as an investment consultant for major hedge funds in London, Moscow and the Middle East.

This is Simon's fifth book for ADVFN Books. Turn over for details of his other four.

Also by Simon Watkins

Trade Financial Markets Like The Pros

There has never been a more difficult time to make money from trading the markets than now. All of the long-standing foundation stones of the global financial system are in a state of flux: engines of growth, monetary policies and the correlation dynamics between asset classes.

Additionally, each of the four core regional growth engines around the world – the US, the Eurozone, China and Japan – face their own sets of problems, undermining the historic relationships between stocks, bonds and currencies even further.

Given this backdrop, it is more important than ever that traders manage and exploit the few remaining factors in global markets that hold good. This is what this book is about: knowing what these are, exploiting them and banking the profits in a risk/reward efficient manner.

Fully illustrated with detailed charts, Trade Financial Markets Like The Pros covers how to balance risk against reward, how to search out correlations between asset classes that offer trading opportunities, and the major factors that could continue to twist financial markets into wildly contradictory modes. It also gives a refresher course in technical analysis and the full range of hedging techniques, including options, to offset possible losses.

Whether you are an experienced trader or just starting out, the information in this book offers you strategies to become one of the winners in the financial markets, and to avoid risking catastrophic losses.

Available in paperback and for the Kindle from Amazon.

The Great Oil Price Fixes And How to Trade Them

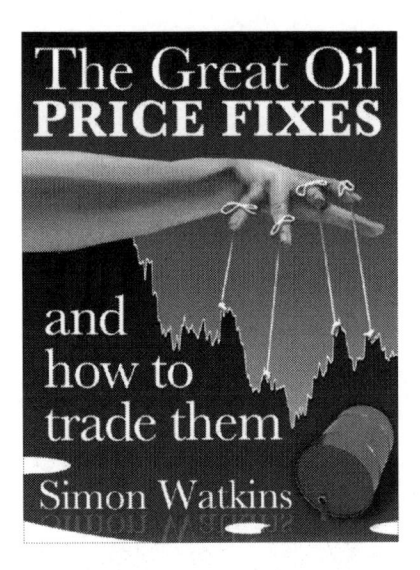

The oil market has been manipulated to an extremely high degree for decades, both overtly and covertly, and given its enduring geopolitical importance that is likely to continue.

Traders need to understand the essential dynamics that drive the global oil market, offering as it does unparalleled opportunities to make returns over and above those of other markets. The oil market is also an essential part of trading FX, equities, bonds and other commodities.

Simon Watkins' book *The Great Oil Price Fixes And How To Trade Them* offers you the knowledge you need. It covers the history of the market, gives you an understanding of the players in the oil game and provides a solid grounding in the market-specific trading nuances required in this particular field.

The essential elements of the general trading methodology, strategies and tactics that underpin top professional traders are covered with reference to how they can be used to trade in the oil market.

Available in paperback and for the Kindle from Amazon.

How To Make Big Money Trading In All Financial Conditions

The markets are going through a period of turbulence right now, but even in periods of low market volatility there's always some asset, somewhere in the world, that oscillates in price sufficiently to offer traders opportunities to make big money. The trick is to know what the asset is, to identify whether it's trading higher or lower than it should be and to have the skill, speed of thought and tenacity to take advantage of it.

In the follow up to his book *Everything You Need To Know About Making Serious Money Trading The Financial Markets*, Simon Watkins covers changing volatility patterns, risk-on/risk-off trading, how to find value in emerging markets and long-term global economic cycles. He outlines more fundamental principles that should guide your trades and trading methodologies to help you succeed.

Fully illustrated with detailed charts, the book shows how you can use technical analysis to make your decisions, how to manage your risk and how to take out hedge positions to offset possible losses.

Available in paperback and for the Kindle from Amazon.

Everything You Need To Know About Making Serious Money Trading The Financial Markets

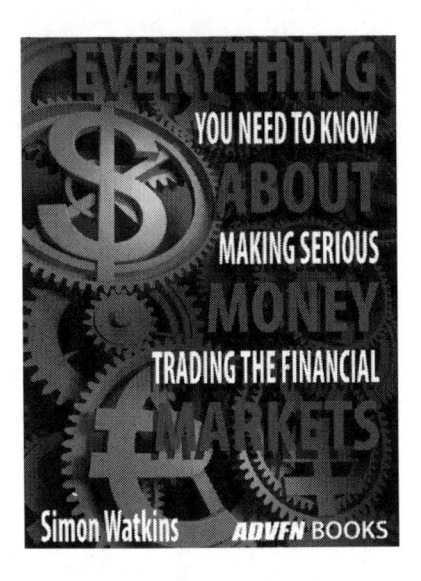

All over the world, people are trading on the financial markets. Some of them make a fortune – and many more lose their shirts. This book tells you how to be one of the winners.

It's a stark and sobering fact that around 90% of retail traders lose all of their trading money within about 90 days. That's because they have little grasp of the realities, technicalities, psychology and nature of the financial markets. In short, they don't know what they are doing.

Everything You Need To Know About Making Serious Money Trading The Financial Markets teaches you how to avoid being one of the 90%, and explains how to stack the odds firmly in your favour so you can become one of the 10% that make life-changing money trading. It's a trading bible that covers all aspects of the subject, from the psychology of trading and the mindset you need to succeed, through the fundamental principles that should guide your trades, to the trading methodologies that will help you succeed.

Fully illustrated with detailed charts, the book shows how you can use technical analysis to make your decisions, how to manage your risk and how to take out hedge positions to offset possible losses.

Available in paperback and for the Kindle from Amazon.

More Books from ADVFN

18 Smart Ways to Improve Your Trading

by Maria Psarra

Any trader or investor that says they have never lost money in the markets is too young, too stupid, too inexperienced, or just plain lying to you. Everyone makes mistakes, particularly when starting out as a trader. It's part of the learning curve.

What matters is that you learn from your mistakes. Even better, learn from the mistakes others have made to avoid making them yourself.

18 Smart Ways to Improve Your Trading explains some of the common mistakes traders make and the routines that winning traders use to avoid those errors. The author draws on her many years' experience of trading, both on institutional proprietary trading desks and for herself, and the knowledge she has gained advising professional clients.

In this book she shares her expertise with you. The *18 Smart Ways* include the habits that separate winning traders from losing ones, the secrets to profitable trading and how to deal with the emotional hiccups that cause you to lose in the markets.

If you absorb these lessons then they should make you a better investor or trader.

Originally published as articles in Master Investor magazine.

Available in paperback and for the Kindle from Amazon.

Simon Watkins

101 Charts for Trading Success

by Zak Mir

Using insider knowledge to reveal the tricks of the trade, Zak Mir's *101 Charts for Trading Success* explains the most complex set ups in the stock market.

Providing a clear way of predicting price action, charting is a way of making money by delivering high probability percentage trades, whilst removing the need to trawl through company accounts and financial ratios.

Illustrated with easy to understand charts this is the accessible, essential guide on how to read, understand and use charts, to buy and sell stocks. *101 Charts* is a must for all future investment millionaires.

Available in paperback and for the Kindle from Amazon.

The Game in Wall Street

by Hoyle and Clem Chambers

As the new century dawned, Wall Street was a game and the stock market was fixed. Ordinary investors were fleeced by big institutions that manipulated the markets to their own advantage and they had no comeback.

The Game in Wall Street shows the ways that the titans of rampant capitalism operated to make money from any source they could control. Their accumulated funds gave the titans enormous power over the market and allowed them to ensure they won the game.

Traders joining the game without knowing the rules are on a road to ruin. It's like gambling without knowing the rules and with no idea of the odds.

The Game in Wall Street sets out in detail exactly how this market manipulation works and shows how to ride the price movements and make a profit.

And guess what? The rules of the game haven't changed since the book was first published in 1898. You can apply the same strategies in your own investing and avoid losing your shirt by gambling against the professionals.

Illustrated with the very first stock charts ever published, the book contains a new preface and a conclusion by stock market guru Clem Chambers which put the text in the context of how Wall Street operates today.

Available in paperback and for the Kindle from Amazon.

For more information go to the ADVFN Books website at www.advfnbooks.com.

Made in the USA
Middletown, DE
09 November 2017